Classic and Contemporary Readings in Physical Anthropology

M. K. SANDFORD, Ph.D.
The University of North Carolina at Greensboro

with

EILEEN M. JACKSON, Ph.D.
Thomas Edison State College

WADSWORTH
CENGAGE Learning·

Australia • Brazil • Japan • Korea • Mexico • Singapore • Spain • United Kingdom • United States

WADSWORTH
CENGAGE Learning

Classic and Contemporary Readings in Physical Anthropology
M. K. Sandford and Eileen M. Jackson

Executive Editor: Marcus Boggs

Development Editor: Lin Marshall

Assistant Editor: Liana Monari

Marketing Manager: Meghan Pease

Marketing Assistant: Mary Anne Payumo

Marketing Communications Manager:
Tami Strang

Project Manager, Editorial Production:
Samen Iqbal

Creative Director: Rob Hugel

Art Director: Caryl Gorska

Print Buyer: Paula Vang

Permissions Editor: Mardell Glinski Schultz

Production Service: Rebecca Logan,
Newgen–Austin

Photo Researcher: Don Schlotman

Copy Editor: Carolyn Haley

Cover Designer: Riezebos Holzbaur
Design Group

Cover Image: Lordkipanidze/National
Museum

Compositor: Newgen

For product information and technology assistance, contact us at **Cengage Learning Customer & Sales Support, 1-800-354-9706.**

For permission to use material from this text or product, submit all requests online at **cengage.com/permissions.** Further permissions questions can be e-mailed to **permissionrequest@cengage.com.**

Library of Congress Control Number: 2008931614

Student Edition:

ISBN-13: 978-0-495-51014-7

ISBN-10: 0-495-51014-9

Wadsworth
10 Davis Drive
Belmont, CA 94002-3098
USA

Cengage Learning is a leading provider of customized learning solutions with office locations around the globe, including Singapore, the United Kingdom, Australia, Mexico, Brazil, and Japan. Locate your local office at **http://international.cengage.com/region.**

Cengage Learning products are represented in Canada by Nelson Education, Ltd.

For your course and learning solutions, visit **academic.cengage.com.** Purchase any of our products at your local college store or at our preferred online store **www.ichapters.com.**

Printed in Canada
1 2 3 4 5 6 7 12 11 10 09 08

To our ancestors,
who continue to teach us

and

to our descendents,
whose survival depends upon
our ability to learn

Contents

Preface

What does it mean to be human?

Quite understandably, this question may send some people into deep personal philosophical and/or spiritual reflection. In physical or biological anthropology, however, we approach this query from a scientific vantage point. Using questions, theory, and methods that are grounded in science, physical anthropologists seek to unravel the very essence of our species: what makes us tick? Why do we look, act, react, hear, sound, think, and feel as we do?

As anthropologists, we organize our efforts toward understanding humankind around two major themes. First, we ask and answer questions about ourselves by investigating the evolution of our species. For example, we seek to know what abilities and characteristics our species has by virtue of our evolutionary relationships with other organisms. Second, we consider human variation—and the underlying reasons for that variation—as essential to understanding ourselves. The two themes are inextricable, of course, for without variation, evolution itself would be impossible. Contemporary physical anthropologists document variation to interpret how evolutionary processes have operated in the past and how they might be playing out in the present or future.

Such questions frame the major topics that are covered in most introductory courses in biological anthropology. These areas—evolutionary theory, nonhuman primates, human evolution, and human variation and adaptation—constitute the major divisions of this collection of readings. Beyond these key subjects, other, equally important considerations guided the selection of individual readings included herein. These areas of emphasis include science itself, as well as the historical development of physical anthropology and the applications of new technology to the discipline.

Scientific principles and methods are stressed throughout this reader for several reasons. It's a pretty safe bet that our species has never, in all of our evolution and history, been so dependent upon science and technology for our very survival. Yet, most people have frighteningly little knowledge of science. In other words, scientific literacy is appallingly low. A recent edition of the report *Science and Engineering Indicators* (National Science Board, 2004) estimated that less than one-fifth of Americans meet minimal standards of scientific literacy. How can our species even begin to confront crises involving overpopulation, hunger, disease, global climate change, ethnic cleansing, and the prospects of biological and/or nuclear warfare with such an uninformed and ill-prepared citizenry? Science is vital for evaluating these problems and every other new bit and byte of information that barrages us via the mass media and the information highway.

The deficient state of our scientific literacy demands the most vigorous efforts to enhance scientific understanding in the contemporary world. To this end, this volume includes an introductory reading, by Dr. Eugenie Scott, that focuses exclusively on the nature and criteria of science. In addition, many other selections were chosen to illustrate specific aspects of scientific inquiry, including testing of alternative hypotheses, stating research questions, and applying new technologies.

A second consideration addressed by the selections in this reader involves the history and development of physical anthropology. To help students truly appreciate some of the early defining moments in physical anthropology, we've included some primary sources. These include an excerpt from Hrdlička's introduction to the discipline published in the first volume of the *American Journal of Physical Anthropology,* as well as Washburn's classic article on the "new physical anthropology." In other sections, we contrast historic and contemporary methods, evidence, and perspectives on the same topics, such as primate behavioral ecology, bipedalism, skin pigmentation, and lactose intolerance. Special attention is also paid to the innovative use of genomic techniques, including using ancient DNA, in addressing old research questions.

Readers should remember that some of the historic articles in the volume—while effectively communicating the tone and aims of earlier anthropologists—also entail some ideas that could offend contemporary sensitivities. Hrdlička's discussion of races and Kretchmer's use of ethnic and tribal terminology should be understood in historical context. The same caveat extends to the virtually ubiquitous use of the word "man" when less gender-laden substitutes like "human" would be more appropriate.

Finally, this reader emphasizes pedagogy. One of the unique features included to facilitate student learning is the use of editor's introductions before each article. These introductions are brief guides that outline key themes and questions for students to consider as they read each selection. Following each reading, lists of discussion questions, as well as terms, names, and other websites to research, may serve as a basis for student review and/or a source for individual or group projects. It is our hope that all of these pedagogical tools will promote active and lifelong student engagement with these subjects, both inside and outside of traditional classrooms.

There is something inherently intriguing about contemplating our evolutionary roots and ultimate destiny. Ultimately, I chose readings—some from my own days as a student—which piqued my interest and imagination. May this book go to the cause of a more complete and integrated understanding of our species' past—and present—and help prepare us to work toward a brighter, more sustainable future.

M. K. Sandford, Ph.D.
Editor
June 2008

Introduction

"Why am I here?"

You may be wondering that very question right at this moment. You may be thinking about your place on the planet, or the role you should play in our world today. More likely, however, your thoughts are closer to home. They are less philosophical and a whole lot more concrete. *"Should I keep reading or go to the gym?"* *"Is it time for dinner yet?"* Here you are, back at school. An open book lies in front of you. You've signed up for a course in physical or biological anthropology, and chances are you're trying to figure out what you'll be learning in this course and what will be expected of you.

It's quite likely that you're taking biological anthropology for one of two reasons. You may be an art, English, theatre, chemistry, or other non-anthropology major, who has signed up for this class because you need a required science course. On the other hand, you may be an anthropology major anxiously awaiting your first overview of physical anthropology—a subject you may already know as one of the four major subfields of anthropology, or the study of humankind.

You may be asking yourself, *"Just what is physical anthropology?"* You may even be feeling a tad apprehensive. Although you have probably never had an opportunity to take a course in this subject before, you may well have had some exposure to the subject matter. You've probably picked up a newspaper, thumbed through a magazine, or turned on the television and heard words and names like *bones, gorilla, DNA, Australopithecus, sickle cell anemia, forensic anthropology, Neandertal, Charles Darwin, skin color,* and *evolution.* Some of these words may sound long, complicated, hard to spell, scary, and/or controversial.

Relax. No matter where you place yourself in the description above, you are likely to find your introduction to physical anthropology course a fascinating and challenging class in which you will hear many new and exciting things about our species. It's even a pretty safe bet that you'll be hearing and thinking about some of the things you learned in this course for the rest of your life.

Taking this class is a very significant act, and it's not just about you. You're also learning physical anthropology for all those friends, coworkers, family members, children, and partners who don't have this opportunity. For two reasons, your education here is vitally important for others. First, as part of anthropology, physical anthropology will help you learn more about who you are as a biological being—as an animal, a vertebrate, a mammal, a primate, and as a human being, just for starters. Second, physical anthropology is a science. As citizens of our contemporary world, we are absolutely dependent upon science and technology for our survival, and yet, the rate of scientific literacy is appallingly low. Said another way, many people lack a true understanding of the most basic scientific concepts and methods. Still fewer could talk about evolution, natural selection, and adaptation with any degree of accuracy. Your presence in a physical anthropology class can help change that.

Let's explore this notion a little further. Biological anthropology is not only relevant to your everyday life, but it will also help you participate more fully and actively in the modern world with all of its challenges. This is true for anthropology in general, which is concerned with all aspects of human existence. Two themes are particularly important in anthropology, however, and you'll be able to see how they play out in biological anthropology. The first is a concern for biological variation—how human beings differ from one another in biological ways that are visible and invisible (but detectable) to the naked eye. A second important theme in anthropology in general, and in biological anthropology in particular, is evolution. Physical anthropologists want to know how human evolution has taken place in the past and how it is operating in the present. There is, in this regard, an inextricable connection between biological variation and evolution; variation is absolutely essential for evolution.

Thus, physical anthropology brings us awareness that our evolutionary heritage is part of our core being. Every time we tell a story, run through an airport to catch a plane, give an infant a bottle, hum the words of our favorite old song, or start the engine of our new car, we are living our evolutionary legacy—both biologically and culturally—in the here and now. In essence we are two human beings at once. One being, the contemporary person, encounters the *new* everyday—we make a new friend, buy a new MP3 player, choose paper or plastic or bring a new green bag, welcome newborns into the world, listen to the news, or read a newspaper. Living inside of us, however, is another being—the one who represents our evolutionary past. This—the old, the past, our evolutionary heritage—enables us at a very basic level to be, to look, to act, to feel, and to function as *Homo sapiens sapiens*. Underlying our contemporary selves are those parts of us that are products of our evolutionary origins as members of the animal kingdom, as vertebrates, as mammals, and as primates.

It is the business of physical anthropology to help us understand how our old self informs our new self. Which of our characteristics do we share with other mammals? What parts of ourselves—biologically and behaviorally—do we have in common with the other members of the taxonomic order primates?

Whenever we see somebody of another skin color, hear about someone's blood type, or read about the spread of MRSA (a resistant strain of infection caused by a bacterium called *Staphylococcus aureus*), we are witness to the complex interplay between biological variation and evolutionary processes. Moreover, in physical anthropology we recognize that human evolution is best viewed through a bio-cultural lens. The biocultural perspective focuses on the ways in which biological, cultural, and environmental factors interact and influence one another in both our past and our present.

How will the articles in this reader help you in your quest to become a better scientific thinker? How will they enhance your understanding of the concepts and methods of biological anthropology in ways that are useful and meaningful for your daily life? The first articles define science in general and then demonstrate how physical anthropology meets the criteria for science. The rest are selections pertaining to major areas of study in physical anthropology. The first section of these readings, called "Evolution and Heredity," initially provides evidence for biological evolution—from fossils to genes—and then explains evolutionary theory and process. The next section, "Primates," consists of case studies of nonhuman primates, from prosimians to chimpanzees. These articles not only illustrate the growth of the field of primatology, they also describe how our perspectives and attitudes about the nonhuman primates have changed. The next section, "Human Evolution," shows how new fossils and techniques can help us sort out old debates and open up new areas of investigation. The last section, "Modern Human Variation," highlights skin color and lactose (milk sugar) intolerance, types of variation that have been investigated by physical anthropologists. You'll be able to see how our knowledge of these topics has been enriched by studies of the human genome as well as of contemporary human populations.

Accompanying each reading are features designed to help you develop a greater understanding of the subject. Each reading is preceded by a short introduction that will draw your attention to key concepts or issues. Discussion questions follow each selection, along with suggestions for further study based on important ideas or scientists.

As you read, pay special attention to the questions that come to you when you are wondering about yourself, your friends and family, and the world around us. Look for science and physical anthropology in the news. Think about the future as well as the past. Consider the ways in which knowledge of science and physical anthropology can help us modern *Homo sapiens sapiens* do better by one another, other species, and this tiny planet.

✳

PART I

The Nature of Science

1

Science: "Truth Without Certainty"

EUGENIE SCOTT

What do you think would happen if you announced that you "love science" to a group of your relatives or close friends? Some might look at you as if you'd just flown in from another galaxy; others might be relieved to have found someone to talk to. The mere mention of science rarely prompts a neutral response. Many people are fascinated by new discoveries in medicine or space; others associate science with a class they slept through in school. In either case, your first course in physical anthropology may turn a page for you toward a lifelong love of science.

Even in a world where scientific and technological knowledge grows every day, the rate of scientific illiteracy is appallingly high. "Science" covers tremendous breadth and depth. It refers to specific methods for learning about the natural world and, at the same time, the bodies of knowledge that those methods reveal. As you begin to study physical anthropology, it is imperative that you thoroughly understand what science is—and is not.

As executive director of the National Center for Science Education, Dr. Eugenie C. Scott is eminently qualified to speak to the definition, characteristics, and methods of scientific inquiry. As a physical anthropologist, Dr. Scott has provided stalwart leadership to fellow scientists and educators in their efforts to teach people the difference between "scientific creationism" and testable science.

In our first selection, Dr. Scott explains science as a way of knowing about the natural world that requires us to test our ideas against nature itself. You will learn the proper meaning of terms such as "theory," "hypothesis," and "fact," as well as the different kinds of scientific testing and verification. You will also learn the ways in which the "big idea" of evolution is subject to scientific predictions and testing.

We live in a universe made up of matter and energy, a *material* universe. To understand and explain this material universe is the goal of science, which is a methodology as well as a body of knowledge obtained through that methodology. As will become clear when we discuss religion, most individuals believe that reality includes something other than matter and energy, but science is limited to the latter two. The methodology of science is a topic on which any college library has dozens of feet of shelves of books and journals, so obviously just one chapter won't go much beyond sketching the bare essentials. Still, I will try to show how science differs from many other ways of knowing and is particularly well-suited to explaining our material universe.

WAYS OF KNOWING

Science requires the testing of explanations of the natural world against nature itself, and discarding

SOURCE: From Eugenie Scott, *Evolution vs. Creationism* (Westport, CT: Greenwood Press, 2004, 3–21).
Reprinted with permission of Greenwood Publishing Group, Inc., Westport, CT.

those explanations that do not work. What distinguishes science from other ways of knowing is its reliance upon the natural world itself as the arbiter of truth. There are many things that people are interested in, are concerned about, or want to know about that science does not address. Whether the music of Madonna or Mozart is superior may be of interest (especially to parents of teenagers), but it is not something that science addresses. Aesthetics is clearly something outside of science. Similarly, literature or music might generate or help to understand or cope with emotions and feelings in a way that science is not equipped to do. But if one wishes to know about the natural world and how it works, science is superior to other ways of knowing. Let's consider some other ways of knowing about the natural world.

Authority

Dr. Jones says, "Male lions taking over a pride will kill young cubs." Should you believe her? You might know that Dr. Jones is a famous specialist in lion behavior who has studied lions for 20 years in the field. *Authority* leads one to believe that Dr. Jones's statement is true. In a public bathroom, I once saw a little girl of perhaps four or five years old marvel at faucets that automatically turned on when hands were placed below the spigot. She asked her mother, "Why does the water come out, Mommy?" Her mother answered brightly, if unhelpfully, "It's magic, dear!" When we are small, we rely on the authority of our parents and other older people, but authority clearly can mislead one, as in the case of the "magic" spigots. And Dr. Jones might be wrong about lion infanticide, even if in the past she has made statements about animal behavior that have been reliable. Yet it is not "wrong" to take some things on authority. In northern California, a popular bumpersticker reads "Question Authority." Whenever I see one of these, I am tempted to pencil in, "but stop at stop signs." We all accept some things on authority, but we should do so critically.

Revelation

Sometimes people believe a statement because they are told it comes from a source that is unquestionable: from God, or the gods, or from some other supernatural power. Seekers of advice from the Greek oracle at Delphi believed what they were told because they believed that the oracle received information directly from Apollo; similarly, Muslims believe the contents of the Koran were revealed to Muhammad by God; and Christians believe the New Testament is true because the authors were directly inspired by God. A problem with revealed truth, however, is that one must accept the worldview of the speaker in order to accept the statement; there is no outside referent. If you don't believe in Apollo, you're not going to trust the Delphic oracle's pronouncements; if you're not a Mormon or a Catholic, you are not likely to believe that God speaks directly to the Mormon President or the Pope. Information obtained through revelation is difficult to verify because there is not an outside referent that all parties are likely to agree upon.

Logic

A way of knowing that is highly reliable is *logic,* which is the foundation for mathematics. Among other things, logic presents rules for how to tell whether something is true or false, and is extremely useful. However, logic in and of itself, with no reference to the "real world," is not complete. It is logically correct to say, "All cows are brown. Bossy is not brown. Therefore Bossy is not a cow." The problem with the statement is the truth of the premise that all cows are brown, when many are not. To know that the proposition about cows is empirically wrong even if logically true requires reference to the real world outside the logical structure of the three sentences. To say, "All wood has carbon atoms. My computer chip has no carbon atoms. Therefore my computer chip is not made of wood" is both logically and empirically true.

Science

Science does include logic—statements that are not logically true cannot be scientifically true—but what distinguishes the scientific way of knowing is the requirement of going to the outside world to verify claims. Statements about the natural world are tested against the natural world, which is the final arbiter. Of course, this approach is not perfect: one's information about the natural world comes from experiencing the natural world through the senses (touch, smell, taste, vision, hearing) and instrumental extensions of these senses (microscopes, telescopes, telemetry, chemical analysis, etc.), any of which can be faulty or incomplete. As a result science, more than any of the other ways of knowing described here, is more tentative in its claims. Ironically, the tentativeness of science ultimately leads to more confidence in scientific understanding: the willingness to change one's explanation with more or better data, or a different way of looking at the same data, is one of the great strengths of the scientific method. The anthropologist Ashley Montagu summarized science rather nicely when he wrote, "The scientist believes in proof without certainty, the bigot in certainty without proof" (Montagu 1984: 9).

Thus science requires deciding among alternative explanations of the natural world by going to the natural world itself to test them. There are many ways of testing an explanation, but virtually all of them involve the idea of holding constant some factors that might influence the explanation, so that some alternate explanations can be eliminated. The most familiar kind of test is the *direct experiment,* which is so familiar that it is even used to sell us products on television.

DIRECT EXPERIMENTATION

Does RealClean detergent make your clothes cleaner? The smiling company representative in the TV commercial takes two identical shirts and pours something messy on each one, and drops them into identical washing machines. RealClean brand detergent goes into one machine, the recommended amount of a rival brand into the other. Each washing machine is set to the same cycle, for the same period of time, and the ad fast-forwards to show the continuously smiling salesperson taking the two shirts out. Guess which one is cleaner.

Now, it would be very easy to rig the demonstration so that RealClean does a better job: the salesperson could use less of the other detergent, use an inferior-performing washing machine, put the RealClean shirt on a soak cycle 45 minutes longer than brand X, employ different temperatures, wash the competitor's shirt on delicate rather than regular cycle—I'm sure you can think of a lot of ways that RealClean's manufacturer could ensure that its product comes out ahead. It would be a bad sales technique, however, because we're familiar with the direct experimental type of test, and someone would very quickly call "Foul!" To convince you that they have a better product, the makers of the commercial have to remove every factor that might possibly explain why the shirt came out cleaner when washed in their product. They have to hold constant or *control* all these other factors—type of machine, length of cycle, temperature of the water, and so on—so that the only reasonable explanation for the cleaner shirt is that RealClean is a better product. The experimental method—performed fairly—is a very good way to persuade people that your explanation is correct. In science, too, someone will call "Foul!" (or at least, "You blew it!") if a test doesn't consider other relevant factors.

Direct experimentation is a very powerful—as well as familiar—research design. As a result, some people think that this is the only way that science works. Actually, in science, what matters is that explanations be *tested,* and direct experimentation is only one kind of testing. The key element to testing an explanation is to hold variables constant, and one can hold variables constant in many ways other than being able to directly manipulate them (as one can water temperature in a washing machine). In fact, the more complicated the science, the less likely an experimenter is to use direct experimentation.

In some tests, variables are controlled statistically; in others, especially in biological field research or in social sciences, one can find circumstances where important variables are controlled by the nature of the experimental situation itself. These observational research designs are another type of direct experimentation.

Noticing that male guppies are brightly colored and smaller than the drab females, you might wonder whether having bright colors makes male guppies easier prey. How would you test this idea? If conditions allowed, you might be able to perform a *direct experiment* by moving brightly colored guppies to a high-predation environment and monitoring them over several generations to see how they do. If not, though, you could still perform an observational experiment by looking for natural populations of the same or related species of guppies in environments where predation was high and other environments where predation was low. You would also want to pick environments where the amount of food was roughly the same—can you explain why? What other environmental factors would you want to hold constant at both sites?

When you find guppy habitats that naturally vary only in the amount of predation and not in other ways, then you're ready to compare the brightness of color in the males. Does the color of male guppies differ in the two environments? If males are less brightly colored in environments with high predation, this would support the idea that brighter guppy color makes males easier prey. (What if in the two kinds of environments, male guppy color is the same?)

Indirect experimentation is used for scientific problems where the phenomena being studied—unlike color in guppies—cannot be directly observed.

INDIRECT
EXPERIMENTATION

In some fields, not only is it impossible to directly control variables, but the phenomena themselves may not be directly observable. A research design known as *indirect experimentation* is often utilized in such fields. Explanations can be tested even if the phenomena being studied are too far away, too small, or too far back in time to be observed

directly. For example, giant planets recently have been discovered orbiting distant stars—though we cannot directly observe them. Their presence is indicated by the gravitational effects they have on the suns around which they revolve: because of what we know about how the theory of gravitation works, we can infer that the passage of a big planet around a sun will make the sun wobble. Through the application of principles and laws in which we have confidence, it is possible to infer that these planetary giants do exist, and to make estimates of their size and speed of revolution.

Similarly, subatomic particles studied by physicists are too small to be observed directly, but particle physicists certainly are able to test their explanations. By applying knowledge about how particles behave, they are able to create indirect experiments to test claims about the nature of particles. Let's say that a physicist wants to ascertain properties of a particle—its mass, charge, or speed. Based on observations of similar particles, he makes an informed estimate of the speed. To test the estimate, he might bombard it with another particle of known mass, because if the unknown particle has a mass of M, it will cause the known particle to ricochet at velocity V. If the known particle does ricochet as predicted, this would support the hypothesis about the mass of the unknown particle. Thus theory is built piece by piece, through inference based on accepted principles.

In truth, most scientific problems are of this "If . . . then . . ." type, whether the phenomena investigated are directly observable or not. If male guppy color is related to predation, then we should see duller males in high-predation environments. If a new drug stimulates the immune system, then individuals taking it should have fewer colds than controls. If human hunters were involved in the destruction of large Australian land mammals, [then] we should see extinction events correlating with the appearance of the first Aborigines. We test by consequence in science all the time. Of course—because scientific problems are never solved so simply—if we get the consequence we predict, this does not mean we have "proven" our explanation. If you found that guppy color does vary in environments where predation differs, this does not mean you've proved yourself right about the relationship between color and predation. To understand why, we need to consider what we mean by proof and disproof in science.

PROOF AND DISPROOF

Proof

Scientists don't usually talk about "proving" themselves right, because "proof" suggests certainty (remember Ashley Montagu's "truth without certainty"!). The testing of explanations is in reality a lot messier than the simplistic descriptions given above. One can rarely be sure that all the possible factors that might explain why a test produced a positive result have been considered. In the guppy case, for example, let's say that you found two habitats that differed in the number of predators but were the same in terms of amount of food, water temperature, and hiding places—you tried to hold constant as many factors as you could think of. If you find that guppies are less colorful in the high-predation environment, you might think you have made the link, but some other scientist may come along and discover that your two environments differ in water turbidity. If turbidity affects predation—or the ability of female guppies to select the more colorful males—this scientist can claim that you were premature to conclude that color is associated with predation. In science we rarely claim to "prove" a theory—but positive results allow us to claim that we are likely to be on the right track. And then you or some other scientist can go out and test some more. Eventually we may achieve a consensus about guppy color being related to predation, but we wouldn't conclude this after one or a few tests. This back-and-forth testing of explanations provides a reliable understanding of nature, but the procedure is neither formulaic nor even especially tidy over the short run. Sometimes it's a matter of two steps forward, a step to the side (maybe down a blind alley), half a step back—but gradually the procedure, and with it human knowledge, lurches forward, leaving us with a clearer knowledge of the natural world and how it works.

In addition, most tests of anything other than the most trivial of scientific claims do not result in slam-dunk, now-I've-nailed-it, put-it-on-the-T-shirt conclusions, but rather in more or less tentative statements: a statement is weakly, moderately, or strongly supported, depending on the quality and completeness of the test. Scientific claims become accepted or rejected depending on how confident the scientific community is about whether the experimental results could have occurred that way just by chance—which is why statistical analysis is so important a part of most scientific tests. Animal behaviorists note that some social species share care of the offspring. Does this make a difference in the survival of the young? Some female African silver-backed jackals, for example, don't breed in a given season, but help to feed and guard the offspring of a breeding adult. If the helper phenomenon is directly related to pup survival, then more pups should survive in families with a helper.

One study tested this claim by comparing the reproductive success of jackal packs with and without helpers, and found that for every extra helper a mother jackal had, she successfully raised one extra pup per litter over the average survival rate (Hrdy 2001). These results might encourage you to accept the claim that helpers contribute to the survival of young, but only one test on one population is not going to be convincing. Other tests on other groups of jackals would have to be conducted to confirm the results, and to be able to generalize to other species the principle that reproductive success is improved by having a helper would require conducting tests on other social species. Such studies in fact have been performed across a large range of birds and mammals, and a consensus is emerging about the basic idea of helpers increasing survivability of the young. But there are many remaining questions, such as whether a genetic relationship always exists between the helper and either the offspring or the helped mother.

Science is quintessentially an open-ended procedure in which ideas are constantly tested, and rejected or modified. Dogma—an idea held by belief or faith—is anathema to science. A friend of mine once was asked to state how he ended up a scientist. His tongue-in-cheek answer illustrates rather nicely the nondogmatic nature of science: "As an adolescent I aspired to lasting fame, I craved factual certainty, and I thirsted for a meaningful vision of human life—so I became a scientist. This is like becoming an archbishop so you can meet girls" (Cartmill 1988: 452).

In principle, all scientific ideas may change, though in reality there are some scientific claims that are held with confidence, even if details may be modified. The physicist James Trefil (1978) suggested that scientific claims can be conceived as arranged in a series of three concentric circles. . . . In the center circle are the core ideas of science: the theories and facts in which we have great confidence because they work so well to explain nature. Heliocentrism, gravitation, atomic theory, and evolution would be examples. The next concentric circle outward is the frontier area of science, where research and debate are actively taking place on new theories or modifications/additions to core theories. Clearly no one is arguing with the basic principle of heliocentrism, but on the frontier, planetary astronomers still are learning things and testing ideas about the solar system. That matter is composed of atoms is not being challenged, but atomic theory is being added to and modified by the discoveries of quantum physics.

The outermost circle is the fringe, a breeding ground for ideas that very few professional scientists are spending time on: unidentified flying objects, telepathy and the like, perpetual motion machines, and so on. Generally the fringe is not a source of new ideas for the frontier, but occasionally (very occasionally!) ideas on the fringe will muster enough support to be considered worthwhile looking at by scientists and will move into the frontier. They may well be rejected and end up back in the fringe or be discarded completely, but occasionally they may move to the frontier, and perhaps eventually into the core. That the continents move began as a fringe idea, moved to the frontier as data began to accumulate in its favor, and finally became a core idea of geology when seafloor spreading was discovered and the theory of plate tectonics was developed.

Indeed, we must be prepared to realize that even core ideas may be wrong, and that somewhere, sometime, there may be a set of circumstances that could refute even our most confidently held theory. But for practical purposes, one needn't fall into a slough of despond over the relative tentativeness of scientific explanation. That the theory of gravitation may be modified or supplemented sometime in the future is no reason to give up riding elevators (or, even less advisedly, to jump off the roof). Science gives us reliable, dependable, and workable explanations of the natural world— even if it is good philosophy of science to keep in mind that in principle anything can change.

On the other hand, even if it is usually not possible absolutely to *prove* a scientific explanation correct—there might always be some set of circumstances or observations somewhere in the universe that would show your explanation wrong—to *disprove* a scientific explanation is possible. If you hypothesize that it is raining outside, and walk out the door to find the sun is shining and the ground is dry, you have indeed disproven your hypothesis (assuming you are not hallucinating). So disproving an explanation is easier than proving one true, and, in fact, progress in scientific explanation has largely come by rejecting alternate explanations. The ones that haven't been disconfirmed yet are the ones we work with—and some of those we feel very confident about.

Disproof

Now, if you are a scientist, obviously you will collect observations that support your explanation, but others are not likely to be persuaded just by a list of confirmations. Like "proving" RealClean detergent washes clothes best, it's easy to find—or concoct— circumstances that favor your view, which is why you have to bend over backward in setting up your test so that it is fair. So you set the temperature on both washing machines to be the same, you use the same volume of water, you use the recommended amount of detergent, and so forth. In the guppy case, you want to hold constant the amount of food in high-predation environments and low-predation environments, and so on. If you are wrong about the ability of RealClean to get the stains out, there won't be any difference between the two loads of clothes, because you have controlled or held constant all the other factors that might explain why one load of clothes emerged with fewer stains. You will have disproved your hypothesis about the alleged superior stain-cleaning qualities of RealClean. You are conducting a fair test of your hypothesis if you set up the test so that everything that might give your hypothesis an advantage has been excluded. If you don't, another scientist will very quickly point out your error, so it's better to do it yourself and save yourself the embarrassment!

What makes science challenging—and sometimes the most difficult part of a scientific investigation—is coming up with a testable statement. Is the African AIDS epidemic the result of tainted oral polio vaccine (OPV) administered to Congolese in the 1950s? Chimpanzees carry simian immunodeficiency virus, which researchers believe is the source for the AIDS-causing virus HIV (human immunodeficiency virus). Was a batch of OPV grown on kidneys from simian immunodeficiency virus-infected chimps the source of African AIDS? If chimpanzee DNA could be found in the 50-year-old vaccine, that would strongly support the hypothesis. If careful analysis could not find chimpanzee DNA, that would fail to support the hypothesis, and you would have less confidence in it. Such a test was conducted, and after very careful analysis, no chimp DNA was found in samples of the old vaccine (Poinar et al. 2001).

This did not *disprove* the hypothesis that African AIDS was caused by tainted OPV (perhaps one of the other batches was tainted), but it is strong evidence against it. Again, as in most science, we are dealing with probabilities: if all four batches of OPV sent to Africa in the 1950s were prepared in the same manner, at the same time, in the same laboratory, what is the probability that one would be completely free of chimp DNA

and one or more other samples tainted? Low, presumably, but because the probability is not 0 percent, we cannot say for certain that the OPV/AIDS link is out of the question. However, it has been made less plausible, and since the positive evidence for the hypothesis was thin to begin with, few people are taking the hypothesis seriously. Both disproof of hypotheses and failure to confirm are critical means by which we eliminate explanations and therefore increase our understanding of the natural world.

Now, you might notice that although I have not defined them, I already have used two scientific terms in this discussion: *theory* and *hypothesis*. You may already know what these terms mean—probably everyone has heard that evolution is "just a theory," and many times you have probably said to someone with whom you disagree, "Well, that's just a hypothesis." You might be surprised to hear that scientists don't use these terms in quite this way.

FACTS, HYPOTHESES, LAWS, AND THEORIES

How do you think scientists would rank the terms *fact, hypothesis, law,* and *theory*? How would *you* list these four from most important to least? Most people list *facts* on top, as the most important, followed by laws, then theories, with hypotheses being least important, at the bottom:

Most important
Facts
Laws
Theories
Hypotheses
Least important

You may be surprised that scientists rearrange this list, as follows:

Most important
Theories
Laws

Hypotheses

Facts

Least important

Why is there this difference? Clearly, scientists must have different definitions of these terms compared to how we use them "on the street." Let's start with facts.

Facts

If someone said to you, "List five scientific facts," you could probably do so with little difficulty. Living things are composed of cells. Gravity causes things to fall. The speed of light is about 186,000 miles/second. Continents move across the surface of Earth. Earth revolves around the sun. And so on. Scientific facts, most people think, are claims that are rock solid, about which scientists will never change their minds. Most people think that facts are just about the most important part of science, and that the job of the scientist is to collect more and more facts.

Actually, facts are useful and important, but they are far from being the most important elements of a scientific explanation. In science, facts are *confirmed observations*. When the same result is obtained after numerous observations, scientists will accept something as a fact and no longer continue to test it. If you hold up a pencil between thumb and forefinger, and then stop supporting it, it will fall to the floor. All of us have experienced unsupported objects falling; we've leaped to catch the table lamp as the toddler accidentally pulls the lamp cord. We consider it a fact that unsupported objects fall. It is always possible, however, that some circumstance may arise when a fact is shown not to be correct. If you were holding that pencil while orbiting Earth on the space shuttle and let it go, it would not fall (it would float). It also would not fall if you were on an elevator with a broken cable that was hurtling at 9.8 meters/second^2 toward the bottom of a skyscraper—but let's not dwell on that scenario. So technically, unsupported objects don't always fall, but the rule holds well enough for ordinary use. One is not frequently on either the

space shuttle or a runaway elevator, or in other circumstances where the confirmed observation of unsupported items falling will not hold. It would in fact be perverse for one to reject the conclusion that unsupported objects fall just because of the existence of helium balloons!

Other scientific "facts" (confirmed observations) have been shown not to be true. For a decade or so back in the 1950s, it was thought that humans had 24 chromosome pairs, but better cell staining techniques have revealed that we actually have 23 pairs. A fact has changed, in this case with more accurate means of measurement. At one point, we had confirmed observations of 24 chromosome pairs, but now there are more confirmations of 23 pairs, so we accept the latter—although at different times, both were considered "facts." Another example of something considered a fact—an observation—was that the continents of the Earth were stationary, which anyone can see! With better measurement techniques, including using observations from satellites, it is clear that continents do move, albeit very slowly (only a few inches/year).

So facts are important but not immutable; they can change. An observation, though, doesn't tell you very much about how something works. It's a first step toward knowledge, but by itself it doesn't get you very far, which is why scientists put it at the bottom of the hierarchy of explanation.

Hypotheses

Hypotheses are statements of the relationship among things, often taking the form of "if . . . then . . ." statements. If brightly colored male guppies are more likely to attract predators, then in environments with high predation, guppies will be less brightly colored. If levels of lead in the bloodstream of children are inversely associated with IQ scores, then children in environments with larger amounts of lead should have lower IQ scores. Elephant groups are led by matriarchs, the eldest females. If the age (and thus experience) of the matriarch is important for the survival of the group, then groups with younger matriarchs will have higher infant mortality than those led by older ones. Each of these hypotheses is directly testable and can be either disconfirmed or confirmed (note that hypotheses are not "proved right"—any more than any scientific explanation is "proven"). Hypotheses are very important in the development of scientific explanations. Whether rejected or confirmed, tested hypotheses help to build explanations by removing incorrect approaches and encouraging the further testing of fruitful ones. Much hypothesis testing in science depends on demonstrating that a result found in a comparison occurs more or less frequently than would be the case if only chance were operating; statistics and probability are important components of scientific hypothesis testing.

Laws

There are many laws in science (e.g., the laws of thermodynamics, Mendel's laws of heredity, Newton's inverse square law, the Hardy-Weinberg law). Laws are extremely useful empirical generalizations: they state what, under certain conditions, will happen. During cell division, under Mendel's law of independent assortment, we expect genes to act like particles and separate independently of one another. Under conditions found in most places on Earth's surface, masses will attract one another in inverse proportion to the square of the distance between them. If a population of organisms is above a certain size, is not undergoing natural selection, and has random mating, the frequency of genotypes of a two-gene system will be in the proportion $p^2 + 2pq + q^2$. This relationship is called the Hardy-Weinberg law.

Outside of science, we also use the term "law." It is the law that everyone must stop for a stoplight. Laws are uniform, and in that they apply to everyone in the society, they are universal. We don't usually think of laws changing, but of course they do: the legal system has a history, and we can see that the legal code used in the United States has evolved over several centuries primarily from legal codes in England. Still, laws must be relatively stable or people would not be able to conduct business or know which practices will get them in trouble. One will not anticipate that if today everyone drives on

the right side of the street, tomorrow everyone will begin driving on the left. Perhaps because of the stability of societal laws, we tend to think of scientific laws as also stable and unchanging.

However, scientific laws can change, or not hold under some conditions. Mendel's law of independent assortment tells us that the hereditary particles will behave independently as they are passed down from generation to generation. For example, the color of a pea flower is passed on independently from the trait for stem length. But after more study, geneticists found that the law of independent assortment can be "broken" if the genes are very closely associated on the same chromosome. So minimally, this law had to be modified in terms of new information—which is standard behavior in science. Some laws will not hold if certain conditions are changed. Laws, then, can change just as facts can.

Laws are important, but as descriptive generalizations, they rarely *explain* natural phenomena. That is the role of the final stage in the hierarchy of explanation: *theory*. Theories *explain* laws and facts. Theories therefore are more important than laws and facts, and thus scientists place them at the top of the hierarchy of explanation.

Theories

The word "theory" is perhaps the most misunderstood word in science. In everyday usage, the synonym of theory is "guess" or "hunch." Yet according to the National Academy of Sciences, a theory is defined as "a well-substantiated explanation of some aspect of the natural world that can incorporate facts, laws, inferences, and tested hypotheses" (National Academy of Sciences 1998: 7). To explain something scientifically requires an interconnected combination of laws, tested hypotheses, and other theories. This reliance upon inferential reasoning is the hallmark of theorizing.

Many high school (and even, unfortunately, some college) textbooks describe theories as tested hypotheses, as if a hypothesis that is confirmed is somehow promoted to a theory, and a really, really good theory gets crowned as a law. Unfortunately, this is not how scientists use these terms, but most people are not scientists and scientists have not done a very good job of communicating the meanings of these terms to students and the general public. (To be honest, some scientists are not very knowledgeable about the philosophy of science! And—to be scrupulously honest—the presentation of facts, hypotheses, laws, and theories I am presenting here is very, very simplified and unnuanced, for which I apologize to philosophers of science.)

EVOLUTION AND TESTING

What about the theory of evolution? Is it scientific? Some have claimed that since no one was present millions of years ago to see evolution occur, evolution is not a scientific field. Yet we can study evolution in a laboratory even if no one was present to see zebras and horses emerge from a common ancestor. A theory can be scientific even if its phenomena are not directly observable. Evolutionary theory is built in the same way that theory is built in particle physics or any other field that uses indirect testing—and some aspects of evolutionary theory can be directly tested. I will devote [a different] chapter . . . to discussing evolution in detail, but let me concentrate here on the question of whether it is testable—and especially if it is falsifiable.

The "big idea" of biological evolution . . . is "descent with modification." Evolution is a statement about history and refers to something that happened, to the branching of species through time from common ancestors. The pattern that this branching takes and the mechanisms that bring it about are other components of evolution. We can therefore look at the testing of evolution in three senses: Can the "big idea" of evolution (descent with modification, common ancestry) be tested? Can the pattern of evolution be tested? Can the mechanisms of evolution be tested?

Testing the Big Idea

Hypotheses about evolutionary phenomena are tested just like hypotheses about other scientific topics: the trick (as in most science!) is to figure out how to formulate your question so it can be tested. The big idea of evolution, that living things have shared common ancestors, can be tested using the "if . . . then . . ." approach—testing by consequences—used by all scientists. The biologist John A. Moore suggested a number of these "if . . . then . . ." statements that could be used to test whether evolution occurred:

1. If living things descended with modification from common ancestors, then we would expect that "species that lived in the remote past must be different from the species alive today" (Moore 1984: 486). When we look at the geological record, this is indeed what we see. There are a few standout species that seem to have changed very little over hundreds of millions of years, but the rule is that the farther back in time one looks, the more creatures differ from present forms.

2. If evolution occurred, we "would expect to find only the simplest organisms in the very oldest fossiliferous [fossil-containing] strata and the more complex ones to appear in more recent strata" (Moore 1984: 486). Again going to the fossil record, we find this is true. In the oldest strata, we find single-celled organisms, then simple multicelled organisms, and then simple versions of more complex invertebrate multicelled organisms (during the early Cambrian period). In later strata, we see the invasion of the land by simple plants, and then the evolution of complex seed-bearing plants, and then the development of the land vertebrates.

3. If evolution occurred, then "there should have been connecting forms between the major groups (phyla, classes, orders)" (Moore 1984: 489). To test this requires going again to the fossil record, but matters are complicated by the fact that not all connecting forms have the same probability of being preserved. For example, connecting forms between the very earliest invertebrate groups (which all are marine) are less likely to be found because of their soft bodies, which do not preserve as well as hard

body parts such as shells and bones that can be fossilized. These early invertebrates also lived in shallow marine environments, where the probability of a creature's preservation is different depending on whether it lived under or on the surface of the sea floor: surface-living forms have a better record of fossilization due to surface sediments being glued together by bacteria. Fossilized burrowing forms haven't been found—although their burrows have. Connections between vertebrate groups might be expected to be found, because vertebrates are large animals with large calcium-rich bones and teeth that have a higher probability of fossilization than the soft body parts of the earliest invertebrates. There are, in fact, good transitions between fish and amphibians, and there are especially good transitions between reptiles and mammals. More and more fossils are being found that show structural transitions between reptiles (dinosaurs) and birds. Within a vertebrate lineage, there are often fossils showing good transitional structures. We have good evidence of transitional structures showing the evolution of whales from land mammals, and modern, large, single-hoofed horses from small, three-toed ancestors. Other examples can be found in reference books on vertebrate evolution such as Carroll (1998) or Prothero (1998).

In addition to the "if . . . then . . ." statements predicting what one would find if evolution occurred, one can also make predictions about what one would *not* find. If evolution occurred and living things have branched off the tree of life as lineages split from common ancestors, one would *not* find a major branch of the tree totally out of place. That is, if evolution occurred, paleontologists would not find mammals in the Devonian age of fishes, or seed-bearing plants back in the Cambrian. Geologists are daily examining strata around the world as they search for minerals, or oil, or other resources, and at no time has a major branch of the tree of life been found seriously out of place. Reports of "man tracks" being found with dinosaur

footprints have been shown to be carvings, or eroded dinosaur tracks, or natural erosional features. If indeed there had not been an evolutionary, gradual emergence of branches of the tree of life, then there is no scientific reason why all strata would not show remains of living things all jumbled together.

In fact, one of the strongest sources of evidence for evolution is the consistency of the fossil record around the world. Similarly, . . . when we look at the relationships among living things, we see that it is possible to group organisms in gradually broader classifications. There is a naturally occurring hierarchy of organisms that has been recognized since the seventeenth century: species can be grouped into genera, genera can be grouped into families, and on into higher categories. The splitting process of evolution generates hierarchy; the fact that animals and plants can be arranged in a "tree of life" is predicted by and explained by the inference of common descent.

Not only the "big idea" of evolution can be tested; so can more specific claims within that big idea. Such claims concern pattern and process, which require explanations of their own.

Pattern and Process

Pattern. Consider that if evolution is fundamentally an aspect of history, then certain things happened and other things didn't. It is the job of evolutionary biologists and geologists to reconstruct the past as best they can, and try to ascertain what actually happened as the tree of life developed and branched. This is the *pattern* of evolution, and indeed, along with the general agreement about the gradual appearance of modern forms over the last 3.8 billion years, the scientific literature is replete with disputes among scientists about specific details of the tree of life, about which structures represent transitions between groups and how different groups are related. For instance, whales are known to be related to the group of hoofed mammals called artiodactyls, but are they more closely related to the hippopotamus branch of artiodactyls (suggested by molecular data) or the cattle branch (suggested by skeletal data)? Morphologically, most Neanderthal physical traits can be placed within the range of variation of living humans, but there are tests on fossil mitochondrial DNA that suggest modern humans and Neanderthals shared a common ancestor very, very long ago—no more recently than 300,000 years ago (Ovchinnikov et al. 2000). So are Neanderthals ancestral to modern humans, or not? There is plenty of room for argument about exactly what happened in evolution! But how do you test such statements?

Tests of hypotheses of relationship commonly use the fossil record. Unfortunately, sometimes one has to wait a long time before hypotheses can be tested. The fossil evidence has to exist (i.e., be capable of being preserved and actually *be* preserved), be discovered, and then painstakingly (and expensively) extracted. Only then can the analysis begin. Fortunately, we can test hypotheses about the pattern of evolution—and the idea of descent with modification itself—using not only the fossil record but also anatomical, embryological, or biochemical evidence from living groups. One reason why evolution—the inference of common descent—is such a robust scientific idea is that so many different sources of information lead to the same conclusions.

We can use different sources of information to test a hypothesis about the evolution of the first primitive amphibians that colonized land. There are two main types of bony fish: the very large group of familiar ray-finned fish (fish such as trout, salmon, and sunfish) and the lobe-finned fish, represented today by only three species of lungfish and one species of coelacanth. In the Devonian, though, there were 19 families of lungfish and 3 families of coelacanths. Because of their many anatomical specializations, we know that ray-finned fish are not part of tetrapod (four-legged land vertebrate) ancestry; we and all other land vertebrates are descended from the lobefin line. Early tetrapods and lobefins both had teeth with wrinkly enamel, and shared characteristics of the shoulder girdle and jaws, plus a sac off the gut used for breathing (Prothero 1998: 358). But are we tetrapods more closely related to lungfish or coelacanths?

. . . It isn't that tetrapods evolved from lungfish, of course, but that lungfish and tetrapods shared a common ancestor, and shared a common ancestor with one another more recently than they shared a common ancestor with coelacanths. There is a large series of fossils filling the morphological gaps between ancestors of lungfish and tetrapods (Carroll 1998) and more are being discovered ([such as the] tiktaalik).

Another interesting puzzle about the pattern of evolution is ascertaining the relationships among the phyla, which are very large groupings of kinds of animals. All the many kinds of fish, amphibians, reptiles, birds, and mammals are lumped together in one phylum (Chordata) with some invertebrate animals such as sea squirts and the wormlike lancelet (amphioxus). Another phylum (Arthropoda) consists of a very diverse group of invertebrates that includes insects, crustaceans, spiders, millipedes, horseshoe crabs, and the extinct trilobites. So you can see that phyla contain a lot of diversity. Figuring out how such large groups might be related to one another is a challenging undertaking.

Phyla are diagnosed based on basic anatomical body plans—the presence of such features as segmentation, possession of shells, possession of jointed appendages, and so forth. Fossil evidence for most of these transitions is not presently available, so scientists have looked for other ways to ascertain relationships among these large groups. The recent explosions of knowledge in molecular biology and developmental biology are opening up new avenues to test hypotheses of relationships—including those generated from anatomical and fossil data. Chordates for a long time have been thought to be related to echinoderms based on anatomical comparisons (larvae of some echinoderms are very similar to primitive chordates) and this relationship is being confirmed through biochemical comparisons (e.g., ribosomal RNA) (Runnegar 1992). Ideas about the pattern of evolution can be and are being tested.

Process. Scientists studying evolution want to know not only the pattern of evolution but also the processes behind it: the mechanisms that cause cumulative biological change through time. The most important is natural selection . . . , but there are other mechanisms (mostly operating in small populations, like genetic drift) that also are thought to bring about change. One interesting current debate, for example, is over the role of genetic factors operating early in embryological development. How important are they in determining differences among—and the evolution of—the basic body plans of living things? Are the similarities of early-acting developmental genes in annelid worms and in primitive chordates like amphioxus indicative of a shared common ancestry? Another debate has to do with the rate and pace of evolution: Do changes in most lineages proceed slowly and gradually, or do most lineages remain much the same for long periods that once in a while are "punctuated" with periods of rapid evolution? We know that individuals in a population compete with each other, and that populations of a species may outbreed each other, but can there be natural selection between lineages of species through time? Are there rules that govern the branching of a lineage through time? Members of many vertebrate lineages have tended to increase in size through time; is there a general rule governing size or other trends? All of these issues and many more constitute the processes or mechanisms of evolution. Researchers are attempting to understand these processes by testing hypotheses against the fossil and geological records as well as other sources of information from molecular biology and developmental biology (embryology).

Natural selection and other genetically based mechanisms are regularly tested and regularly are shown to work. By now there are copious examples of natural selection operating in our modern world, and it is not unreasonable to extend its operation into the past. Farmers and agricultural experts are very aware of natural selection as insects, fungi, and other crop pests become resistant to chemical controls. Physicians similarly are very aware of natural selection as they try to counter antibiotic-resistant microbes. The operation of natural selection is not disputed in the creation/evolution controversy: both supporters and detractors of evolution accept that natural selection works.

Creationists, however, claim that natural selection cannot bring about differences from one "kind" to another.

Pattern and process are both of interest in evolutionary biology, and each can be evaluated independently. Disputes about the pattern of evolutionary change are largely independent of disputes about the process. That is, arguments among specialists about how fast evolution can operate, or whether it is gradual or punctuated, are irrelevant to arguments over whether Neanderthals are ancestral to modern Europeans and vice versa. Similarly, arguments about either process or pattern are irrelevant to *whether* evolution took place (the "big idea" of descent with modification). This is relevant to the creation/evolution controversy because some of the arguments about pattern or process are erroneously used to support the claim that descent with modification did not occur. Such arguments confuse different levels of understanding.

CREATIONISM AND TESTING

The topic of religion constitutes [another] chapter . . . , and creationism is a religious concept. Religion will be defined as a set of ideas concerning a nonmaterial reality; thus it would appear that—given science's concern for material explanations—science and creationism would have little in common. Yet the controversy that this book considers, the creationism/evolution controversy, includes the claim made by some that creationism is scientific, or can be made scientific, or has scientific elements. The question naturally arises, then, "Is creationism testable?"

As discussed, science operates by testing explanations of natural phenomena against the natural world. Explanations that are disproved are rejected; explanations that are not disproved—that are corroborated—are provisionally accepted (though at a later time they may be rejected or modified with new information). An important element of testing is being able to hold constant some of the conditions of the test, so that a causative effect can be correctly assigned.

The ultimate statement of creationism—that the present universe came about as the result of the action or actions of a divine Creator—is thus outside the abilities of science to test. If there is an omnipotent force in the universe, it would by definition be impossible to hold constant (to control) its effects. A scientist could control for the effects of temperature, light, humidity, or predators—but it would be impossible to control the actions of God!

The question of whether God created cannot be evaluated by science. Most believers conceive of God as omnipotent, so He can create everything as we see it today, a theological position known as "special creationism"; or He can create through the process of natural law, a theological position known as "theistic evolution." An omnipotent being could create the universe to appear as if it had evolved, but actually have created everything five minutes ago. The reason that the ultimate statement of creationism cannot be tested is simple: any action of an omnipotent Creator is compatible with any and all scientific explanations of the natural world. The methods of science cannot choose among the possible actions of an omnipotent Creator.

Science is thus powerless to test the ultimate claim of creationism, and must be agnostic about whether God did or did not create the material world. However, some types of creationism go beyond the basic statement "God created" to make claims of fact about the natural world. Many times these fact claims, such as those concerning the age of Earth, are greatly at variance with observations of science, and creationists sometimes evoke scientific support to support these fact claims. One creationist claim, for example, is that the Grand Canyon was laid down by the receding waters of Noah's Flood. In cases like this, scientific methods *can* be used to test creationist claims, because the claims are claims of fact. Of course, it is always possible to claim that the Creator performed miracles (that the Grand Canyon stratigraphy—which virtually all geologists consider to be impossible to have been laid down during a year's time—was created through the special actions of an omnipotent Creator), but at this point one passes from science to some other way of knowing. If fact claims are made—assuming the claimer argues scientific support for such claims—then such claims can be tested by the methods of science; some scientific views are better supported than others, and some will be rejected as a result of comparing data and methodology. But such occasions leave the realm of science for that of religion if miracles are invoked.

CONCLUSION/SUMMARY

Science is an especially good way of knowing about the natural world. It involves testing explanations against the natural world, discarding the ones that don't work and provisionally accepting the ones that do.

Theory-building is the goal of science. Theories explain natural phenomena and are logically constructed of facts, laws, and confirmed hypotheses. Knowledge in science, whether expressed in theories, laws, tested hypotheses, or facts, is provisional, though reliable. Although any scientific explanation may be modified, there are core ideas of science that have been tested so many times that we feel very confident about them and believe that there is an extremely low probability of their being discarded. The willingness of scientists to modify their explanations (theories) is one of the strengths of the method of science, and it is the major reason that knowledge of the natural world has increased exponentially over the last couple of hundred years.

Evolution, like other sciences, requires that natural explanations be tested against the natural world. Indirect observation and experimentation, involving "if . . . then . . ." structuring of questions and testing by consequence, are the normal mode of testing in sciences such as particle physics and evolution, where phenomena cannot be directly observed.

The three elements of biological evolution—descent with modification, the pattern of evolution, and the process or mechanisms of evolution—can all be tested through the methods of science. The heart of creationism—that an omnipotent being created— is not testable by science, but fact claims about the natural world made by creationists can be. . . .

REFERENCES

Carroll, Robert L. 1998. *Vertebrate Paleontology and Evolution.* New York: W. H. Freeman.

Cartmill, Matt. 1988. Seventy-five Reasons to Become a Scientist: *American Scientist* Celebrates Its Seventy-fifth Anniversary. *American Scientist* 76: 450–463.

Hrdy, Sarah Blaffer. 2001. Mothers and Others. *Natural History,* May: 50–62.

Montagu, M. F. Ashley. 1984. *Science and Creationism.* New York: Oxford University Press.

Moore, John A. 1984. Science as a Way of Knowing—Evolutionary Biology. *American Zoologist* 24 (2): 467–534.

National Academy of Sciences. 1998. *Teaching About Evolution and the Nature of Science.* Washington, DC: National Academy Press.

Ovchinnikov, I. V., A. Gotherstrom, G. P. Romanova, V. M. Kharitonov, K. Liden, and W. Goodwin. 2000. Molecular Analysis of Neanderthal DNA from the Northern Caucasus. *Nature* 404: 490–493.

Poinar, Hendrik, Melanie Kuch, and Svante Pääbo. 2001. Molecular Analysis of Oral Polio Vaccine Samples. *Science* 292 (5517): 743–744.

Prothero, Donald R. 1998. *Bringing Fossils to Life: An Introduction to Paleontology.* Boston: WCB McGraw-Hill.

Runnegar, Bruce. 1992. Evolution of the Earliest Animals. In *Major Events in the History of Life,* edited by J. W. Schopf. Boston: Jones and Bartlett.

Trefil, James. 1978. A Consumer's Guide to Pseudo-science. *Saturday Review,* April 29: 16–21.

DISCUSSION QUESTIONS

1. At a family reunion, you tell a distantly related cousin that you are studying evolution this semester. Your cousin responds by saying, "Well, that's all 'just a *theory.*'" How do you respond? Is your cousin using the concept of "theory" correctly? What do scientists actually mean when they refer to or formulate a "theory"?

2. The same cousin argues that evolution isn't scientific because we can't see it taking place. Give specific examples you would use to illustrate that evolution is, in fact, a scientific theory.

3. Can "creationism" be considered as science? Provide two to three specific reasons to support your answer.

 **INTERNET RESOURCES**

After reading this selection you may wish to research the following individuals.

- Charles R. Darwin
- Thomas Henry Huxley

To learn more about Dr. Eugenie Scott's work, visit the website for the National Center for Science Education at http://www.natcenscied.org.

 **InfoTrac College Edition**

(infotrac-college.com)

You can find many other readings pertinent to this topic by consulting online databases including InfoTrac College Edition. Some suggested search terms for this article are as follows.

- Evolution
- Science
- Theory

2

Physical Anthropology: Its Scope and Aims; Its History and Present Status in America

ALEŠ HRDLIČKA

Every academic discipline emerges from a particular historical setting—or context—through the pioneering efforts of key individuals. This selection is an intellectual time machine that will transport you back to the founding of physical anthropology. Dr. Aleš Hrdlička, the father of physical anthropology in the United States, published this article in 1918, in the very first issue of the American Journal of Physical Anthropology—*a journal he inaugurated and edited until his death in 1943. A decade after launching the journal, he became a founder of the American Association of Physical Anthropologists.*

Most of physical anthropology's earliest pioneers came from the fields of medicine, anatomy, and natural history, and Hrdlička was no exception. He obtained degrees in medicine in New York before turning his attention to the study of anatomical variation. He began his professional anthropological career by obtaining an appointment at the Smithsonian Institution, where he ultimately served as Curator of Physical Anthropology at the National Museum of Natural History. He traveled to places like South America and Siberia, visiting archaeological sites and amassing skeletal and anatomical collections. These materials subsequently provided training and research projects for many budding physical anthropologists.

In this selection, Hrdlička outlines his vision of physical anthropology. Of particular importance is his discussion of French scientist Paul Broca, who defined anthropology as "the natural history" of humankind. Also, look for Hrdlička's description of the distinguishing characteristics of physical anthropology. What did he see as the roles of evolution, variation, and the comparative method in the science of physical anthropology?

Many contemporary anthropologists take issue with some of the concepts and methods that were employed by our earliest academic ancestors. These include an emphasis on description and measurement as well as the use of "race" as an appropriate category for humans. But the basic idea that human beings should be studied using methods developed for other species was, in itself, quite revolutionary. Humans were often described as occupying a place apart from, rather than a part of, the animal kingdom. Physical anthropologists have played a key role in changing that idea. Our work in this regard continues to this day.

SOURCE: Aleš Hrdlička, "Physical Anthropology: Its Scope and Aims; Its History and Present Status in America," *American Journal of Physical Anthropology* 1, no. 1 (January/February 1918): 3–23.

A. PHYSICAL ANTHROPOLOGY, ITS SCOPE AND AIMS[1]

I. Definitions

An understanding of whatsoever exists, formulated and preserved in memory or in writing, is knowledge; and systematic search for *knowledge*, on the basis of existing foundations of learning, is *science*. Being of the utmost utility, science constitutes the most important intellectual function of mankind.

A branch of science may be defined as a portion of systematized research that extends to closely related phenomena and has become the special function of a class of qualified observers. One of the most interesting and far-reaching of such branches is Anthropology. This has been frequently but somewhat vaguely defined as "the science of man"; perhaps a more fitting definition would be "the comparative science of man," for its main characteristic, the [criterion] in fact, which differentiates it from many closely related branches of science, is that of comparison. More specifically Anthropology may also be defined as that portion of systematic research which deals with the differences, and causes of the differences, in structure, in function, and in all other manifestations of mankind, according to time, variety, place, and condition.

In the course of its development, or since the beginning of the last century, Anthropology has become differentiated into a number of important branches, which follow correlated yet separate aims, and which, while often cooperating, are developing in large measure independently and through distinct personnel. In America since Powell's time the recognized main subdivisions of Anthropology are: Archeology, or the study of man's products and material accomplishments in the past; Ethnology, or the study of man's intellectual, linguistic, and present material activities; and Physical Anthropology, or the study of racial anatomy, physiology, and pathology.

It is the last-named branch, or Physical Anthropology, which interests us exclusively in this place. Formerly known simply as "Anthropology,"

it was defined by its principal founder and promoter, Paul Broca, as "the natural history of the genus homo," or, more in detail, as "that science which has for its object the study of mankind as a whole, in its parts, and in its relation with the rest of nature."[2] It can be defined to-day in the briefest form as the *study of man's variation.* It is that part of Anthropology which occupies itself in a comparative way with the study of the human body and its inseparable functions. It deals with the causes and ways of human evolution, and with the development, transmission, classification, effects, and tendencies of man's bodily and functional differences. It is, briefly and comprehensively, the research into man's anatomical and physiological variation.

The comparative element shows clearly the position of Physical Anthropology in relation to general human anatomy and physiology, and general biology. The objects of general human anatomy and physiology are essentially the pursuit of knowledge regarding structure and function in the average man of the present day; while the chief aims of general biology are to trace the structural and functional relations of the various species of living beings to one another, and to seek the general causes and processes of organic variation and evolution. Physical Anthropology is a continuation—and extension—of all these to the chronological, racial, social, and even pathological groupings of mankind, and it reaches with its investigations beyond man only in so far as may be necessary to an understanding of the phenomena which it encounters. If it had not its present designation it could well be called "advanced human anatomy, physiology, and biology."

II. Historical

Physical Anthropology is a comparatively recent branch of science, though its roots extend far back in the development of human reflection. It is interesting to know that one of its main incentives was the discovery of America, with its new race of people, no mention of which occurred in any of the old accounts or traditions. This most sensational event was followed by discoveries of other lands and peoples in the Pacific, and this was succeeded by rapidly increasing knowledge of organized beings in general, including the anthropoid apes. All this led irresistibly to new lines of thought by scientific men, as well as to a general doubt as to the correctness of the old theories of creation; and the mental fermentation, though greatly impeded by old dogmas, lack of precise data and collections, and the backward state of many collateral branches of science, progressed until it finally pierced the clouds of the past and manifested itself in anthropological publications. Peyrère's "Preadamites" appeared in 1655, and, notwithstanding prohibitions and the small real worth of the book, it was received with eagerness and read very extensively. In 1699 was published Tyson's classic on "Comparative Anatomy of Man and Monkey." And in 1735 one of the actual corner stones of modern anthropology was laid by Linnaeus. It was in the "Systema Naturae" of this great naturalist that man for the first time was placed within the line of living beings in general, and that his close organic relations with the rest of the primates was authoritatively expressed. Then followed Buffon, the precursor of Lamarck, with whom the new branch of the natural science of man took more definite form, and thenceforward the progress toward Anthropology, as differentiated to-day, has been continuous.

Those who contributed more directly toward the development of Physical Anthropology are too numerous to mention: they really include all the prominent naturalists and anatomists of the latter half of the eighteenth and the first half of the nineteenth century, such as Daubenton, Camper, Lamarck, Blumenbach, Soemmering, Lacépède, Cuvier, Retzius, the brothers Geoffroy, Lawrence, Edwards, Serres, Prichard, Morton, and many others.[3] Even the teachings of Gall, however erroneous in application, have aided its growth, for they stimulated research into the variations of the head, skull, and brain, gave rise to various craniological collections, and were the main incentive to Morton's ultimate and remarkable work, the "Crania Americana." The discussions of the monogenists and polygenists, particularly those of the nineteenth century, were also of much importance and assistance.

The first effort toward an organization of forces in the new field was made as early as 1800, when a small body of scientific men formed themselves, in Paris, into a Society of Students of Man (*Société des observateurs de l'homme*). It was in this little circle that the term Anthropology (used previously as a title for some works on man of philosophical and in a few instances of simple anatomical nature) was employed in something like its present significance. This attempt at organization, however, was premature and was abandoned two years later (1803), after little had been accomplished.

In 1832 the Museum of Natural History in Paris, under the influence of Prof. William Edwards, transformed its chair of Anatomy into that of Natural History of Man, and to this Serres, in 1839, added Anthropology. These were in many respects remarkable steps forward, but the time was not yet ripe for the subject to assume much importance. There were no large collections, no material evidence of man's antiquity or evolution, and the public mind was still to a considerable degree medieval.

From 1839 to 1848 Paris had a Société d'Ethnologie, which included Physical Anthropology, but again with little lasting result. In 1843 the Ethnological Society was founded in England.[4] It included men like Prichard and Richard Owen, and its main object was the study of primitive races. But it was not until after the beginning of the second half of the nineteenth century, with the advent of Paul Broca and his collaborators, and the founding of the Société d'Anthropologie in Paris (1859),[5] that the actual birth of the new branch of science may be said to have taken place. This is less than sixty years ago; and how difficult the beginnings were, even then, will be appreciated from the fact that when permission to establish the society was sought, the Minister of Public Instruction, notwithstanding the rank of those who, with Broca, applied for the sanction, refused to countenance the matter. Finally the petition was sent to the Prefect of Police, but that official was equally unwilling, and returned the document to the Ministry. It was not until after the influential intervention of Ambroise Tardieu that one of the chiefs of the police department became convinced that the scientific gentlemen were not quite so dangerous to the welfare of the empire or to society as was suspected, and not finding, more-over, any law that forbade the gathering of fewer than twenty persons, the eighteen future anthropol-ogists were finally informed that their meetings would be tolerated. But Broca was made personally responsible for anything that might be said at the meetings against the government or religion, and for further safety every meeting was to be attended by an officer in plain clothes.

From the establishment of the Société d'Anthro-pologie in Paris, the progress of the new branch of research was rapid. Before long similar societies came into existence in England (1863), in Germany (1869), and other countries, some of the leading men in medical circles taking active part; the publi-cation of anthropological journals was commenced; an efficient system of anthropometry, with the required instruments, was devised, principally by Broca, and detailed instructions in the system were published by the same author; collections were be-gun and important lines of investigation undertaken in different parts of Europe as well as in the United States; and in 1876 the École d'Anthropologie was founded in Paris for academic instruction and training in the new branch of research. Finally, in 1885, appeared Paul Topinard's great textbook, the "Éléments d'Anthropologie générale," which to this day is a respected and indispensable volume in our laboratories. Much progress was also made during this period in the differentiation of Anthropology as a whole into its present main subdivisions.

But this quarter century of the history of Anthropology as a separate branch of learning—a period of the greatest and most hopeful activity, the detailed and still unwritten history of which is of absorbing interest—was not one of uninterrupted progress. Unexpectedly, and it now seems unjustifi-ably, a crisis was encountered which seriously affected progress, and from the effects of which Physical Anthropology is only now beginning to recover. This crisis was the result of a schism in anthropometry, begun in 1874 by von Ihering and

completed by the German anthropologists at Frankfurt in 1882. This is not a suitable place for a discussion of the causes or the details of the case; suffice it to say that the division resulted in great loss of effort and had a generally untoward influence on the progress of the science. It is only quite recently that international commissions, composed of foremost anthropologists of all countries, have endeavored to adjust the differences and, by impar-tially selecting the best from existing methods in anthropometry, to effect a much needed uniformity. Two conferences have been held, one in 1906 at Monaco and the other in 1912 at Geneva,[6] with much harmony and most encouraging results. A complete agreement on anthropometric methods will be of the greatest importance to the branch and mark an epoch in Physical Anthropology.

This chapter, necessarily condensed and inade-quate, may be appropriately concluded with a few words concerning the actual status of Physical Anthropology. The subject, like the entire history of the science, calls for thorough presentation, but this is out of the question at the present time.

Physical Anthropology to-day numbers distin-guished followers wherever science flourishes. It has already a bibliography that reaches into tens of thousands of titles. It maintains a number of well-equipped laboratories, where students are trained or may conduct investigations. It possesses most important collections of material, which from year to year increase in numbers and value. It sustains or contributes a large body of original material to anthropological journals of high standing, such as the *Bulletins et Mémoires de la Société d'Anthropologie de Paris, L'Anthropologie,* the Journal of the Royal Anthropological Institute of Great Britain and Ireland, *Man,* the *Biometrica,* the *Archivio per l'Antropologia,* the *Giornale per la Morfologia dell'Uomo e dei Primati,* the *Archiv für Anthropologie,* the *Zeitschrift für Morphologie und Anthropologie,* etc. Numerous other results of investigations are disseminated through periodicals devoted to anat-omy, general biology, and other subdivisions of anthropology. Finally, it is a subject of instruc-tion in the École d'Anthropologie of Paris, in the Anthropological Institute of the University of

Zurich, in various large museums, and in many of the principal universities of both hemispheres. It is still struggling with numerous difficulties, but it has now a solid foundation, has repeatedly shown itself to be of public and national utility, and has surely before it a future of great importance. . . .

NOTES

1. Published in preliminary form in *Science,* N. S., XXVIII, July 10, 1908, 33–43; and *The Anatomical Record,* 11, no. 5, 1908, 182–195.

2. Article "Anthropologie" in Dict. encycl. d. sci. méd., vol. V, p. 276, Paris, 1866; also in Broca's *Mémoires d'Anthropologie,* Paris, 1871, vol. I, p. 1. References to numerous definitions in R. Martin, System d. (physischen) Anthropologie, etc., *Korr.-Bl. d. d. Anthr. Ges.,* 1907, Nr. 9/12, and in his Lehrbuchd. Anthr., Jena, 1914. See also L. Manouvrier, *Rev. de l'École d'Anthr.,* 1904, pp. 397–410; F. Boas, "Anthropology," pp. 1–28, Columbia University Press, N. Y., 1908; and F. Frassetto, *Lezioni di Antropologia,* 3 vol., Rome, 1909–13.

3. For details concerning the history of anthropology, see T. Benlyshe, *Mem. Anthr. Soc.,* London, vol. I, 1863–64, pp. 335–458; P. Topinard's *Éléments d'Anthropologie générale,* Paris, 1885, pp. 1–148; L. Niederle, *Athenaeum,* Prague, 1889 (repr. pp. 1–19); F. Boas, *Science,* October 21, 1904, pp. 513–524; references to more or less direct contributions to the subject in R. Martin, op. cit., and in "Recent Progress in American Anthropology," *Amer. Anthr.,* vol. VIII, no. 3, 1906, pp. 441–556.

4. See A. Keith, Presidential Address (Roy. Anthr. Inst.), *Jour. Roy. Anthr. Inst.,* XLVII, 1917, 12–30.

5. L'École d'Anthropologie de Paris, 1876–1906, Paris (F. Alcan), 1907.

6. See F. v. Luschan, Die Konferenz von Monaco, *Korr.-Bl. d. d. Ges. f. Anthr.* etc., Juli, 1906, pp. 53 et seq., in *Archiv. f. Anthr.,* 1906, H. 1–2; and "Entente internationale pour l'unification des mesures craniométriques et céphalométriques," *L'Anthropologie,* 1906, 559–572; ibid., 1912, 623–627; also "The international agreement for the unification of anthropometric measurements," etc., reported by W. L. H. Duckworth, Univ. of Cambridge, 1912, pp. 1–11.

DISCUSSION QUESTIONS

1. Where and when does Hrdlička place the formal beginnings of physical anthropology? Who did Hrdlička see as the founder of physical anthropology?

2. Which fields of study are most similar to physical anthropology? According to Hrdlička, how do the perspectives and emphases of physical anthropology differ from those disciplines?

3. What sort of social circumstances helped to fuel the beginnings of anthropology? What kind of impact did natural history have on the founding of anthropology?

 **INTERNET RESOURCES**

After reading this article, you may wish to do some additional research on the following individuals.

- Paul Broca
- Carolus Linnaeus
- Edward Tyson

You can learn more about the Smithsonian Institution's National Museum of Natural History and anthropology department by visiting their websites at http://www.mnh.si.edu and http://www.anthropology.si.edu.

InfoTrac College Edition

(infotrac-college.com)
You can find many other readings pertinent to this topic by consulting online databases including InfoTrac College Edition. Some suggested search terms for this article are as follows.

- Anthropometry
- Natural history

3

The New Physical Anthropology

SHERWOOD H. WASHBURN

Scientific knowledge changes over time; likewise, fields of study, including physical anthropology, are dynamic as well. New discoveries, technologies, and changes in society as a whole can alter the questions we ask, the methods we use, and the subjects that we study. At times scientists need to fundamentally alter their approach and apply new models to the natural world. Such changes are often referred to as "paradigm shifts."

The following article, written by the late Dr. Sherwood H. Washburn, represented a bold call for a paradigm shift in physical anthropology. Washburn argues that traditional physical anthropology focused too much on the description, measurement, and classification of human variation. In contrast, the "new physical anthropology" should look for the processes responsible for human variation and evolution.

What had happened in just over three decades between the founding of physical anthropology in 1918 and Washburn's classic paper?

Hrdlička and his peers had worked to define physical anthropology as a distinctive science and not just "anatomy for doctors." They accomplished this by focusing on describing, measuring, and classifying human variation. Dr. Earnest A. Hooton, of Harvard University, championed this cause. Hooton trained 28 Ph.D. students—including Sherwood Washburn—by documenting and interpreting variation among both prehistoric skeletons and living peoples. Although his students often found their first academic jobs teaching anatomy, they could explain—in theory—how biological variation relates to an understanding of human evolution.

By 1950, Sherwood Washburn argued that physical anthropologists should move away from their emphases on description and measurement to more problem-based, analytical, and theoretical work. Revolutionary work was taking place in other fields: concepts from genetics and statistics were being used to understand how populations evolve. Washburn believed that studies of primate behavior and comparative anatomy also could help answer questions about human evolution. He and his students subsequently helped shift physical anthropology. He emphasized how skeletal anatomy or "form" reflected its "function," often seeing the latter as evolutionary adaptations. Dr. Washburn's paper, which shifted physical anthropology toward a more problem-oriented approach, continues to influence and inspire physical anthropologists today.

SOURCE: Sherwood H. Washburn, "The New Physical Anthropology," *Transactions of the New York Academy of Sciences*, series II, vol. 13 (1951), 298–304. Reprinted by permission of the New York Academy of Sciences.

Recently, evolutionary studies have been revitalized and revolutionized by an infusion of genetics into paleontology and systematics. The change is fundamentally one of point of view, which is made possible by an understanding of the way the genetic constitution of populations changes. The new systematics is concerned primarily with process and with the mechanism of evolutionary change, whereas the older point of view was chiefly concerned with sorting the results of evolution. Physical anthropology is now undergoing the same sort of change. Population genetics presents the anthropologist with a clearly formulated, experimentally verified, conceptual scheme. The application of this theory to the primates is the immediate task of physical anthropology.

In the past, physical anthropology has been considered primarily as a technique. Training consisted in learning to take carefully defined measurements and in computing indices and statistics. The methods of observation, measurement, and comparison were essentially the same, whether the object of the study was the description of evolution, races, growth, criminals, constitutional types, or army personnel. Measurements were adjusted for various purposes, but measurement of the outside of the body, classification, and correlation remained the anthropologist's primary tools. The techniques of physical anthropology were applied to a limited group of problems, and any definition or statement of traditional anthropology must include both the metrical methods and the problems for which the methods were used. Further, anthropology was characterized by theories, or rather by a group of attitudes and assumptions.

There has been almost no development of theory in physical anthropology itself, but the dominant attitude may be described as static, with emphasis on classification based on types. Any such characterization is oversimplified, and is intended only to give an indication of the dominant techniques, interests, and attitudes of the physical anthropologist. Except for emphasis on particular animals, physical anthropology shared much with the zoology of the times when it developed. Much of the method was developed before the acceptance of the idea of evolution, and all of it before the science of genetics.

Physical anthropology should change, just as systematic zoology has changed. The difficulties which accompany the necessary modifications can be greatly reduced if their nature is clearly understood. Naturally, in a time of rapid flux there will be numerous doubts and disagreements as to what should be done. This is natural, and what I have to offer is a tentative outline to indicate how parts of the new physical anthropology may differ from the old.

The old physical anthropology was primarily a technique. The common core of the science was measurement of external form with calipers. The new physical anthropology is primarily an area of interest, the desire to understand the process of primate evolution and human variation by the most efficient techniques available.

The process of evolution, as understood by the geneticist, is the same for all mammals. The genetic composition of a population may be described in terms of gene frequencies. The modification of these frequencies results in evolution which is caused by selection, mutations, drift, and migrations. Mutations and migrations introduce new genetic elements into the population. But selection on the phenotype, adapting animals to their environment, is the primary cause of alteration in gene frequencies.

This is essentially a return to Darwinism, but with this important difference: Darwin wrote in a pregenetic era. Therefore, he did not understand the mechanism which makes possible the production of variation and the possibility of selection. Since Darwin's ideas could not be proved in detail by the techniques available in his time, the concept of selection did not become fully effective. Therefore, some pre-evolutionary ideas continued in full force. More Linnaean species were described from types after Darwin than before. The idea of evolution created interest in species, but the species were described in pre-evolutionary terms. Further, it is possible for people to hold a variety of theories in place of, or in addition to, Darwin's. For example, Lamarckian ideas have continued right down to today. Orthogenesis has been widely believed and irreversibility has been regarded as a law.

It has been claimed that evolution should be described in terms of nonadaptive traits, yet this is impossible if evolution is largely due to selection. The first great achievement of the synthesis of genetics, paleontology, and systematics is in clearing away a mass of antiquated theories and attitudes which permeate the writings of the older students of evolution. Further, the new evolutionary theory shows which aspects of past work are worth using, extending, and strengthening. This is possible because much of the mechanism of evolutionary change is now understood, clearly formulated, and *experimentally verified*. The logic of Darwin's great theory could only become fully effective when techniques had been developed to prove that selection was right and that other ideas of evolution were wrong. A change in theory, no matter how popular, is not enough. The new ideas must be implemented by effective techniques.

If a new physical anthropology is to differ effectively from the old, it must be more than the adoption of a little genetic terminology. It must change its ways of doing things to conform with the implications of modern evolutionary theory. For example, races must be based on the study of populations. There is no way to justify the division of a breeding population into a series of racial types. It is not enough to state that races should be based on genetic traits; races which can not be reconciled with genetics should be removed from consideration. If we consider the causes of changes in gene frequency as outlined above, and if we are concerned with the process of evolution, the task of the anthropologist becomes clear. He has nothing to offer on mutation, but can make contributions with regard to migration, drift, and selection.

The migrations of man made possible by culture have vastly confused the genetic picture. Before selection can be investigated, it is necessary to know how long a people has been in an area and under what conditions they have been living. For example, the spread of European people, of Bantu speakers, or of Eskimo, all have changed the distribution of the blood groups. The interpretation of the genetic situation demands an understanding of history. Whether people became adapted to cold by selection or by change in their way of life completely alters the interpretation of the distribution of physical traits. This has been widely recognized by anthropologists, and the solution of this difficulty requires the active collaboration of archeologists, ethnologists, linguists, and students of the physical man.

Drift is related to population size, and this depends on the way of life. Again, as in the case of migration, the situation in which drift may have taken place cannot be specified by the physical anthropologist alone, but requires the active collaboration of many specialists. The adoption of modern evolutionary theory will force a far closer and more realistic collaboration between the branches of anthropology than ever before.

Although much of the present distribution of races may be explained by migration and although drift probably accounts for some differences, selection must be the explanation of long-term evolutionary trends and of many patterned variations as well. Anthropologists have always stressed the importance of adaptation in accounting for the differences between apes and men, and sometimes have used the idea in interpreting racial divergences. But suggestions of adaptations are not enough. It is easy to guess that a form is adaptive, but the real problem is to determine the precise nature of a particular adaptation. The work in which I have been interested is designed to demonstrate the relation of form to function. My feeling has been that it is impossible to do more than guess about this matter using traditional anthropological measurements, and that the literature is already too full of uncontrolled speculations. Therefore, I would like to take this opportunity to present an outline, a beginning, of an analysis of the human body into complexes which may vary independently.

In this work, the guiding principle has been that the major force in evolution is selection of functional complexes. A variety of methods has been used to demonstrate the adaptive complexes. The four major methods for factoring complexes out of the body are: (1) comparison and evolution; (2) development; (3) variability; and (4) experiment. All these have been used by numerous investigators, but, to the best of my knowledge, they have not been combined into a working system. All must be used to gain an understanding of the human body.

The major regions of the body seem to have had remarkable independence in recent evolutionary history. The complex to attain its present pattern first is that of the arms and thorax. This complex is associated with arm swinging in the trees, the way of life called "brachiation." It is associat[ed] with a reduction in the deep back muscles and in the number of lumbar vertebrae and consequent shortening of the trunk and elongation of all parts of the upper extremity, adaptation of the joints and muscles to greater pronation, supination in the forearm, and flexion and abduction at the shoulder. Many changes in the positions of the viscera are associated with the shorter trunk. We share this complex with the living gibbons and apes. The bipedal complex was the next to develop and seems to have been fundamentally human in the South African man-apes. The major changes are in the ilium and in the gluteal muscles. Just as in the arm, the change is in a bone-muscle complex, which makes a different way of life possible. The head seems to have attained essentially its present form during the fourth glacial advance, perhaps 50,000 years ago. The brain continued to enlarge until the end of the last interglacial period, and the face decreased in size for some time after that. The great increase in the size of the brain and decrease in the face were after the use of tools.

Evolution, in a sense, has dissected the body for us, and has shown that great changes may occur in arms and trunk, pelvis and legs, and brain case, or face, accompanied by little change in the rest of the body. The first two complexes to change are related to brachiation and bipedal locomotion. The final changes in the head may well be related to changed selection after the use of tools.

To carry the analysis further, it is necessary to deal with one of the areas suggested by this preliminary dividing of the body. Let us consider the face, and especially the lower jaw. The coronoid process varies with the temporal muscle. The angle of the jaw varies with the masseter and internal pterygoid muscle. The tooth-supporting area varies with the teeth. The main core of the jaw is affected by hormones which do not affect the other parts, as

shown in acromegaly. Alizarin dye, which stains the growing bone, reveals the pattern of growth. The split-line technique (Benninghoff) shows the mechanical arrangement.

After making an analysis of this kind, comparisons of a different sort are possible. The simple statement, that a trait is or is not there, is replaced by the attempt to understand under what conditions it might be present. For example, if the simian shelf is developed in monkeys and apes when the jaws are long and the anterior teeth large, then the South African man-apes and other fossil men would not be expected to have such a shelf. The dental characters necessary to bring out the expression of the shelf are absent in all. It can be argued that we have the potential for a simian shelf but that we do not have the necessary tooth and jaw size to make it evident. Trying to understand the process which produces a trait leads to very different evaluations than does a listing of presence or absence.

In the light of this sort of information, let us look at the skull of an Eocene lemur, *Notharctus*. The jaw is long, in conformity with the length of the teeth. It is low, and there is a large angular region. This region has been described as lemuroid. If this angle has remained there for 50 million years, however, over countless generations of lemurs, it must have more of a function than to mark the jaw as primitive or to help us in identifying lemur jaws. If the mandible of a remarkably similar modern [lemur] (genus *Lemur*) is examined, it is found that the internal pterygoid muscle inserts at the end of the angle, but that the masseter muscle inserts only on the lateral side of the ascending ramus, leaving the angle bar of muscle. An internal pterygoid muscle inserting in this position is a protruder of the jaw. The function of the angle of the lemur jaw is to provide insertion for a large, functionally important muscle. The dependence of the angular process on the internal pterygoid and the exact function of the internal pterygoid need to be experimentally verified.

The only point to be stressed now is that the theory that such a process is of adaptive significance, and that it is maintained by selection, leads one to look for a functional complex. If such a process is regarded simply as a taxonomic aid, or as nonfunctional, no guide is available for research or future understanding.

The post-orbital bar of this same lemur again illustrates the advantage of assuming, until it is proved otherwise, that a part is functionally important. Originally, the complete bony ring around the orbit may have been for protection or for some other unknown function. Once the ring is established, however, the skeletal framework for radical modification of the skull is present. The change from the lemur skull, with a wide interorbital region, to the monkey skull, with reduced olfactory mechanism and reduced interorbital space, is mechanically possible because pressure, tension, and buttressing of the sides of the face is provided by the complete rings of bone around the orbits. Structures which probably develop as part of a protective mechanism were preadaptive for a reorganization of the face.

Classic Neanderthal man differs from other fossil men in that the angle of the lower jaw is poorly developed, the part of the malar bone associated with the origin of the largest part of the masseter muscle is small, and the lateral part of the browridge is less sharply demarcated. All these differences may be related, and certainly the association of the small angle and malar suggests that the masseter muscle was small compared to the temporal muscle. Differences of this sort should be described in terms of the variation in the groups being compared. Since similar differences may be found in living men, the development of appropriate quantitative, descriptive methods is merely a matter of time and technique. The procedure is: (1) diagnose the complex; (2) develop methods appropriate to describe variations in it; and (3) try to discover the genetic background of these variations.

So far, we are still engaged in finding the complexes, but even at this level it is possible to make suggestions about fossil men. Probably some Mongoloid groups will have the highest frequency of the big masseter complex, and some of the Negro groups the lowest. This is merely stating some traditional physical anthropology in a somewhat different way by relating statements about the face to those on the lower jaw and relating both to a large and important muscle. It differs from the traditional in the

technique of analysis and avoids speculation of the sort which says that the characteristics of the Mongoloid face are due to adaptation to cold.

In this preliminary analysis of the lower jaw, the attempt has been made to divide a single bone into relatively independent systems and to show that the differences make sense in terms of differing adaptations. Eventually, it may be possible to understand the genetic mechanisms involved. If this type of analysis is at all correct, it is theoretically impossible to make any progress in genetic understanding by taking the traditional measurements on the mandible. They are all complex resultants of the interrelation of two or more of the variables. The measurements average the anatomy in such a way that it is as futile to look for the mode of inheritance of the length of the jaw as it is to look for the genes of the cephalic index.

The implications for anthropology of this type of analysis may be made clearer by some comparisons of the skulls of monkeys. If the skulls of adult male and adult female vervets are compared, many differences may be seen. The male skull is larger in all dimensions, particularly those of the face. If, however, an adult female is compared to a juvenile male with the same cranial capacity and the same weight of temporal muscle, all the differences disappear, except that in the size of the canine tooth. What would appear to be a very large number of unrelated differences, if traditional methods were used, are only aspects of one fundamental difference in the size of the face. If a large-faced monkey is compared with a small-faced one, both of the genus *Cercopithecus,* there appear to be many differences. Yet again, if animals of the same cranial capacity and the same temporal muscle size are compared, almost all the measurements are the same. The species difference is in quantity of face, although this appears in many different forms. If these two skulls were fossil men, differing in the same way, and if they were treated by the usual anthropological methods, they would be found to differ in numerous observations, measurements, and indices. Yet one may be transformed into the other by a simple reduction in mass of face, including teeth, bones, muscles. Perhaps many fossils are far less different than we have supposed. The methods used created the number of differences, just as a metrical treatment of these monkeys would make the adults appear very distinct.

The purpose of this paper has been to call attention to the changes which are taking place in physical anthropology. Under the influence of modern genetic theory, the field is changing from the form it assumed in the latter part of the nineteenth century into a part of modern science. The change is essentially one of emphasis. If traditional physical anthropology was 80 per cent measurement and 20 per cent concerned with heredity, process, and anatomy, in the new physical anthropology the proportions may be approximately reversed. I have stressed the impact of genetics on anthropology, but the process need not be all one way. If the form of the human face can be thoroughly analyzed, this will open the way to understanding its development, the interpretation of abnormalities and mal-

occlusion, and may lead to advances in genetics, anatomy, and medicine. Although evolution is fascinating in itself, the understanding of the functional anatomy which may be gained from it is of more than philosophical importance. The kind of systemic anatomy in which bones, muscles, ligaments, etc., are treated separately became obsolete with the publication of the *Origin of Species* in 1859. The anatomy of life, of integrated function, does not know the artificial boundaries which still govern the dissection of a corpse. The new physical anthropology has much to offer to anyone interested in the structure or evolution of man, but this is only a beginning. To build it, we must collaborate with social scientists, geneticists, anatomists, and paleontologists. We need new ideas, new methods, new workers. There is nothing we do today which will not be done better tomorrow.

DISCUSSION QUESTIONS

1. How would you define the "old," or traditional, physical anthropology? How did Washburn envision the "new" physical anthropology?

2. Discuss some examples where Washburn used "form and function," as well as adaptive complexes. How does this differ from the way traits

were studied in traditional physical anthropology?

3. What were some questions about human evolution that Washburn believed that the "new" physical anthropology" should focus on?

INTERNET RESOURCES

After reading this article, you might wish to investigate the following individuals.

- Earnest Hooton
- Sherwood Washburn

InfoTrac College Edition

(infotrac-college.com)
You can find many other readings pertinent to this topic by consulting online databases including

InfoTrac College Edition. Some suggested search terms for this article are as follows.

- Brachiation
- Population genetics
- Bipedalism

✳

PART II

Evolution and Heredity

4

Patterns

NILES ELDREDGE

In this article, Niles Eldredge, Curator of Paleontology at the American Museum of Natural History, describes his role in planning an exhibit to honor Charles R. Darwin. April 12, 2009, is Darwin's 200th birthday, while the year 2009 marks the 150th anniversary of his monumental work, On the Origin of Species. *As of this writing, events are being planned around the world—including Shrewsbury, Darwin's birthplace in England, and the famous Down House, near London, where Darwin lived with his wife and children, corresponded with fellow scholars, and synthesized the volumes of information he collected during his five years aboard the HMS* Beagle.

On the Origin of Species sold out the very day it became available in 1859, for Darwin had accomplished the unprecedented: he had described an actual mechanism— natural selection—that drives evolutionary change. Natural selection rapidly became the phrase heard 'round the world. Darwin's close friend, scientist Thomas Henry Huxley, remarked, "How terribly stupid not to have thought of that sooner" upon learning how natural selection operates. At the opposite extreme, one proper Victorian lady is said to have exclaimed, "Descended from the apes. . . . Let us hope it is not true; but, if it is, let us pray it does not become generally known!" Such excitement is hardly surprising. Darwin's contributions to science, and the continuing impact of his work in contemporary society, can scarcely be overstated. From the origins of modern Homo sapiens *to the development of resistant strains of tuberculosis, natural selection continues to provide a common denominator for our understanding of evolution.*

In this selection, Eldredge imagines the journey aboard the Beagle *through Darwin's eyes, seeking those observations that convinced him of the reality of evolutionary change. What did Darwin know, and when did he know it? Eldredge argues that Darwin's recognition of patterns is critical to understanding his insights about the natural world. Darwin successfully explained one such pattern in his own lifetime, whereas future generations of scientists accounted for others. As you read this article, try to imagine how Darwin felt while seeing giant tortoises and lizards, climbing to the top of volcanoes, or prying giant fossilized scales out of the ground. What sorts of patterns in nature do such things suggest?*

When I set out to organize the "Darwin" exhibition, as part of the American Museum of Natural History's great scientists series —and as an early start on Darwin's birthday celebration in 2009—I began with a simple question: What exactly did Darwin see on his famous voyage

SOURCE: Niles Eldredge, "Patterns," *Natural History* 114, no. 9 (November 2005): 80–81. Copyright © Natural History Magazine, Inc., 2005.

around the world (1831–36) that led him to his theory of evolution?

The answer to this question is "patterns." Darwin saw patterns in nature that cried out for explanation. In South America, he discovered the bony plates of glyptodonts—creatures reminiscent of armadillos, but much larger—and (at a separate site) the fossil bones of giant ground sloths. South America was also home to living species of armadillos and sloths. Why would fossil remains and modern species found on the same continent resemble each other?

His second observation was the pattern of distribution of some living species in South America. He saw the common rhea—an ostrichlike bird—living in Argentina. Then he found a smaller Argentinean species living farther south, its range just barely overlapping that of the larger bird. Why do those flightless birds, unique to South America, seem to replace each other in adjoining regions?

A third pattern Darwin noted was that distinct forms of otherwise similar animals occur on the various islands of the Galapagos archipelago. He observed several unique species of mockingbirds on the islands, and surmised that they must all be related to the mockingbirds of mainland South America, 600 ocean miles away. (He noted the pattern of the famous finches only after he returned to London and an ornithologist called it to his attention.) Darwin also learned that locals could tell from which islands giant tortoises had come by the shapes of the reptiles' shells. While still aboard the *Beagle,* he speculated about whether similar patterns of distribution might hold in other island groups. If so, he noted, it would tend to "undermine the stability of Species"—the earliest hint of the idea of evolution in his writings.

I believe that by the time he returned to England, Darwin had become a confirmed evolutionist. He was now speculating not about whether species had evolved, but how. Departing from his plan to compile additional examples of his original three patterns, he looked for other patterns that would make sense if evolution was true.

Darwin reexamined one pattern that was well known to the naturalists of his day: the Linnaean system for classifying plants and animals, in which sets of species are nested within ever-larger groupings. In his Notebook B, Darwin sketched out a branching tree of species . . . adding in a note that the nearest branches (closest relatives) would resemble each other more closely than they would their remote relatives. Darwin realized that Linnaeus's hierarchical system could be viewed not merely as groupings of similar types, but as patterns of evolutionary relationships and descent.

Of the three patterns he observed during his *Beagle* voyage, Darwin arrived at a fully satisfactory explanation for one: the Galapagos birds and tortoises evolved according to local conditions when they were isolated for long periods on the islands of the archipelago. But he had difficulty imagining how isolation could operate on vast open stretches of continents. His attempt to explain divergence by natural selection in the case of such species as the two rheas was intriguing but incomplete. Evolutionary biologists now understand that past climatic and geologic changes have often created barriers that split up populations. When those physical obstacles later disappear, the two related species may once more share the same ranges. As for South America's extinct and living sloths and armadillos, Darwin correctly concluded that they were related, but was uncomfortable with the fossil evidence, which did not fit his view of gradual evolution through natural selection.

Darwin's theory has itself evolved over the years. Yet it is worth recalling that modern evolutionary biology was founded when a young naturalist—a creationist at the time—was struck by three puzzling patterns in nature. To him, the patterns all pointed toward a single, great truth. "I cannot possibly believe," Darwin wrote in 1859, "that a false theory would explain so many classes of facts."

DISCUSSION QUESTIONS

1. What do scientists mean by "patterns" and why are patterns significant in scientific inquiry? (See also the discussion of patterns in Eugenie Scott's article.)

2. Review the categories of the Linnaean system of classification as they relate to humans. How would Linneaus explain the basis for these groupings? What alternative explanation does Darwinian evolution offer for the inherent patterns in nature?

3. Why was Darwin able to explain only one of the three patterns that Eldredge discusses?

 **INTERNET RESOURCES**

You can learn more about the events surrounding the anniversary of Darwin's birthday and the publication of *On the Origin of Species* by visiting http://darwin-online.org.uk and http://www.darwin200.org.

 **InfoTrac College Edition**

(infotrac-college.com)
You can find many other readings pertinent to this topic by consulting online databases including InfoTrac College Edition. Some suggested search terms for this article are as follows.

- Paleontology
- Natural selection
- Linnaean system of classification

5

The Fossils Say Yes

DONALD R. PROTHERO

Discoveries of fossils are often announced with much fanfare. You may have heard about some ancient species through television news or a feature documentary. Perhaps intriguing headlines or a colorful photograph caught your eye. The phrases "transitional form" or "missing link"—when used in connection with new fossil finds—tend to garner even more attention, attracting reporters like paparazzi to rock stars. Both descriptors refer to the place of a fossil on a hypothetical evolutionary tree, or phylogeny. When a fossil is said to be "transitional" this means that it bridges a gap between its evolutionary ancestors and descendants by possessing characteristics of both groups. Transitional forms are especially useful for learning about large-scale, or macroevolutionary, trends, such as the origins of the earliest birds, mammals, or primates.

In this selection, paleontologist Donald R. Prothero introduces us to some noteworthy transitional forms. As you read through the article, don't be intimidated by (or try to memorize) all of the long names of fossils. Instead, think about what particular transitional forms have taught us about the evolution of life.

It is also important to compare our understanding of the fossil record today to that of Charles Darwin's time. Darwin clearly understood the significance of fossils. He uncovered mineralized outer plates of glyptodonts and noted their resemblance to contemporary armadillos. He predicted that the fossilized remains of other ancient species would be forthcoming. Indeed, his idea that evolutionary change was slow, gradual, and continual predicted that there would be fossils linked to one another over time through "numerous gradations."

Contemporary creationists often argue that the "gaps" in the fossil record support their religious beliefs about the development of life. Prothero convincingly dispenses with these arguments. Through reading this selection, you'll learn more about the relationships between birds and dinosaurs and the terrestrial origins of aquatic mammals (like whales), as well as the evolutionary beginnings of amphibians, mammals, and even Homo sapiens.

> It has been asserted over and over again, by writers who believe in the immutability of species, that geology yields no linking forms. This assertion . . . is certainly erroneous. . . . What geological research has not revealed, is the former existence of infinitely numerous gradations . . . connecting together nearly all existing and extinct species.
>
> —CHARLES DARWIN, THE *ORIGIN OF SPECIES*

SOURCE: Donald R. Prothero, "The Fossils Say Yes," *Natural History* 114, no. 9 (November 2005): 52–56.

When Darwin first proposed the idea of evolution by natural selection in 1859, the fossil record offered little support for his ideas. Darwin even devoted two entire chapters of the *Origin of Species* to the imperfection of the geologic record, because he was well aware it was one of the weakest links in his arguments. Then, just two years after his book was published, the first specimen of Archaeopteryx was discovered, hailed by many as the "missing link" between birds and reptiles. By the late nineteenth century, fossils helped demonstrate how the modern thoroughbred horse evolved from a dog-size, three-toed creature with low-crowned teeth. (The understanding of those fossils has since been much refined.)

Fossil evidence supporting evolution has continued to mount, particularly in the past few decades. DNA analysis, moreover, has helped make sense of how the evidence fits together in the family tree of life on Earth. Unfortunately, many people still think, quite erroneously, that the fossil record shows no "transitional forms." In large part, that misconception is the product of the campaign of misinformation—or disinformation—spread by the creationist movement.

The fossil record is far from perfect, of course. By most estimates, less than 1 percent of all the species that have ever lived are preserved as fossils. The reason for the scarcity is simply that the physical conditions needed to turn a dead organism into a fossil lasting millions of years are unusual.

Nevertheless, there are numerous excellent specimens that reflect transitional stages between major groups of organisms. Many more fossils exhibit how "infinitely numerous gradations" connect the species. The one caveat is that when a sequence of fossils appears to follow a direct line of descent, the chances are slim that they actually bear such precise interrelations. Paleontologists recognize that when one fossil looks ancestral to another, the first fossil is more safely described as being closely related to the actual ancestor.

The classic story of the evolution of the horse is a good example. The various known fossils were once arranged—simplistically, it turns out—into a single lineage leading from "*Eohippus*" to *Equus*.

When more fossils became available, paleontologists revised that simple lineage. The fossils now give a branching and very bushy picture of equine evolution, with numerous now-extinct lineages living side by side. One quarry in Nebraska has yielded a dozen distinct species of fossil horses, in rock about 12 million years old. The earliest horses, such as *Protorohippus* (from early in the Eocene epoch, about 53 million years ago), are virtually indistinguishable from *Homogalax*, the earliest member of the lineage, which also gave rise to tapirs and rhinoceroses. Very early in my career, when I was taking an undergraduate paleontology class, I discovered just how tough it is to sort out those two ancient genera.

Perhaps the most remarkable recent discoveries are the numerous fossils that connect whales with their four-legged terrestrial ancestors. If you look at dolphins, orcas, and blue whales, all fully aquatic animals, you would have a hard time imagining them walking on land. Yet even living whales retain vestiges of their hips and thighbones, deeply buried in the muscles along their spines. Paleontologists have known for a long time, on the basis of detailed features of the skull and teeth, that whales are closely related to hoofed mammals. But creationists long touted the absence of transitional fossils for whales as evidence against evolution.

The balance has now changed. In 1983 specimens of *Pakicetus* were discovered in Pakistan in early Eocene beds about 52 million years old. Although the body of *Pakicetus* was primarily terrestrial, it had the skull and teeth of the ancient archaeocetes, the earliest family of whales—which swam the world's oceans in the Middle Eocene epoch, about 50 million years ago.

Then, in 1994, *Ambulocetus natans* (literally, the "walking whale that swims") was discovered, also in Pakistan. . . . The animal was the size of a large sea lion, with broad webbed feet on both fore- and hind limbs, so it could both walk and swim. Yet it still had tiny hooves on its toes and the primitive skull and teeth of the archaeocete. *Ambulocetus* apparently swam much like an otter, with an up-and-down motion of the spine, the precursor to the motion of the flukes of a whale's tail. In 1995 yet a third transitional creature was discovered, *Dalanistes,* with shorter legs than *Ambulocetus,* webbed feet, a longer tail, and a much larger and more whalelike skull.

Today more than a dozen transitional whale fossils have been unearthed—an excellent series for such rarely fossilized animals. DNA from the living species suggests that whales are descended from even-toed hoofed mammals known as artiodactyls and, in particular, are most closely related to the hippopotamus. That hypothesis was dramatically confirmed by the discoveries in 2001 of the "double-pulley" anklebone, which is characteristic of artiodactyls, in two kinds of primitive whales.

Whales are not the only aquatic mammals with terrestrial ancestors. Modern sirenians (manatees and dugongs) are large, docile, aquatic herbivores that have flippers for forelimbs and no hind limbs. In 2001 Daryl Domning, a marine mammal paleontologist at Howard University in Washington, D.C., described a remarkably complete skeleton of *Pezosiren portelli* from Jamaican deposits about 50 million years old. That animal had the typical skull and teeth of a sirenian, and even the thick sirenian ribs made of dense bone, which serve as ballast. Yet it had four legs as well, all with feet, not flippers. Strong transitional fossils also link seals and sea lions to bearlike ancestors.

The origin of mammals is well documented. Mammals and their extinct relatives belong to a larger group known as the Synapsida. The earliest members of the group were once known as "mammal-like reptiles," even though they were not true reptiles but had already evolved to become a separate branch of animals. Among them was *Dimetrodon,* the largest predator on Earth about 280 million years ago. (Its sail-shaped back is familiar from toy-dinosaur kits for children, even though it was not a true dinosaur.) Although it was a primitive form, *Dimetrodon* had large, stabbing canine teeth and some of the specialized skull features of mammals.

For the next 80 million years, synapsids evolved into various wolflike and bearlike predators, as well as into an array of peculiar piglike herbivores. Along the way, they acquired progressively more mammalian features: additional jaw muscles

that enabled complex chewing motions; a secondary palate covering the old reptilian palate and nasal region, which enabled them to breathe and eat at the same time; multicusped molars for chewing rather than gulping their food; enlarged brains; relatively upright (rather than sprawling) posture; and a muscular diaphragm in the rib cage for efficient breathing. There are even signs that they had hair, a quintessentially mammalian feature. The story of the synapsids culminates in the appearance of the earliest true mammals—shrew-size creatures—in fossil beds about 200 million years old in China, South Africa, and Texas.

Among the most remarkable transformations that took place as the mammals emerged are the ones that can be observed in fossils of the lower jaws. In reptiles and primitive synapsids, the right and left lower jaws are each made up of a number of bones, one of which is the dentary, or tooth-bearing, bone. As synapsids evolved, the dentary bone grew progressively larger until it took over the role of hinging the jaw to the skull. One of the other reptilian jawbones shrank until it vanished, whereas the other two shifted to the middle ear. There they became the anvil and the hammer, minute bones that transmit sound from the eardrum to the stirrup bone and, ultimately, to the inner ear. The shift in function seems bizarre until you realize that in reptiles, sound vibrations from the lower jaw travel through the skull bones to the inner ear, and that, along with the vibrations that travel from the eardrum, those vibrations are important sources of sensation.

Excellent "missing links" now exist for other major groups as well. Many fossil species show the transition from dinosaurs to birds. *Archaeopteryx,* for instance, discovered in Europe in Late Jurassic fossil beds about 150 million years old, had teeth. Slightly younger fossils, from the Chinese Lower Cretaceous, about 140 million years ago, had more birdlike features. *Sinornis,* for instance, had wings it could fold against its body, grasping feet with an opposable toe, and tailbones fused into a single element. *Confuciusornis* sported the first toothless beak. Lower Cretaceous rocks in Spain, about 130 million years old, have yielded *Iberomesornis,* which had a large, keeled breastbone to which powerful flight muscles were anchored. Still, the creature had the primitive long backbone of a dinosaur.

Such bird fossils are now joined in the web of ancient life-forms by numerous, recently discovered fossils of nonflying, nonavian dinosaurs, closely related to *Velociraptor* of Jurassic Park fame. Those fossils, such as *Microraptor* and *Caudipteryx,* had well-developed feathers, suggesting that feathers originally served other functions, such as insulation, long before they became useful for flight. . . .

Another transition that is now well documented is the conquest of the land by the amphibians. For decades the only good intermediate fossil between fishes and amphibians was *Ichthyostega,* from the Late Devonian epoch (about 360 million years ago) of Greenland and Spitzbergen. Although *Ichthyostega* resembled many amphibians in having well-developed legs, a complete shoulder girdle, and hips fused to the backbone, it still had fishlike gill slits, a sensory system on its face for detecting underwater currents, and a long, fishlike tail fin.

More recent discoveries, such as *Acanthostega* from the same beds, show that the picture is much more complicated and interesting. . . . *Acanthostega* had ear bones that were still adapted for underwater hearing, a longer tail fin than *Ichthyostega,* and better-developed gills, making it more primitive and aquatic than *Ichthyostega*. *Acanthostega* also had as many as eight toes on each of its four feet—rather than five, which became the standard in most early four-footed creatures. Apparently, its limbs were primarily adapted for swimming and walking along the bottom of a lake, rather than for crawling on land. Contrary to the popular story that four legs evolved because they enabled animals to crawl out onto the land (to escape drying ponds, chase new food sources, and so forth), it now appears that legs evolved for walking underwater (as most salamanders still do today). They became secondarily useful on land, because they were already in place.

What about the transitional forms that led to our favorite species, *Homo sapiens?* Not long ago, the fossil record of the human family was severely limited, and readily thrown into confusion by a single fraudulent "fossil" such as the 1912 hoax known as Piltdown Man. But in the past three decades new findings have exploded. In Chad, fossils of *Sahelanthropus* were discovered in beds between 6 million and 7 million years old. In Ethiopia, the new genus *Ardipithecus* and two new species of *Australopithecus* (*A. anamensis* and *A. bahrelghazali*) were unearthed in beds between 2 million and 5 million years old. Several species of our own genus, *Homo,* which goes back at least 2 million years, have now been identified.

In short, the human fossil record has become quite dense and complete, and the newfound samples have led to some surprises. For example, contrary to the expectations of earlier anthropologists, the fossils show that bipedalism arose before enlarged brains, which came quite late in human evolution.

The origin of vertebrates as a whole once also presented a frustrating gap in the fossil record. Biologists could examine the many living animals (such as lancelets and sea squirts) that represented stages in the transition from the invertebrates to the earliest jawless fishes. Until recently, however, few good fossils had been identified from beds older than about 480 million years, near the beginning of the Ordovician period. What's more, they were only scattered bony scales and plates.

But recent discoveries in China from the Middle Cambrian epoch, between 510 million and 500 million years ago, have included not only the earliest relatives of the lancelets, but also some soft-bodied specimens that appear to be the earliest vertebrates. Thus, backboned animals can now be traced all the way back to the Cambrian, when most of the modern branches of animals originated.

As the 150th anniversary of Darwin's *Origin* approaches, the fossil evidence now available would make Darwin proud, rather than apologetic. Evolutionary biologists can also look forward to many more discoveries. Some will come as a surprise, like the early small-brained bipedal hominids. Some will force paleontologists to revise their ideas about evolutionary events. But the fossil record is no longer the embarrassment that it was in Darwin's day.

DISCUSSION QUESTIONS

1. If you are interested in human evolution, is it important to study the evolution of other species? How might the investigation of other mammals, such as horses and whales, or the evolution of other taxonomic groups (such as birds and fishes), help us learn more about evolutionary principles and processes? Provide examples to illustrate your answer.

2. After reading this article, how would you define the term "transitional form?" What characteristics make a fossil "transitional"? What are some examples of transitional forms and why are they important?

3. What do evolutionists mean by "adaptation"? How can transitional forms contribute to our understanding of adaptation?

 **INTERNET RESOURCES**

After reading this article, you might wish to do further research on the following individuals.

- Donald R. Prothero
- Ernst Mayr

InfoTrac College Edition

(infotrac-college.com)
You can find many other readings pertinent to this topic by consulting online databases including

InfoTrac College Edition. Some suggested search terms for this article are as follows.

- Synapsida
- Eocene epoch
- Eohippus

6

The Origins of Form

SEAN B. CARROLL

As we celebrate Charles Darwin's 200th birthday—and the 150th anniversary of On the Origin of Species—*it is good to take stock of just how much we've learned about evolutionary change since Darwin's extraordinary life and work. When one looks not only at the innumerable fossils that have been discovered but also at the contributions of developmental biology and genetics, it is nothing short of amazing. As biologist Sean Carroll explains in this selection, scientists now have identified specific genes that played crucial roles in the evolution of life, including complex anatomical structures.*

Carroll introduces us to "evo-devo," or evolutionary developmental biology, a field that synthesizes molecular genetics, paleontology, evolutionary theory, and developmental biology. The roots of evo-devo trace back to Darwin, for he recognized that embryos of entirely different organisms may be quite similar, or share the same structures, at certain stages of development. Darwin argued that embryonic development somehow reflected evolutionary kinship.

The contemporary field of evo-devo helps us understand the basis for Darwin's observation. It turns out that widely different organisms share a set of genes—what Carroll calls a common "body-building" and "organ-forming tool kit"—that account for anatomical similarities. Alterations in these genes, over the expanse of evolutionary time, can rearrange or renumber the bones of the skeleton or reshape the intricacies of a complex structure, like the eye.

Carroll points out that an earlier synthesis of genetics and evolutionary theory (the "modern synthesis") helped us understand microevolution, or small-scale evolutionary changes. In this selection, you'll see how evo-devo helps explain macroevolution, which refers to more monumental changes over time. Be sure to note the particular importance of Hox genes and the PAX6 genes and their roles in both development and evolution.

> When we no longer look at an organic being as a savage looks at a ship, as at something wholly beyond his comprehension; when we regard every production of nature as one which has had a history; when we contemplate every complex structure and instinct as the summing up of many contrivances, each useful to the possessor . . . how far more interesting, I speak from experience, will the study of natural history become!
>
> —CHARLES DARWIN, THE *ORIGIN OF SPECIES,* 1859

SOURCE: Sean B. Carroll, "The Origins of Form," *Natural History* 114, no. 9 (November 2005): 58–64.

Darwin closed the most important book in the history of biology by inspiring his readers to see the grandeur in his new vision of nature—in how "from so simple a beginning endless forms most beautiful and most wonderful have been, and are being, evolved." For the next century, many kinds of biologists—geneticists, paleontologists, taxonomists—sought to test and expand that vision. The result of their work was the so-called modern synthesis, which organized the basic principles that have guided evolutionary biology for the past fifty years.

In spite of the labels "modern" and "synthesis," however, an important element was still missing from evolutionary theory. Biologists could say, with confidence, that forms change, and that natural selection is an important force for change. Yet they could say nothing about how that change is accomplished. How bodies or body parts change, or how new structures arise, remained complete mysteries.

Contemporary biologists are no longer savages staring at passing ships. In the past twenty years biologists have gained a revolutionary new understanding of how animal and plant forms and their complex structures arise and evolve. The key to the new understanding is development, the way a single cell becomes a complex, multibillion- or trillion-celled organism. And development is intimately linked to evolution, because all changes in form come about through changes in development. As an animal embryo grows, it must make countless "decisions" about the number, position, size, and color patterns of body parts. The endless combinations of such decisions made during development have led to the great variety of animal forms of the past and present.

Advances in the new science of evolutionary developmental biology—dubbed "evo-devo" for short—have enabled biologists to see beyond the external beauty of organic forms into the mechanisms that shape their diversity. Much of what has been learned, about animal forms in particular, has been so stunning and unexpected that it has profoundly expanded and reshaped the picture of how evolution works. In the same stroke, evo-devo delivers some crushing blows against the outdated rhetoric of those who doubt that complex structures and organisms arise through natural selection.

Darwin always insisted that embryology was crucial to understanding evolution. In a letter to the American botanist Asa Gray, shortly after the publication of the *Origin of Species,* he lamented, "Embryology is to me by far the strongest single class of facts in favor of change of forms, and not one, I think, of my reviewers has alluded to this." Yet the puzzle of how a single egg gives rise to a complete individual long stood as one of the most elusive questions in all of biology.

Many biologists once despaired that development was hopelessly complex. Each kind of animal, they thought, would require its own unique developmental explanation. With the advent of genetics, biologists came to realize that genes must be at the center of the mysteries of both development and evolution. After all, butterflies look like butterflies, elephants look like elephants, and we look the way we do because of the genes we each carry. Those physical resemblances, and many other attributes, would surely be traceable to the genes within each species.

The challenge, given such a focus on genes, was that until relatively recently no one knew which of the thousands of genes in every animal shape its formation and appearance. The impasse was finally broken by the humble fruit fly. Geneticists devised schemes to find the relatively small fraction of genes that control the patterning of the fly's body and the formation of its parts.

Just as the invention of the telescope revolutionized astronomy, new technologies were pivotal to conceptual breakthroughs in developmental biology. New techniques for cloning and manipulating genes, together with new kinds of microscopes, enabled the body-building genes to be observed in action. Chemical changes in an embryo could be visualized long before the appearance of physical structures. Workers could thereby directly observe the earliest events in the formation of segments, limbs, or a brain. . . .

I realize it may be hard to get excited about how a maggot develops. What can that teach us about the more majestic creatures people care about, such as mammals, the rest of the animal kingdom, our own species? Indeed, the common perception twenty years ago—reinforced by a wide cultural divide between biologists who worked with furry animals and those who worked with bugs or worms—was that the rules of development would differ enormously among such different forms.

The body parts of fruit flies, for instance, would not appear to have much in common with our own. We don't have antennae or wings. We walk around on two long, bony legs, not six little ones reinforced by an exoskeleton. We have a single pair of movable, camera-type eyes, not compound bug eyes staring out from a fixed position. Our blood is pumped by a four-chambered heart through a closed circulatory system with arteries and veins; it does not just slosh around in our body cavity. Given such great differences in structure and appearance, one might well conclude that there is nothing to learn from the study of a fly about how our own organs and body parts are formed. But that would be so wrong.

The first and perhaps most important lesson from evo-devo is that looks can be quite deceiving. Virtually no biologist expected to find what turned out to be the case: most of the genes first identified as body-building and organ-forming genes in the fruit fly have exact counterparts, performing similar jobs, in most mammals, including humans. The very first shots fired in the evo-devo revolution revealed that despite their great differences in appearance, almost all animals share a common "tool kit" of body-building genes. That discovery—actually a series of discoveries—vaporized many previous ideas about how animals differ from one another.

For example, the origin of eyes has received a lot of attention throughout the history of evolutionary biology. Darwin devoted considerable effort in *Origin* to explaining how such "organs of extreme perfection" could evolve by natural selection. What has puzzled and intrigued biologists ever since Darwin is the variety of eye types in the animal kingdom. We and other vertebrates have camera-type eyes with a single lens. Flies, crabs, and other arthropods have compound eyes in which many, sometimes hundreds, of individual ommatidia, or unit eyes, gather visual information. Even though they are not close relatives of ours, squids and octopuses also have camera-type eyes, whereas their own close relatives, the clams and the scallops, have three kinds of eyes—camera, compound, and a mirror-type.

The great diversity and crazy-quilt distribution of eyes throughout the animal kingdom was, for more than a century, thought to be the result of the independent invention of eyes in various animal groups. The late evolutionary biologist Ernst Mayr and his colleague L. von Salvini-Plawen suggested, on the basis of cellular anatomy, that eyes had been invented independently between some forty and sixty-five times. Discoveries in evo-devo have forced a thorough reexamination of this accepted idea.

In 1994 Walter Gehring and his colleagues at the University of Basel, Switzerland, discovered that a gene required for eye formation in fruit flies is the exact counterpart of a gene required for eye formation in humans and mice. The gene, dubbed *Pax-6,* was subsequently found to play a role in eye formation in a host of other animals, including a species of squid. . . . Those discoveries suggested that despite their vast differences in structure and optical properties, the evolution of different eyes has involved a common genetic ingredient.

Ernst Mayr once wrote:

If there is only one efficient solution for a certain functional demand, very different gene complexes will come up with the same solution, no matter how different the pathway by which it is achieved. The saying "Many roads lead to Rome" is as true in evolution as in daily affairs.

But Mayr's view is incorrect. The architects of the modern synthesis expected the genomes of vastly different species to differ vastly. They had no idea that such different forms could be built with similar sets of genes. Stephen Jay Gould, in his monumental work, *The Structure of Evolutionary Theory,* saw the unexpected discovery of common body-building genes as overturning a major tenet of the modern synthesis.

There are not as many roads to Rome—or in other words, evolutionary paths to eyes and other complex structures—as biologists once thought. Natural selection has not repeatedly forged eyes from scratch. Rather, eye formation has common genetic ingredients, and a wide range of eye types incorporate parts, such as photoreceptor cells and light-sensing proteins, that have long been under the command of the *Pax-6* gene.

Other tool-kit genes have been identified that take part in building various kinds of limbs, hearts, and other structures. Because parts of the genetic tool kit are shared among most branches of the animal kingdom, they must date back, at least, to some common ancestor of those branches. That would place their origin far back in time, before the Cambrian explosion that marked the emergence of large, complex animal bodies, more than 500 million years ago.

Here, then, is another somewhat counterintuitive insight from evo-devo: One might think that increases in animal complexity and diversity would be driven by the evolution of new genes. But it is now clear that most body-building genes were in place long before most kinds of animal body plans and complex organs emerged.

The discovery of such an ancient genetic tool kit, as exciting and rewarding as it is, raises a conundrum. If the sets of body-building genes among animals are so similar, how do such vast differences in forms arise?

Studies of many animal groups have shown that the diversity arises not so much from the content of the tool kit, but from how it is used. Various animal architectures are the products of applying the same genetic tools in different ways. For example, one of the most obvious features of large, complex animals such as vertebrates (fishes, amphibians, reptiles, birds, mammals) and arthropods (centipedes, spiders, crustaceans, insects) is their construction from repeating parts. Segments are the building blocks of arthropod bodies, vertebrae the building blocks of backbones. In both cases, important structures

emerge from subsets of these building blocks—the many appendages of arthropods from their segments, the ribs of vertebrates from the vertebrae.

One of the dominant themes in the large-scale evolution of these animal bodies is change in the number and kind of repeating parts. The major features that distinguish classes of arthropods are the number of segments and the number and kind of appendages. Similarly, vertebrates differ fundamentally in the number and kind of vertebrae (cervical, thoracic, lumbar, sacral).

Extensive study of arthropod and vertebrate development has shown that those major features depend on a set of tool-kit genes called Hox genes. In general, Hox genes shape the number and appearance of repeated structures along the main body axes of both groups of animals. Individual Hox genes govern the identity of particular zones along that main body axis, and determine where various structures will form. A large body of work—on birds, frogs, mammals, and snakes, as well as insects, shrimp, and spiders—has proved that shifts in where Hox genes are expressed in embryos are responsible for the major differences among both vertebrates and arthropods.

Those shifts account, for instance, for the way a snake forms its unique long body, with hundreds of rib-bearing vertebrae and essentially no neck, in contrast to other vertebrates. . . . The shifts explain why insects have just six legs and other arthropods have eight or more. The new imagery of evo-devo can pinpoint when and how the development of these animals diverges. The study of Hox genes has shown how, at an entirely new and fundamental level, these animals are the products of variations on ancient body plans—not wholly independent inventions.

Shifts in the expression of tool-kit genes during development not only account for large-scale differences in animal forms; they can also explain differences among closely related species, or even populations of the same species. For example, the three-spined stickleback fish occurs in two forms in many lakes in northern North America. . . . One is a short-spined, shallow-water, bottom-dwelling form. The other is long-spined and lives in open water. The two forms have evolved rapidly in these lakes since the end of the last ice age, about 10,000 years ago. The length of the fishes' pelvic spine is under pressure from predation. In the open water, long spines help protect the stickleback from being swallowed by large predators. But on the lake bottom, long pelvic spines are a liability: dragonfly larvae seize and feed on young sticklebacks by grabbing them by their spines.

Pelvic spines are part of the fishes' pelvic fin skeleton. Short spines in bottom-dwelling populations can be traced to a reduction in the development of the pelvic-fin bud in the embryo. David Kingsley, a geneticist at Stanford University, Dolph Schluter, a biologist at the University of British Columbia in Vancouver, and their collaborators have demonstrated that the change in spine length in short-spined sticklebacks can be traced to one specific tool-kit gene. The expression of the gene is altered so as to reduce the pelvic fin bud and, ultimately, the pelvic skeleton. The research has connected a change in DNA to a specific event in embryonic development, which in turn gives rise to a major adaptive change in body form that directly affects the ecology of a species.

The insights from the little three-spined stickleback may reach far beyond the fish's particular natural history. The pelvic fin is the evolutionary precursor of the vertebrate hind limb. Hind-limb reduction is not at all rare in vertebrates. In two groups of mammals—the cetaceans (dolphins and whales) and the manatees—the hind limbs became greatly reduced in size as the animals evolved from their land-dwelling ancestors into fully aquatic forms. Similarly, legless lizards have evolved many times. The study of sticklebacks has shown how natural selection can lead to changes in major features of animal skeletons in a relatively short time.

In addition to showing how evolution can change the number and kind of repeated body structures, evo-devo is shedding light on how novel structures and new patterns evolve. Bird feathers, for instance, are prominent examples of novelties that have emerged from changes in the ways tool-kit genes are expressed. So are the hands and feet of four-legged vertebrates, the insect wing, and the geometric color patterns on the wings of butterflies. It is easy to imagine that insects invented "wing" genes, or birds "feather" genes, or vertebrates "hand" and "finger" genes. But there is no evidence that such genes ever arose. On the contrary, innovation seems to be more a matter of teaching old genes new tricks.

The implications of that insight are particularly significant for understanding human evolution. We humans have long supposed that we hold some unique position in the animal kingdom. Surely we must be the most genetically well-endowed species. Yet the reality, as molecular biologists now know from sequencing the genomes of our own and other species, is that the genes of human beings are very similar in number and kind to the genes of the chimpanzee and of the mouse—in fact, of all other vertebrates. No one should expect to account for the evolution of bipedalism, language, speech, or other human traits by finding novel genes. A more likely explanation will come from understanding how our "old" genes, shared with other primates, mammals, vertebrates, and more distant animal relatives, have found new applications.

Darwin knew very well the difficulty people would have in picturing how complex structures or "contrivances" arose. In fact, as scholars such as the late Stephen Jay Gould and Randy Moore, a biologist at the University of Minnesota in Minneapolis, have pointed out, Darwin's choice of the term "contrivances," which appears fifteen times in *Origin,* was a deliberate one, used for rhetorical effect. It evoked a term the Reverend William Paley used in his 1802 book, *Natural Theology.* Paley saw the fashioning of "contrivances" in nature for specific purposes as revelations of God's design:

> Contrivance must have had a contriver;
> design, a designer. . . . It is only by the
> display of contrivance, that the existence,
> the agency, the wisdom of the Deity,
> could be testified to his rational creatures.

Paley's argument is the essence of the idea of "intelligent design," now being touted as a new "alternative" to evolutionary science. Darwin admired Paley's book, and declared that he had virtually committed parts of it to memory. He then structured much of his argument in *Origin* as a direct refutation of Paley. Where Paley compared the design of the eye with the design of the telescope, Darwin explained how such contrivances arose by natural selection, without the intervention of a divine contriver.

But Darwin's explanation, no matter how brilliant, was founded on the extrapolation of natural selection over vast periods of time. He had no access to fundamental knowledge about the development of eyes or their detailed evolutionary history. The new knowledge of tool-kit genes makes it clear how such complex structures are built. Evo-devo makes it possible to connect this everyday, observable, and experimentally accessible process to the long-term process of evolutionary change. Evo-devo shows how complex forms and structures evolve, not only in ways that lead from one species to the next, but also in ways, such as the making of body plans, that have shaped the major differences in the higher taxonomic ranks.

The major tenet of the modern evolutionary synthesis is that the evolution of forms above the species level ("macroevolution") can be extrapolated from processes operating at the level of populations, within species ("microevolution"). For those who have doubted that the modern evolutionary synthesis could explain macroevolution, the new insights from evo-devo should resolve the question. Through the lens of evolutionary developmental biology, biologists can finally see beyond external forms into the very processes that forge them, completing the picture of how the endless forms of nature have been, and are being, evolved.

DISCUSSION QUESTIONS

1. Explain the basic principles of evolutionary developmental biology (evo-devo). How does this field contribute to our understanding of the evolution of complex structures in diverse animal and plant forms?

2. How do new findings from evo-devo differ from what the authors of the modern synthesis, like Ernst Mayr, envisioned about evolutionary processes? How have discoveries relating to developmental genes and genetic mechanisms shed light on these evolutionary processes?

3. You are discussing evolutionary change with a friend who tells you that the human eye is so complex a structure that it simply couldn't have arisen through evolutionary change. Your friend believes that the design of the eye implies the existence of a divine creator. Using information about evo-devo, what arguments could you offer that contradict your friend's position?

INTERNET RESOURCES

This reading mentions the work and writings of other individuals whom you might wish to learn more about, including:

- Stephen Jay Gould
- Ernst Mayr
- Charles Darwin

InfoTrac College Edition

(infotrac-college.com)
You can find many other readings pertinent to this topic by consulting online databases including InfoTrac College Edition. Some suggested search terms for this article are as follows.

- Macroevolution
- Hox genes
- Intelligent design

7

Evolution in Action

JONATHAN WEINER

It's not uncommon for an introductory student to ask, "If natural selection occurred, why isn't it still happening?" You may have thought this to yourself. The problem, though, is not with natural selection. Rather, the question starts from an incorrect premise. It turns out that natural selection is happening. *Just as it operated in the past, it is occurring right now—in some cases, quite rapidly—as you read the words on this page. Remember, if certain conditions exist, natural selection has to happen. It is inevitable. Of course—short of cartoons or the movies—we can't watch a reptilian-looking bird morph into a pileated woodpecker or a fish crawl up onto a sandy beach. Numerous lines of evidence—many presented in this reader—demonstrate evolution's occurrence in the past. How, then, do we see the evolution in the contemporary world?*

In this selection science writer Jonathan Weiner takes us to both remote locations and familiar settings to demonstrate the reality of evolutionary change in everyday life. He travels to a desert island in the Galápagos Islands where biologists Peter and Rosemary Grant are documenting natural selection among finch populations. They have determined that natural selection can take place quite rapidly, responding to environmental fluctuations. Most remarkably, they've been able to bring bench science outdoors to study the genes underlying beak shape and size. Pay particular attention to what they have accomplished with respect to BMP4, or bone morphogenic protein. If Darwin were alive today, he'd be able to follow natural selection in action—from gene, to protein, to trait, to change over time.

Weiner also asks us to think about the impact of human behavior on natural selection. He explores how populations of bighorn sheep respond biologically, over time, to trophy hunters. This and other examples—from commercial fishing to antibiotic use—provide ample evidence for biological change over time, or, as Darwin might say, "descent with modification." You might find yourself contemplating the future of our own species, as well as others on the Earth. In thinking about the consequences of human behavior for natural selection, we would do well to heed Weiner's observation: "We often seem to lose out wherever we fight our hardest to control nature."

Charles Darwin's wife, Emma, was terrified that they would be separated for eternity, because she would go to heaven and he would not. Emma confessed her fears in a letter that Charles kept and treasured, with his reply to her scribbled in the margin: "When I am dead, know that many times, I have kissed and cryed over this."

Close as they were, the two could hardly bear to talk about Darwin's view of life. And today, those of us who live in the United States, by many measures

SOURCE: Jonathan Weiner, "Evolution in Action," *Natural History* 114, no. 9 (November 2005): 47–52.

the world's leading scientific nation, find ourselves in a house divided. Half of us accept Darwin's theory, half of us reject it, and many people are convinced that Darwin burns in hell. I find that old debate particularly strange, because I've spent some of the best years of my life as a science writer peering over the shoulders of biologists who actually watch Darwin's process in action. What they can see casts the whole debate in a new light—or it should.

Darwin himself never tried to watch evolution happen. "It may metaphorically be said," he wrote in the *Origin of Species,*

> that natural selection is daily and hourly scrutinising, throughout the world, the slightest variations; rejecting those that are bad, preserving and adding up all that are good; silently and insensibly working, whenever and wherever opportunity offers. . . . We see nothing of these slow changes in progress, until the hand of time has marked the lapse of ages.

Darwin was a modest man who thought of himself as a plodder (one of his favorite mottoes was, "It's dogged as does it"). He thought evolution plodded too. If so, it would be more boring to watch evolution than to watch drying paint. As a result, for several generations after Darwin's death, almost nobody tried. For most of the twentieth century the only well-known example of evolution in action was the case of peppered moths in industrial England. The moth had its picture in all the textbooks, as a kind of special case.

Then, in 1973, a married pair of evolutionary biologists, Peter and Rosemary Grant, now at Princeton University, began a study of Darwin's process in Darwin's islands, the Galápagos, watching Darwin's finches. At first, they assumed that they would have to infer the history of evolution in the islands from the distribution of the various finch species, varieties, and populations across the archipelago. That is pretty much what Darwin had done, in broad strokes, after the *Beagle*'s five-week survey of the islands in 1835. But the Grants soon discovered that at their main study site, a tiny desert island called Daphne Major, near the center of the archipelago, the finches were evolving rapidly. Conditions on the island swung wildly back and forth from wet years to dry years, and finches on Daphne adapted to each swing, from generation to generation. With the help of a series of graduate students, the Grants began to spend a good part of every year on Daphne, watching evolution in action as it shaped and reshaped the finches' beaks.

At the same time, a few biologists began making similar discoveries elsewhere in the world. One of them was John A. Endler, an evolutionary biologist at the University of California, Santa Barbara, who studied Trinidadian guppies. In 1986 Endler published a little book called *Natural Selection in the Wild,* in which he collected and reviewed all of the studies of evolution in action that had been published to that date. Dozens of new field projects were in progress. Biologists finally began to realize that Darwin had been too modest. Evolution by natural selection can happen rapidly enough to watch.

Now the field is exploding. More than 250 people around the world are observing and documenting evolution, not only in finches and guppies, but also in aphids, flies, grayling, monkeyflowers, salmon, and sticklebacks. Some workers are even documenting pairs of species—symbiotic insects and plants—that have recently found each other, and observing the pairs as they drift off into their own world together like lovers in a novel by D.H. Lawrence.

The Grants' own study gets more sophisticated every year. A few years ago, a group of molecular biologists working with the Grants nailed down a gene that plays a key role in shaping the beaks of the finches. The gene codes for a signaling molecule called bone morphogenic protein 4 (BMP4). Finches with bigger beaks tend to have more BMP4, and finches with smaller beaks have less. In the laboratory, the biologists demonstrated that they could sculpt the beaks themselves by adding or subtracting BMP4. The same gene that shapes the beak of the finch in the egg also shapes the human face in the womb.

Some of the most dramatic stories of evolution in action result from the pressures that human beings are imposing on the planet. As Stephen Palumbi, an evolutionary biologist at Stanford University, points out, we are changing the course of evolution for virtually every living species everywhere, with consequences that are sometimes the opposite of what we might have predicted, or desired.

Take trophy hunting. Wild populations of bighorn mountain sheep are carefully managed in North America for hunters who want a chance to shoot a ram with a trophy set of horns. Hunting permits can cost well into the six figures. On Ram Mountain, in Alberta, Canada, hunters have shot the biggest of the bighorn rams for more than thirty years. And the result? Evolution has made the hunters' quarry scarce. The runts have had a better chance than the giants of passing on their genes. So on Ram Mountain the rams have gotten smaller, and their horns are proportionately smaller yet.

Or take fishing, which is economically much more consequential. The populations of Atlantic cod that swam for centuries off the coasts of Labrador and Newfoundland began a terrible crash in the late 1980s. In the years leading up to the crash, the cod had been evolving much like the sheep on Ram Mountain. Fish that matured relatively fast and reproduced relatively young had the better chance of passing on their genes; so did the fish that stayed small. So even before the population crashed, the average cod had been shrinking.

We often seem to lose out wherever we fight hardest to control nature. Antibiotics drive the evolution of drug-resistant bacteria at a frightening pace. Sulfonamides were introduced in the 1930s, and resistance to them was first observed a decade later. Penicillin was deployed in 1943, and the first penicillin resistance was observed in 1946. In the same way, pesticides and herbicides create resistant bugs and weeds.

Palumbi estimates that the annual bill for such unintended human-induced evolution runs to more than $100 billion in the U.S. alone. Worldwide, the pressure of global warming, fragmented habitats, heightened levels of carbon dioxide, acid rain, and the other myriad perturbations people impose on the chemistry and climate of the planet—all change the terms of the struggle for existence in the air, in the water, and on land. Biologists have begun to worry about those perturbations, but global change may be racing ahead of them.

To me, the most interesting news in the global evolution watch concerns what Darwin called "that mystery of mysteries, the origin of species."

The process whereby a population acquires small, inherited changes through natural selection is known as microevolution. Finches get bigger, fish gets smaller, but a finch is still a finch and a fish is still a fish. For people who reject Darwin's theory, that's the end of the story: no matter how many small, inherited changes accumulate, they believe, natural selection can never make a new kind of living thing. The kinds, the species, are eternal.

Darwin argued otherwise. He thought that many small changes could cause two lines of life to diverge. Whenever animals and plants find their way to a new home, for instance, they suffer, like émigrés in new countries. Some individuals fail, others adapt and prosper. As the more successful individuals reproduce, Darwin maintained, the new population begins to differ from the ancestral one. If the two populations diverge widely enough, they become separate species. Change on that scale is known as macroevolution.

In *Origin,* Darwin estimated that a new species might take between ten thousand and fourteen thousand generations to arise. Until recently, most biologists assumed it would take at least that many, or maybe even millions of generations, before microevolutionary changes led to the origin of new species. So they assumed they could watch evolution by natural selection, but not the divergence of one species into separate, reproductively isolated species. Now that view is changing too.

Not long ago, a young evolution-watcher named Andrew Hendry, a biologist at McGill University in Montreal, reported the results of a striking study of sockeye salmon. . . . Sockeye tend to reproduce either in streams or along lake beaches. When the glaciers of the last ice age melted and retreated, about ten thousand years ago, they left behind thousands of new lakes.

Salmon from streams swam into the lakes and stayed. Today their descendants tend to breed among themselves rather than with sockeyes that live in the streams. The fish in the lakes and streams are reproductively isolated from each other. So how fast did that happen?

In the 1930s and 1940s, sockeye salmon were introduced into Lake Washington, in Washington State. Hundreds of thousands of their descendants now live and breed in Cedar River, which feeds the lake. By 1957 some of the introduced sockeye also colonized a beach along the lake called Pleasure Point, about four miles from the mouth of Cedar River.

Hendry could tell whether a full-grown, breeding salmon had been born in the river or at the beach by examining the rings on its otoliths, or ear stones. Otolith rings reflect variations in water temperature while a fish embryo is developing. Water temperatures at the beach are relatively constant compared with the river temperatures. Hendry and his colleagues checked the otoliths and collected DNA samples from the fish—and found that more than a third of the sockeye breeding at Pleasure Point had grown up in the river. They were immigrants.

With such a large number of immigrants, the two populations at Pleasure Point should have blended back together. But they hadn't. So at breeding time many of the river sockeye that swam over to the beach must have been relatively unsuccessful at passing on their genes.

Hendry could also tell the stream fish and the beach fish apart just by looking at them. Where the sockeye's breeding waters are swift-flowing, such as in Cedar River, the males tend to be slender. Their courtship ritual and competition with other males requires them to turn sideways in strong current—an awkward maneuver for a male with a deep, roundish body. So in strong current, slender males have the better chance of passing on their genes. But in still waters, males with the deepest bodies have the best chance of getting mates. So beach males tend to be rounder—their dimensions greater from the top of the back to the bottom of the belly—than river males.

What about females? In the river, where currents and floods are forever shifting and swirling the gravel, females have to dig deep nests for their eggs. So the females in the river tend to be bigger than their lake-dwelling counterparts, because bigger females can dig deeper nests. Where the water is calmer, the gravel stays put, and shallower nests will do.

So all of the beachgoers, male and female, have adapted to life at Pleasure Point. Their adaptations are strong enough that reproductive isolation has evolved. How long did the evolution take? Hendry began studying the salmon's reproductive isolation in 1992. At that time, the sockeyes in the stream and the ones at Pleasure Point had been breeding in their respective habitats for at most thirteen generations. That is so fast that, as Hendry and his colleagues point out, it may be possible someday soon to catch the next step, the origin of a new species.

And it's not just the sockeye salmon. Consider the three-spined stickleback. After the glaciers melted at the end of the last ice age, many sticklebacks swam out of the sea and into new glacial lakes—just as the salmon did. In the sea, sticklebacks wear heavy, bony body armor. In a lake they wear light armor. . . . In a certain new pond in Bergen, Norway, during the past century, sticklebacks evolved toward the lighter armor in just thirty-one years. In Loberg Lake, Alaska, the same kind of change took only a dozen years. A generation for sticklebacks is two years. So that dramatic evolution took just six generations.

Dolph Schluter, a former finch-watcher from the Galápagos and currently a biologist at the University of British Columbia in Vancouver, has shown that, along with the evolution of new body types, sticklebacks also evolve a taste for mates with the new traits. In other words, the adaptive push of sexual selection is going hand-in-hand with natural selection. Schluter has built experimental ponds in Vancouver to observe the phenomenon under controlled conditions, and the same patterns he found in isolated lakes repeat themselves in his ponds. So adaptation can sometimes drive sexual selection and accelerate reproductive isolation.

There are other developments in the evolution watch, too many to mention in this small space. Some of the fastest action is microscopic. Richard Lenski, a biologist at Michigan State University in East Lansing, watches the evolution of *Escherichia coli*. Because one generation takes only twenty minutes, and billions of *E. coli* can fit in a petri dish, the bacteria make ideal subjects for experimental evolution. Throw some *E. coli* into a new dish, for instance, with food they haven't encountered before, and they will evolve and adapt—quickly at first and then more slowly, as they refine their fit with their new environment.

And then there are the controversies. Science progresses and evolves by controversy, by internal debate and revision. In the United States these days one almost hates to mention that there are arguments among evolutionists. So often, they are taken out of context and hyperamplified to suggest that nothing about Darwinism is solid—that Darwin is dead. But research is messy because nature is messy, and fieldwork is some of the messiest research of all. It is precisely here at its jagged cutting edge that Darwinism is most vigorously alive.

Not long ago, one of the most famous icons of the evolution watch toppled over: the story of the peppered moths, familiar to anyone who remembers biology 101. About half a century ago, the British evolutionist Bernard Kettlewell noted that certain moths in the British Isles had evolved into darker forms when the trunks of trees darkened with industrial pollution. When the trees lightened again, after clean air acts were passed, the moths had evolved into light forms again. Kettlewell claimed that dark moths resting on dark tree trunks were harder for birds to see; in each decade, moths of the right color were safer.

But in the past few years, workers have shown that Kettlewell's explanation was too simplistic. For one thing, the moths don't normally rest on tree trunks. In forty years of observation, only twice have moths been seen resting there. Nobody knows where they do rest. The moths did evolve rapidly, but no one can be certain why.

To me what remains most interesting is the light that studies such as Hendry's, or the Grants', may throw on the origin of species. It's extraordinary that scientists are now examining the very beginnings of the process, at the level of beaks and fins, at the level of the genes. The explosion of evolution-watchers is a remarkable development in Darwin's science. Even as the popular debate about evolution in America is reaching its most heated moment since the trial of John Scopes, evolutionary biologists are pursuing one of the most significant and surprising voyages of discovery since the young Darwin sailed into the Galápagos Archipelago aboard Her Majesty's Ship *Beagle*.

Not long ago I asked Hendry if his studies have changed the way he thinks about the origin of species. "Yes," he replied without hesitation, "I think it's occurring all over the place."

DISCUSSION QUESTIONS

1. Some of the examples of the evolutionary process provided in this article differ from Darwin's predictions. Describe these findings, and explain how they might have surprised Darwin.

2. The article illustrates that human culture can affect the evolution of other species. Using an example or two from the article (or one that you may have found from another source), describe how human activity can alter the evolutionary course of other species. Beyond extinction, how might global climate change and environmental pollution affect other species?

3. How has biotechnology contributed to our understanding of the genetic mechanisms that underlie some phenotypic variation?

INTERNET RESOURCES

This reading mentions the work and writings of other individuals about whom you might wish to learn more, including:

- Peter and Rosemary Grant
- Andrew Hendry
- Dolph Schluter

After reading this article, you might want to investigate the website of the University of Nebraska State Museum at http://explore-evolution.unl.edu/.

InfoTrac College Edition

(infotrac-college.com)

You can find many other readings pertinent to this topic by consulting online databases including InfoTrac College Edition. Some suggested search terms for this article are as follows.

- Microevolution
- Drug-resistant antibiotics
- Sexual selection

8

A Terrible Scrooge

OLIVIA JUDSON

Anthropologists are forever making comparisons. Indeed, all subfields of anthropology use the comparative approach. Cultural anthropologists compare behaviors of peoples around the world. They try to identify "universals"—practices that occur everywhere—and to understand how cultures function as adaptations to diverse environments. Archaeologists, in turn, compare artifacts and other facets of past societies to gain insights on how cultures change over time.

Biological anthropologists also rely on the comparative method. When we look at human behavior and anatomy compared to that of nonhuman primates, we learn about the degrees of biological relatedness that connect us. Such comparisons also help us envision features of human biological evolution. Following publication of Darwin's On the Origin of Species, *anatomical comparisons became especially critical for evaluating our evolutionary relationships with different species. Charles Darwin's close friend and advocate, Thomas Henry Huxley, made tremendous strides in that arena. Huxley dissected various apes and monkeys and added what was then known about their behaviors. In his book,* Man's Place in Nature, *Huxley reported on how the behavior, gross anatomy, and skeletons of various nonhuman primates compare with those of human beings. He found particularly striking similarities among humans and great apes—a point that supported the concept of an extremely close evolutionary kinship between humans and our cousins, the apes.*

In this article, scientist Olivia Judson takes us to a new and exciting venue for the comparative approach: our own genetic makeup, or genome. Genome sequencing gives us the chance to conduct gene by gene comparisons with other species, thus obtaining another measure of evolutionary relatedness. Knowledge of the genome also provides us with the means to assess the effects of natural selection. Judson reviews the relationships between our biological characteristics, the corresponding proteins, and the basic, underlying chemicals responsible for proteins known as amino acids. Though scientists have long suspected that natural selection operates directly on protein function, Judson presents new evidence that suggests the cost, or amount of energy used in producing a protein, also is subject to natural selection. As you read the article, focus on how this mechanism works, paying special attention to the role of amino acids.

Honeybees. Sea urchins. Black cottonwood trees. Those are just three of the species that had their genomes published last year. It's amazing to think that a dozen years ago, the sequencing of any whole genome was a sensational event. Back then, just a few viruses and one puny bacterium had had theirs done. Now DNA sequencing is almost as automated as sausage-making, and geneticists have whole-genome sequences for a menagerie that includes dogs, rice, humans, chimpanzees, roundworms, mosquitoes, chickens, silkworms, red algae, at least four species of fruit fly, scores of fungi, hundreds of bacteria, and hordes of viruses. More exciting still, whole-genome sequences for species that don't even walk the planet any more, such as the Neanderthal, the dodo, and the woolly mammoth, will soon be available.

Each genome is a treasure trove of surprise and revelation. Sea urchins turn out to have genes for a large and complicated immune system, which may explain why some of them manage to live well beyond their hundredth birthdays. A glance at the genome of trypanosomes—the single-celled parasites that cause sleeping sickness and Chagas' disease—shows why they are so good at evading the human immune system. About a quarter of their 12,000 genes is a disguise kit, the molecular equivalent of wigs, hats, sunglasses, and false mustaches. Just when the immune system knows what it's looking for, the trypanosomes change their appearance.

But it's not just the individual genomes that are fascinating. It's the comparisons. Without comparisons, you don't know which attributes of a sea urchin are unique, which are shared by close relatives such as starfish, and which are common to all organisms, from bacteria to people.

More important, you can't detect evolutionary patterns and trends. It was only by comparing teeth from many different animals, from horses to the fruit-eating fish of South America, that anatomists learned that diet reliably affects the evolution of tooth shape. Only by comparing the genomes of parasitic bacteria with those of their free-living relations did biologists discover that becoming a parasite has predictable effects on genome evolution. The genomes of the parasites are smaller and more streamlined than those of their free-living relatives. Which makes sense: if you live inside another organism, you don't have to bother much about finding food.

Indeed, it was by comparing everything, from the miniature males of certain species of barnacle to the beaks of the finches living in the Galápagos Islands, that Charles Darwin discovered natural selection in the first place. In each generation, some organisms have more offspring than others. Some offspring die before they make it to adulthood; others make it to adulthood but aren't very good at reproducing. Darwin reasoned that if those differences were due to certain heritable traits, those traits would be subject to natural selection. Natural selection is not the only force in evolution, but it is the most important one: it is the sculptor of beaks, and songs, and immune systems.

Just as comparative anatomy formed the basis of evolutionary thought in the nineteenth century, comparative genomics appears set to form the basis of evolutionary biology in the twenty-first. Darwin didn't know about genes, but ultimately, it is on genomes that natural selection leaves its fingerprints. And a close look at those fingerprints shows natural selection acting in a new way. That matters, because until recently it's been an open question whether natural selection is as pervasive and powerful at shaping molecules as it is at shaping bodies.

At its most elemental level, natural selection acts on genes. And a gene is nothing more than an instruction to make a protein. Proteins are essential building blocks of the body (along with fats and sugars); they are large molecules that come in a wide range of shapes and sizes and have a variety of jobs. Some, such as hemoglobin, carry oxygen around in the blood. Others, such as alcohol dehydrogenase, help digest alcohol. Still others form the scaffolding that helps cells stay in the right shape. If you're a finch, the protein calmodulin affects the shape of your beak. Cells make thousands of proteins—if you dry out a cell, the proteins will make up more than half the remaining mass.

But whether big or small, working in blood or beaks, each protein is just a chain of dozens or even hundreds of smaller molecules called amino acids. And each gene in DNA is an ordered list of the amino acids needed for making a particular protein.

It's no longer news that natural selection acts on protein function, that is, on how well proteins work. Mutations—changes in the DNA sequence of a gene—that improve how a protein does its job tend to spread: the owners of the mutations tend to produce more descendants. The bar-headed goose is a good example. This small, elegant goose from Central Asia has a white face and two dark bars, or stripes, on its head. But what makes the bird remarkable is that it has evolved a form of hemoglobin so sensitive to oxygen that it can breathe the thin air above the Himalayas.

Conversely, a mutation that disables a protein needed for survival may appear from time to time, but it cannot spread. If you've got a faulty collagen—the stuff of which cartilage and bones are made—you're likely to die as a baby, or even before you're born.

How well a protein does its job—its ability to carry oxygen or digest alcohol or act as scaffolding—depends to a great extent on its having a particular shape. Hemoglobin carries oxygen because the hemoglobin molecule has a little "pocket" that attracts and loosely holds oxygen molecules—a bit like one of those magnetic cups for paper clips. The shape of a protein depends on the way the string of amino acids folds up, which in turn depends on the properties of the amino acids in question. There are just twenty standard amino acids, and each is useful in particular ways, like the various shapes of Lego bricks. The amino acid glycine, for instance, is small and simple; it can serve as a hinge. Tryptophan is huge and bulky. Cysteine lends stability to a protein. And so on.

But often, only a few of the amino acids in a protein are essential to its function. At position 122, say, you must have glycine and no other—whereas the rest are interchangeable, at least to some extent. (Occasionally any of the twenty will work; more typically it'll be a choice between the two, or five, or ten that for the purposes of the protein have broadly similar properties.)

The question, then, is what determines which amino acids the cell evolves to use in the less critical parts of a protein? Until recently, the choice was put down to mutation—and assumed to be more or less random. Now investigators—among them Hiroshi Akashi of Pennsylvania State University in University Park, Jonathan Swire of Imperial College London, and Takashi Gojobori

of the National Institute of Genetics in Mishima, Japan—have discovered it is not random, but to a large extent predictable. And it comes down to how much proteins cost to manufacture.

To see how cost comes into the picture, think of your cells as factories, churning out proteins much as an assembly line churns out cups for paper clips. The components—in this case, the amino acids—of the final product have to be built, or acquired. That takes energy. Furthermore, not all amino acids cost the same energy to make. Bulky, complicated tryptophan is particularly expensive; small and simple glycine is notably cheap.

If cells are sensitive to cost, you would expect them to evolve to use cheap amino acids wherever possible—particularly in the proteins they mass produce, compared with the ones they make only occasionally. The reason is straightforward: if you make protein A thousands of times more often than you make protein B, a mutation that enables you to make a cheaper version of protein A will have a far more pronounced effect than a similar mutation in protein B. The organism with the cheaper (but equally effective) version of A will get more substantial savings on its energy bills. If reducing cost is important—if the more miserly, cost-efficient creatures are more likely to survive and reproduce—then such a mutation is more likely to spread.

Sure enough, cost matters. You can look within the genomes of organisms that have one cell—such as brewer's yeast, or that common resident of the human gut, the bacterium *Escherichia coli*. Or you can look within the genomes of animals such as fruit flies, roundworms, and people, which have lots of different cells. But either way, you find that selection to reduce cost has been pervasive. Given a choice among several amino acids, genomes reliably evolve to use the cheapest ones. In brewer's yeast, for instance, proteins that play a role in metabolism are made in large numbers, and are cheap, whereas transcription factors (proteins that control whether or not a particular gene gets turned on or not) are made in small quantities, and are generally expensive.

That "cost accounting" explains subtle but systematic differences in the ways various organisms build their proteins. For example, the energy it takes to make a given amino acid is different for creatures, like us, that live on the Earth's surface, than it is for denizens of the sulfurous vents in the deepest seas. There, the water is infernally hot, the pressure is immense, and life and its protein-building machinery are bathed in a volcanic brew. That changes the dynamics of chemical reactions. Some amino acids that are cheap for us surface-dwellers become expensive, and vice versa.

Those discoveries are exciting, for three reasons. First, selection to reduce cost operates differently from selection on how well a protein works. Without knowing a great deal about a particular protein, it's hard to predict whether a given mutation will affect how well it does its job. But cost selection is something that applies to every position in a protein, and in a clear way. Each amino acid has a known price tag, so you can just go down the list of amino acids that a gene specifies, and work out which mutations would lead to cost savings, and by how much. It's a weaker force: a mutation that reduces cost can spread only if it doesn't mess up how well a protein does its job. After all, it's no good making proteins cheaply if they don't work. Cost selection is therefore most pronounced in the parts of the protein that are least critical to its function.

Second, cost selection opens up a new way to understand how evolution proceeds, molecule by molecule. It shows that natural selection is as powerful and pervasive in the sculpting of proteins as it is in the sculpting of beaks. But it also shows that comparing beaks and comparing genomes are not simply questions of scale. Processes that are invisible to the beakologist nonetheless exert profound effects on the very molecules from which the beak is made.

Finally, it's not every day that a new facet of natural selection is discovered. Since the publication of Darwin's *Origin of Species,* only three or four have come to light. There's sexual selection, which explains the evolution of extravagant traits, such as peacocks' tails, that increase mating success at the expense of surviving. There's kin selection, which explains such odd phenomena as the fact that worker bees cooperate in rearing offspring that are not their own. (They do so because they share many of the same genes.) There's selection on protein function. And now, there's selection on protein cost.

When it comes to making proteins, Mother Nature, it seems, is a terrible Scrooge.

DISCUSSION QUESTIONS

1. What are some specific things we can learn by comparing the genomes of different species?

2. What exactly are proteins? Using information provided in the article, provide examples of actual proteins, and explain the relationships between genes, proteins, and characteristics.

3. Explain how proteins are selected for with respect to the cost of their manufacture.

INTERNET RESOURCES

InfoTrac College Edition

(infotrac-college.com)
You can find many other readings pertinent to this topic by consulting online databases including InfoTrac College Edition. Some suggested search terms for this article are as follows.

- Genome
- Amino acid
- Proteins

9

Reading the Book of Jim

SHARON BEGLEY

If you won a contest to have your entire genome sequenced (simply for donating a vial of blood), would you want to do this? It's now possible, and a growing number of people are interested in learning the exact genes they carry for an extensive list of biological traits. The cost, for most of us, is still prohibitively high; but if you won a chance to find out the contents of your genome, how do you think you would you feel?

In this selection, science writer Sharon Begley reports on the movement toward personal genomic sequencing using the case of the well-known Dr. James Watson, a man she refers to as "the bad boy of molecular biology." (In fact, he has often expressed controversial views.) As you may know, Dr. Watson was one of three individuals, along with Francis Crick and Maurice Wilkins, who were awarded a Nobel Prize in 1962 for determining the molecular structure of DNA. This revolutionary discovery propelled the study of human genetics forward because it provided the molecular framework for the inheritance of biological characteristics.

The basic DNA skeleton may well be familiar to you: DNA chemical bases (identified by their first letter as A, T, G, or C) are components of nucleotides, which are stacked on top of one another to form a chain which is joined to another nucleotide chain. These two strands are twisted to form a double helix that has been described as looking like a twisted ladder. Specific amino acids are spelled out by three bases in sequence. Strings of amino acids are known, in turn, as polypeptide chains. Polypeptides make up particular proteins or parts of proteins, the chemical compounds that underlie all of our traits.

It seems fitting that one of DNA's co-discoverers would be among the first people to have their entire genome sequenced. Watson's genome is now available online for scientists to study and compare with other genetic sequences obtained during the Human Genome Project. Through such comparisons we can begin to understand the normal ranges of variation—at the molecular level—for various traits. Using this technology, we can also identify genes that are involved in particular diseases and characteristics. As you read this article, ask yourself, "What are the potential benefits of personal genome sequencing to science, society, and individuals?" Do you foresee any problems that might arise because of personal genome sequencing? Should we run right out and get our personal genome sequenced?

It would be a mistake to think that reaching the age of 79 has mellowed James Watson. Fifty-four years after he discovered, with Francis Crick, the structure of DNA, and 45 years after sharing the Nobel Prize for it, he delights in provocation just as much as when he made his reputation as the bad boy of molecular biology, bulldozing colleagues and competitors (and using crucial data generated by one, Rosalind Franklin) in his headlong race to the double helix. In the years since, Watson built Cold Spring Harbor Laboratory in New York into a biology powerhouse, briefly led the Human Genome Project—and endorsed designer babies, genetic engineering to make "all girls pretty" and curing "stupidity" through genetics. Which makes his words this rainy May morning at the lab all the more surprising.

Two years ago Watson agreed to become the first person to have his genome sequenced and made public. A biotech company, 454 Life Sciences, has now determined, from a blood sample, every one of the 6 billion chemical "letters" (designated A, T, C and G) that make up the DNA in Watson's cells. He will see his genetic blueprint on May 30[, 2007]. The next day it will be posted in a National Institutes of Health database for all the world to look at and, in the case of experts, deduce whether his genes have spellings (ATTCGT . . .) associated with diseases, intelligence, neuroticism, risk-taking, belief in God, shyness and all the other traits that biologists have linked to genes. "I always wanted to be a hero," Watson says almost apologetically; he's doing this to encourage others to have their own genome sequenced. He thinks it will "make people healthier" by giving them information that could prevent disease. But he has another hope. If personal-genome sequencing becomes widespread, he says, "it will make people more compassionate."

"We'll understand why people can't do certain things," he continues. "Instead of asking a child to shape up, we'll stop having unrealistic expectations." If a child's genome shows that his awkwardness or inattention or limited intelligence has a genetic basis, "we'll want to help rather than be mad. If a child doesn't finish high school, we treat that as a failure, as his fault. But knowing someone's full genetic information will keep us from making him do things he'll fail at." For a clue to this softer side of Watson, one need look no farther than his office next door to the room where he is speaking. There, along with the Nobel citation and other honors, hangs a poster-size framed photo of his two sons when they were

little. One suffers from a mental illness that causes symptoms of both autism and schizophrenia.

It remains to be seen whether society will look more kindly on people, like his son, who are different if those differences are traced to DNA. Homophobia didn't exactly vanish after sexual orientation was shown to have a genetic basis. And the notion that genes are destiny raises possibilities more disturbing than Watson's impish suggestion that we use genetic engineering to beautify the female half of the species. Most obviously, people may believe that what is written in their code of life determines not only their health but also their intelligence, character, talents and personality. "Will our genetic profiles make us self-limiting, and will we allow them to?" asks Elaine Ostrander of the National Human Genome Research Institute, part of the National Institutes of Health.

Ready or not, personal-genome sequencing is just around the corner. "Project Jim," as 454 calls it, took 67 days of sequencing time and cost $1 million. But with new technology "we are on our way to the $10,000 genome and soon the $1,000 genome," says Jonathan Rothberg, 454's founder and chairman. And unlike other medical tests, which must be done regularly to detect changes, your genome need be sequenced only once.

If Rothberg is right about the $1,000, that would be cheaper than a battery of genetic tests, which cost between $300 and several thousand dollars each. A personal genome offers another advantage. Most conventional genetic tests probe for known mutations. "If yours is one of the rare ones you're out of luck," says geneticist Richard Gibbs of Baylor University, who first suggested that 454 approach Watson about sequencing his genome. A full sequence, in contrast, can be compared to the benchmark genome—sort of an average of the genomes of the people who ponied up DNA samples for the Human Genome Project—so if you have any misspelling at all it will be detected.

The biggest potential benefit of having your genome fully sequenced is likely to come from the fact that no gene is an island. With the exception of diseases that arise from defects in a single gene, such as Huntington's and cystic fibrosis, the effect of one gene depends on your other genes. "We know it's not just your genes or your environment" that determines your health, says 454's Rothberg, "but the other genes in your genome." After all, the fact that identical twins—who have identical genomes—are identical for disease only 60 percent of the time (on average) shows that having a particular DNA sequence doesn't mean you will definitely develop the disease. One reason not every woman with a BRCA1 mutation develops breast cancer (some 30 percent do not) is almost certainly that some carry "modifier" genes that weaken the effect of the disease genes. A full genome sequence would pick up these modifier genes. "I think if we can identify those modifiers," says Baylor's Gibbs, "we'll be able to tell if you're in the 30 percent or the 70 percent," which today's genetic tests cannot.

The value of a personal genome depends on its accuracy, of course. At this early stage the error rate is a huge unknown. Watson's biggest concern is that he'll be told incorrectly that he has one chemical letter instead of another—a C instead of a G, say—somewhere and that the misspelling is associated with a disease, raising alarms unnecessarily.

An equal problem is that gene-disease claims have a lousy track record. Of those for complex diseases involving multiple genes, notably mental illness, few have been confirmed. And when scientists have tried to validate a claim the results have been sobering. Geneticists led by Thomas Morgan of Washington University recently examined 85 variants (that is, "spellings" of A, T, C and G that are different from the norm) in 70 genes that studies had linked to an increased risk of cardiovascular disease. Exactly zero of the variants were more frequent in heart patients than in healthy people, they reported last month in the *Journal of the American Medical Association*. That means the variants do not increase risk of heart disease as claimed. Yet companies offer genetic tests for at least seven of them. "An unfortunate number of claims based on candidate [disease] genes have not held up," admits Francis Collins, who led the Human Genome Project to the finish line in 2003 and is now director of the genome institute at NIH.

Even assuming the sequencing is accurate and the link to disease correct, the value of a personal genome sequence is debatable. At least 90 percent

of the human genome is "junk DNA" that has no clear function. An even higher percentage seems to have nothing to do with health. Genetic variations linked to disease are sprinkled across 0.01 percent of the genome, estimates George Church of Harvard University, who has been pushing technology to make genome sequencing affordable. Those regions could be sequenced for $1,000, he estimates, "and would give you 95 percent of the heavy-hitting mutations" linked to health.

Watson hopes that if people learn they harbor genes that raise the risk of any diseases, they will take steps to minimize that risk starting from birth. That way, a kid at risk for type-2 diabetes, say, will keep her weight in check and thus her diabetes risk lower before she becomes even a pudgy toddler. (Watson, though, concedes that if he has a gene variant that raises the risk of some disease 20 percent, and that the risk can be lowered by giving up chocolate, count him out.) But it is not at all clear how people will react to knowing their genetic blueprints. Many are genetic fatalists, says Angela Trepanier, president-elect of the National Society of Genetic Counselors. That is, they believe that health and even intellectual and emotional destiny is written in their DNA. Rather than reacting to the news that they have genes that raise the risk of colon cancer by having regular colonoscopies, some will say, "To hell with it, I'm doomed anyway. Where's the cheesecake?"

That would be especially unfortunate given that many genes linked to disease raise the risk of that disease 20 percent or 40 percent or even 200 percent—but well short of "you will definitely get it." The overall chance of getting schizophrenia, for instance, is 1 percent; a 200 percent extra risk due to a genetic variation means your risk is still just 3 percent. And the uncertainty about the consequences of having a particular gene variant is even greater for traits such as aggression, neuroticism, shyness and intelligence. Fatalism when it comes to those could be tragic, making parents give up on kids who struggle academically or resign themselves to sociopathic behavior despite reams of evidence showing that DNA is not destiny. With the spectacular advances in genetics since the discovery of the double helix, says the genome institute's Lawrence Brody, "we've convinced the public that genetics is important and deterministic. Now we have to back off a little and say it's not that deterministic."

Not even experts are immune from the sovereignty of DNA, though. Watson remains scientifically active and intellectually engaged, only occasionally forgetting a name, he says. But there is one part of his genome he has asked 454 to keep private, even from him: whether he carries gene variants associated with Alzheimer's disease. He fears that if he knew he did, he would interpret each slip of memory as impending dementia.

Coincidentally, just as the personal genome arrives, so does another novel way to detect disease early. Called biomarkers, they are proteins in the blood that reveal the presence of disease before it even causes symptoms, offering a good chance for successful treatment. The PSA test for prostate cancer is a biomarker, but others promise to be much more useful (the PSA test has not been shown to save lives). "Genetic tests just tell you you have a chance of getting this condition sometime," says Mark Chandler, chairman and CEO of Biophysical Corp., which sells a $3,500 test that screens for 250 biomarkers indicative of scores of diseases. "With biomarkers, it's not just potential anymore; it's real."

Despite the concerns over its usefulness, if 454 is right about the $1,000 or even the $10,000 cost, the personal genome sequence will likely become a must-have novelty—even if for now it's just "recreational genetics," as Brody calls it, amusing but not terribly useful. As he prepared to fly to Baylor for the official unveiling of his genome, Watson expressed nary a doubt that everyone should learn the 6 billion chemical letters that spell their own genetic blueprint. "It's going to be an extraordinary period," he says. For better or worse.

DISCUSSION QUESTIONS

1. What reasons led Dr. James Watson to volunteer to have his entire genome sequenced?

2. What are some difficulties in interpreting the results of a person's entire genomic sequence?

3. In general, how closely would you say that genes relate to specific biological characteristics, behaviors, or diseases?

4. Given the opportunity (and the money), would you want to know the contents of your personal genome? Why or why not?

INTERNET RESOURCES

This reading mentions the work and writings of individuals whom you might wish to learn more about, including:

■   Rosalind Franklin

■   Francis Crick

■   James Watson

After reading this article, you may wish to consult Cracking the Code of Life, a web page maintained by PBS's NOVA Online, at http://www.pbs.org/wgbh/nova/genome.

InfoTrac College Edition

(infotrac-college.com)

You can find many other readings pertinent to this topic by consulting online databases including Info-Trac College Edition. Some suggested search terms for this article are as follows.

■   Human Genome Project

■   Junk DNA

■   Twin studies

PART III

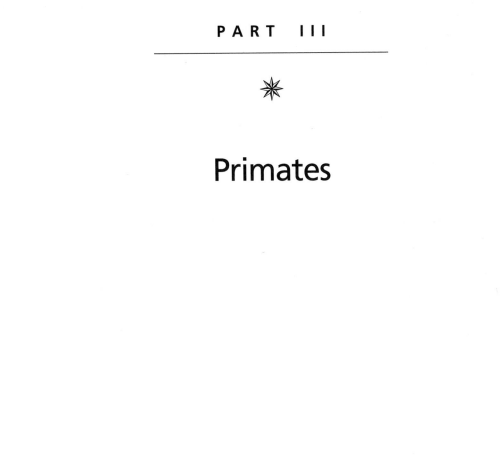

Primates

10

The Social Life of Baboons

S. L. WASHBURN AND IRVEN DEVORE

By all measures, this selection by Sherwood Washburn and Irven DeVore is a classic in anthropology. In 1950, Washburn called upon physical anthropologists to follow new directions by pursuing problem-oriented research aimed at achieving a better understanding of human evolution. This article demonstrates one of the ways in which Washburn "walked his talk." By initiating field studies of nonhuman primates (and encouraging his students to do the same), Washburn established himself as a pioneer in the modern specialization of primatology, or the study of the behavior, anatomy, and evolution of the order primates.

Washburn and DeVore launched an investigation that helped define studies of non-human primates in field settings for generations to come. As you read the selection, note how the authors systematically describe certain aspects of baboon society, like the size and composition of their troops, their interactions with other species, their diet, and their environment. Careful observation of baboon troops over a significant period of time helped Washburn and DeVore delineate the consistent aspects of baboon behavior as compared with those features that vary somewhat from troop to troop. Above all, Washburn viewed the natural world through an evolutionary lens, and he looked for ways that both behaviors and anatomical features represented adaptations. Note, for example, how important environmental variables are—such as food, water, and predators—in understanding savanna baboons. By interpreting behaviors like dominance, troop structure, and grooming in the light of specific environmental challenges, Washburn and DeVore pioneered a perspective known as behavioral ecology in primate studies.

Washburn and DeVore's landmark study also helped refute some incorrect conclusions about baboon behavior that had been reached by earlier researchers. Pay particular attention, for example, to their discussion of the sex lives of baboons and the role other investigators had attributed to sex in keeping baboon societies together. Taken as a whole this article demonstrates how a new and important area of research took hold in anthropology and, in the process, corrected old assertions about the nature of primate behavior.

The behavior of monkeys and apes has always held great fascination for men. In recent years plain curiosity about their behavior has been reinforced by the desire to understand human behavior. Anthropologists have come to understand that the evolution of man's behavior, particularly his social behavior, has played an integral role in his biological evolution. In the attempt to reconstruct the life of man as it was shaped through the ages, many studies of primate behavior are now under way in the

SOURCE: S. L. Washburn and Irven Devore, "The Social Life of Baboons," *Scientific American*, June 1961.

laboratory and in the field. As the contrasts and similarities between the behavior of primates and man—especially preagricultural, primitive man—become clearer, they should give useful insights into the kind of social behavior that characterized the ancestors of man a million years ago.

With these objectives in mind we decided to undertake a study of the baboon. We chose this animal because it is a ground-living primate and as such is confronted with the same kind of problem that faced our ancestors when they left the trees. Our observations of some 30 troops of baboons, ranging in average membership from 40 to 80 individuals, in their natural setting in Africa show that the social behavior of the baboon is one of the species' principal adaptations for survival. Most of a baboon's life is spent within a few feet of other baboons. The troop affords protection from predators and an intimate group knowledge of the territory it occupies. Viewed from the inside, the troop is composed not of neutral creatures but of strongly emotional, highly motivated members. Our data offer little support for the theory that sexuality provides the primary bond of the primate troop. It is the intensely social nature of the baboon, expressed in a diversity of inter-individual relationships, that keeps the troop together. This conclusion calls for further observation and experimental investigation of the different social bonds. It is clear, however, that these bonds are essential to compact group living and that for a baboon life in the troop is the only way of life that is feasible.

Many game reserves in Africa support baboon populations but not all were suited to our purpose. We had to be able to locate and recognize particular troops and their individual members and to follow them in their peregrinations day after day. In some reserves the brush is so thick that such systematic observation is impossible. A small park near Nairobi, in Kenya, offered most of the conditions we needed. Here 12 troops of baboons, consisting of more than 450 members, ranged the open savanna. The animals were quite tame; they clambered onto our car and even allowed us to walk beside them. In only 10 months of study, one of us (DeVore) was able to recognize most of the members of four troops and to become moderately famil-

iar with many more. The Nairobi park, however, is small and so close to the city that the pattern of baboon life is somewhat altered. To carry on our work in an area less disturbed by humans and large enough to contain elephants, rhinoceroses, buffaloes and other ungulates as well as larger and less tame troops of baboons, we went to the Amboseli game reserve and spent two months camped at the foot of Mount Kilimanjaro. In the small part of Amboseli that we studied intensively there were 15 troops with a total of 1,200 members, the troops ranging in size from 13 to 185 members. The fact that the average size of the troops in Amboseli (80) is twice that of the troops in Nairobi shows the need to study the animals in several localities before generalizing.

A baboon troop may range an area of three to six square miles but it utilizes only parts of its range intensively. When water and food are widely distributed, troops rarely come within sight of each other. The ranges of neighboring troops overlap nonetheless, often extensively. This could be seen best in Amboseli at the end of the dry season. Water was concentrated in certain areas, and several troops often came to the same water hole, both to drink and to eat the lush vegetation near the water. We spent many days near these water holes, watching the baboons and the numerous other animals that came there.

On one occasion we counted more than 400 baboons around a single water hole at one time. To the casual observer they would have appeared to be one troop, but actually three large troops were feeding side by side. The troops came and went without mixing, even though members of different troops sat or foraged within a few feet of each other. Once we saw a juvenile baboon cross over to the next troop, play briefly and return to his own troop. But such behavior is rare, even in troops that come together at the same water hole day after day. At the water hole we saw no fighting between troops, but small troops slowly gave way before large ones. Troops that did not see each other frequently showed great interest in each other.

When one first sees a troop of baboons, it appears to have little order, but this is a superficial impression. The basic structure of the troop is most apparent when a large troop moves away from the safety of trees and out onto open plains. As the troop moves the less dominant adult males and perhaps a large juvenile or two occupy the van. Females and more of the older juveniles follow, and in the center of the troop are the females with infants, the young juveniles and the most dominant males. The back of the troop is a mirror image of its front, with less dominant males at the rear. Thus, without any fixed or formal order, the arrangement of the troop is such that the females and young are protected at the center. No matter from what direction a predator approaches the troop, it must first encounter the adult males.

When a predator is sighted, the adult males play an even more active role in defense of the troop. One day we saw two dogs run barking at a troop. The females and juveniles hurried, but the males continued to walk slowly. In a moment an irregular group of some 20 adult males was interposed between the dogs and the rest of the troop. When a male turned on the dogs, they ran off. We saw baboons close to hyenas, cheetahs and jackals, and usually the baboons seemed unconcerned—the other animals kept their distance. Lions were the only animals we saw putting a troop of baboons to flight. Twice we saw lions near baboons, whereupon the baboons climbed trees. From the safety of the trees the baboons barked and threatened the lions, but they offered no resistance to them on the ground.

With nonpredators the baboons' relations are largely neutral. It is common to see baboons walking among topi, eland, sable and roan antelopes, gazelles, zebras, hartebeests, gnus, giraffes and buffaloes, depending on which ungulates are common locally. When elephants or rhinoceroses walk through an area where the baboons are feeding, the baboons move out of the way at the last moment. We have seen wart hogs chasing each other, and a running rhinoceros go right through a troop, with the baboons merely stepping out of the way. We have seen male impalas fighting while baboons fed beside them. Once we saw a baboon chase a giraffe, but it seemed to be more in play than aggression.

Only rarely did we see baboons engage in hostilities against other species. On one occasion, however, we saw a baboon kill a small vervet monkey and eat it. The vervets frequented the same water holes as the baboons and usually they moved near them or even among them without incident. But one troop of baboons we observed at Victoria Falls pursued vervets on sight and attempted, without success, to keep them out of certain fruit trees. The vervets easily escaped in the small branches of the trees.

The baboons' food is almost entirely vegetable, although they do eat meat on rare occasions. We saw dominant males kill and eat two newborn Thomson's gazelles. Baboons are said to be fond of fledglings and birds' eggs and have even been reported digging up crocodile eggs. They also eat insects. But their diet consists principally of grass, fruit, buds and plant shoots of many kinds; in the Nairobi area alone they consume more than 50 species of plant.

For baboons, as for many herbivores, association with other species on the range often provides mutual protection. In open country their closest relations are with impalas, while in forest areas the bushbucks play a similar role. The ungulates have a keen sense of smell, and baboons have keen eyesight. Baboons are visually alert, constantly looking in all directions as they feed. If they see predators, they utter warning barks that alert not only the other baboons but also any other animals that may be in the vicinity. Similarly, a warning bark by a bushbuck or an impala will put a baboon troop to flight. A mixed herd of impalas and baboons is almost impossible to take by surprise.

Impalas are a favorite prey of cheetahs. Yet once we saw impalas, grazing in the company of baboons, make no effort to escape from a trio of approaching cheetahs. The impalas just watched as an adult male baboon stepped toward the cheetahs, uttered a cry of defiance and sent them trotting away.

The interdependence of the different species is plainly evident at a water hole, particularly where the bush is thick and visibility poor. If giraffes are drinking, zebras will run to the water. But the first animals to arrive at the water hole approach with extreme caution. In the Wankie reserve, where we also observed baboons, there are large water holes surrounded by wide areas of open sand between the water and the bushes. The baboons approached the water with great care, often resting and playing for some time in the bushes before making a hurried trip for a drink. Clearly, many animals know each other's behavior and alarm signals.

A baboon troop finds its ultimate safety, however, in the trees. It is no exaggeration to say that trees limit the distribution of baboons as much as the availability of food and water. We observed an area by a marsh in Amboseli where there was water and plenty of food. But there were lions and no trees and so there were no baboons. Only a quarter of a mile away, where lions were seen even more frequently, there were trees. Here baboons were numerous; three large troops frequented the area.

At night, when the carnivores and snakes are most active, baboons sleep high up in big trees. This is one of the baboon's primary behavioral adaptations. Diurnal living, together with an arboreal refuge at night, is an extremely effective way for them to avoid danger. The callused areas on a baboon's haunches allow it to sleep sitting up, even on small branches; a large troop can thus find sleeping places in a few trees. It is known that Colobus monkeys have a cycle of sleeping and waking throughout the night; baboons probably have a similar pattern. In any case, baboons are terrified of the dark. They arrive at the trees before night falls and stay in the branches until it is fully light. Fear of the dark, fear of falling and fear of snakes seem to be basic parts of the primate heritage.

Whether by day or night, individual baboons do not wander away from the troop, even for a few hours. The importance of the troop in ensuring the survival of its members is dramatized by the fate of those that are badly injured or too sick to keep up with their fellows. Each day the troop travels on a circuit of two to four miles; it moves from the sleeping trees to a feeding area, feeds, rests and moves again. The pace is not rapid, but the troop does not wait for sick or injured members. A baby baboon rides its mother, but all other members of the troop must keep up on their own. Once an animal is separated from the troop the chances of death are high. Sickness and injuries severe enough to be easily seen are frequent. For example, we saw a baboon with a broken forearm. The hand swung uselessly, and blood showed that the injury was recent. This baboon was gone the next morning and was not seen again. A sickness was widespread in the

Amboseli troops, and we saw individuals dragging themselves along, making tremendous efforts to stay with the troop but falling behind. Some of these may have rejoined their troops; we are sure that at least five did not. One sick little juvenile lagged for four days and then apparently recovered. In the somewhat less natural setting of Nairobi park we saw some baboons that had lost a leg. So even severe injury does not mean inevitable death. Nonetheless, it must greatly decrease the chance of survival.

Thus, viewed from the outside, the troop is seen to be an effective way of life and one that is essential to the survival of its individual members. What do the internal events of troop life reveal about the drives and motivations that cause individual baboons to "seek safety in numbers"? One of the best ways to approach an understanding of the behavior patterns within the troop is to watch the baboons when they are resting and feeding quietly.

Most of the troop will be gathered in small groups, grooming each other's fur or simply sitting. A typical group will contain two females with their young offspring, or an adult male with one or more females and juveniles grooming him. Many of these groups tend to persist, with the same animals that have been grooming each other walking together when the troop moves. The nucleus of such a "grooming cluster" is most often a dominant male or a mother with a very young infant. The most powerful males are highly attractive to the other troop members and are actively sought by them. In marked contrast, the males in many ungulate species, such as impalas, must constantly herd the members of their group together. But baboon males have no need to force the other troop members to stay with them. On the contrary, their presence alone ensures that the troop will stay with them at all times.

Young infants are equally important in the formation of grooming clusters. The newborn infant is the center of social attraction. The most dominant adult males sit by the mother and walk close beside her. When the troop is resting, adult females and juveniles come to the mother, groom her and attempt to groom the infant. Other members of the troop are drawn toward the center thus formed, both by the presence of the protective adult males and by their intense interest in the young infants.

In addition, many baboons, especially adult females, form preference pairs, and juvenile baboons come together in play groups that persist for several years. The general desire to stay in the troop is strengthened by these "friendships," which express themselves in the daily pattern of troop activity.

Our field observations, which so strongly suggest a high social motivation, are backed up by controlled experiment in the laboratory. Robert A. Butler of Walter Reed Army Hospital has shown that an isolated monkey will work hard when the only reward for his labor is the sight of another monkey. . . . In the troop this social drive is expressed in strong individual preferences, by "friendship," by interest in the infant members of the troop and by the attraction of the dominant males. Field studies show the adaptive value of these social ties. Solitary animals are far more likely to be killed, and over the generations natural selection must have favored all those factors which make learning to be sociable easy.

The learning that brings the individual baboon into full identity and participation in the baboon social system begins with the mother-child relationship. The newborn baboon rides by clinging to the hair on its mother's chest. The mother may scoop the infant on with her hand, but the infant must cling to its mother, even when she runs, from the day it is born. There is no time for this behavior to be learned. Harry F. Harlow of the University of Wisconsin has shown that an infant monkey will automatically cling to an object and much prefers objects with texture more like that of a real mother. . . . Experimental studies demonstrate this clinging reflex; field observations show why it is so important.

In the beginning the baboon mother and infant are in contact 24 hours a day. The attractiveness of the young infant, moreover, assures that he and his mother will always be surrounded by attentive troop members. Experiments show that an isolated infant brought up in a laboratory does not develop normal social patterns. Beyond the first reflexive clinging, the development of social behavior requires learning. Behavior characteristic of the species depends therefore both on the baboon's biology and on the social situations that are present in the troop.

As the infant matures it learns to ride on its mother's back, first clinging and then sitting upright. It begins to eat solid foods and to leave the mother for longer and longer periods to play with other infants. Eventually it plays with the other juveniles many hours a day, and its orientation shifts from the mother to this play group. It is in these play groups that the skills and behavior patterns of adult life are learned and practiced. Adult gestures, such as mounting, are frequent, but most play is a mixture of chasing, tail-pulling and mock fighting. If a juvenile is hurt and cries out, adults come running and stop the play. The presence of an adult male prevents small juveniles from being hurt. In the protected atmosphere of the play group the social bonds of the infant are widely extended.

Grooming, a significant biological function in itself, helps greatly to establish social bonds. The mother begins grooming her infant the day it is born, and the infant will be occupied with grooming for several hours a day for the rest of its life. All the older baboons do a certain amount of grooming, but it is the adult females who do most. They groom the infants, juveniles, adult males and other females. The baboons go to each other and "present" themselves for grooming. The grooming animal picks through the hair, parting it with its hands, removing dirt and parasites, usually by nibbling. Grooming is most often reciprocal, with one animal doing it for a while and then presenting itself for grooming. The animal being groomed relaxes, closes its eyes and gives every indication of complete pleasure. In addition to being pleasurable, grooming serves the important function of keeping the fur clean. Ticks are common in this area and can be seen on many animals such as dogs and lions; a baboon's skin, however, is free of them. Seen in this light, the enormous amount of time baboons spend in grooming each other is understandable. Grooming is pleasurable to the individual, it is the most important expression of close social bonds and it is biologically adaptive.

The adults in a troop are arranged in a dominance hierarchy, explicitly revealed in their relations with other members of the troop. The most dominant males will be more frequently groomed and they occupy feeding and resting positions of their choice. When a dominant animal approaches a subordinate one, the lesser animal moves out of the way. The observer can determine the order of dominance simply by watching the reactions of the baboons as they move past each other. In the tamer troops these observations can be tested by feeding. If food is tossed between two baboons, the more dominant one will take it, whereas the other may not even look at it directly.

The status of a baboon male in the dominance hierarchy depends not only on his physical condition and fighting ability but also on his relationships with other males. Some adult males in every large troop stay together much of the time, and if one of them is threatened, the others are likely to back him up. A group of such males outranks any individual, even though another male outside the group might be able to defeat any member of it separately. The hierarchy has considerable stability and this is due in large part to its dependence on clusters of males rather than the fighting ability of individuals. In troops where the rank order is clearly defined, fighting is rare. We observed frequent bickering or severe fighting in only about 15 per cent of the troops. The usual effect of the hierarchy, once relations among the males are settled, is to decrease disruptions in the troop. The dominant animals, the males in particular, will not let others fight. When bickering breaks out, they usually run to the scene and stop it. Dominant males thus protect the weaker animals against harm from inside as well as outside. Females and juveniles come to the males to groom them or just to sit beside them. So although dominance depends ultimately on force, it leads to peace, order and popularity.

Much has been written about the importance of sex in uniting the troop; it has been said, for example, that "the powerful social magnet of sex was the major impetus to subhuman primate sociability." . . . Our observations lead us to assign to sexuality a much lesser, and even at times a contrary, role. The sexual behavior of baboons depends on the biological cycle of the female. She is receptive for approximately one week out of every month, when she is in estrus. When first receptive, she leaves her infant and her friendship group and goes to the males, mating first with the subordinate males and older juveniles. Later in the period of receptivity she goes to the dominant males and "presents." If a male is not interested, the female is likely to groom him and then

present again. Near the end of estrus the dominant males become very interested, and the female and a male form a consort pair. They may stay together for as little as an hour or for as long as several days. Estrus disrupts all other social relationships, and consort pairs usually move to the edge of the troop. It is at this time that fighting may take place, if the dominance order is not clearly established among the males. Normally there is no fighting over females, and a male, no matter how dominant, does not monopolize a female for long. No male is ever associated with more than one estrus female; there is nothing resembling a family or a harem among baboons.

Much the same seems to be true of other species of monkey. Sexual behavior appears to contribute little to the cohesion of the troop. Some monkeys have breeding seasons, with all mating taking place within less than half the year. But even in these species the troop continues its normal existence during the months when there is no mating. It must be remembered that among baboons a female is not sexually receptive for most of her life. She is juvenile, pregnant or lactating; estrus is a rare event in her life. Yet she does not leave the troop even for a few minutes. In baboon troops, particularly small ones, many months may pass when no female member comes into estrus; yet no animals leave the troop, and the highly structured relationships within it continue without disorganization.

The sociableness of baboons is expressed in a wide variety of behavior patterns that reinforce each other and give the troop cohesion. As the infant matures the nature of the social bonds changes continually, but the bonds are always strong. The ties between mother and infant, between a juvenile and its peers in a play group, and between a mother and an adult male are quite different from one another. Similarly, the bond between two females in a friendship group, between the male and female in a consort pair or among the members of a cluster of males in the dominance hierarchy is based on diverse biological and behavioral factors, which offer a rich field for experimental investigation.

In addition, the troop shares a considerable social tradition. Each troop has its own range and a secure familiarity with the food and water sources, escape routes, safe refuges and sleeping places inside it. The counterpart of the intensely social life within the troop is the coordination of the activities of all the troop's members throughout their lives. Seen against the background of evolution, it is clear that in the long run only the social baboons have survived.

When comparing the social behavior of baboons with that of man, there is little to be gained from laboring the obvious differences between modern civilization and the society of baboons. The comparison must be drawn against the fundamental social behavior patterns that lie behind the vast variety of human ways of life. For this purpose we have charted the salient features of baboon life in a native habitat alongside those of human life in preagricultural society. . . . Cursory inspection shows that the differences are more numerous and significant than are the similarities.

The size of the local group is the only category in which there is not a major contrast. The degree to which these contrasts are helpful in understanding the evolution of human behavior depends, of course, on the degree to which baboon behavior is characteristic of monkeys and apes in general and therefore probably characteristic of the apes that evolved into men. Different kinds of monkey do behave differently, and many more field studies will have to be made before the precise degree of difference can be understood.

For example, many arboreal monkeys have a much smaller geographical range than baboons do. In fact, there are important differences between the size and type of range for many monkey species. But there is no suggestion that a troop of any species of monkey or ape occupies the hundreds of square miles ordinarily occupied by preagricultural human societies. Some kinds of monkey may resent intruders in their range more than baboons do, but there is no evidence that any species fights for complete control of a territory. Baboons are certainly less vocal than some other monkeys, but no nonhuman primate has even the most rudimentary language. We believe that the fundamental contrasts in our chart would hold for the vast majority of monkeys and apes as compared with the ancestors of man. Further study of primate behavior will sharpen these contrasts and define more clearly the gap that had to be traversed from ape to human behavior. But already we can see that man is as unique in his sharing, co-operation and play patterns as he is in his locomotion, brain and language.

The basis for most of these differences may lie in hunting. Certainly the hunting of large animals must have involved co-operation among the hunters and sharing of the food within the tribe. Similarly, hunting requires an enormous extension of range and the protection of a hunting territory. If this speculation proves to be correct, much of the evolution of human behavior can be reconstructed, because the men of 500,000 years ago were skilled hunters. In locations such as Choukoutien in China and Olduvai Gorge in Africa there is evidence of both the hunters and their campsites. . . . We are confident that the study of the living primates, together with the archaeological record, will eventually make possible a much richer understanding of the evolution of human behavior.

DISCUSSION QUESTIONS

1. Why do the authors feel that the study of nonhuman primates is an important undertaking for anthropologists? Why, in particular, did they choose to study baboons?

2. How might the physical environment of the baboons play a role in shaping the evolution of baboon behavior?

3. How do the size, structure, and daily routine of a baboon troop increase its chances for survival?

INTERNET RESOURCES

After reading this article, you might wish to learn more about the research and writings of other individuals, such as:

- Solly Zuckerman
- Harry Harlow
- Robert Sapolsky

 **InfoTrac College Edition**

(infotrac-college.com)
You can find many other readings pertinent to this topic by consulting online databases including Info-Trac College Edition. Some suggested search terms for this article are as follows.

- Dominance hierarchy
- Grooming
- Mother–infant bond

11

Leading Ladies

JEANNE ALTMANN

Three decades after Sherwood Washburn and Irven DeVore published their landmark study of savanna baboons, Jeanne Altmann wrote this selection, a snapshot of baboon behavior as night falls, predators lurk about, and the troop needs to make its way gingerly toward safe places to sleep. Here in the Amboseli National Park (one of the areas where her predecessors studied common baboons), Altmann conducted her own 20-year investigation of this species.

In both focus and tone, Altmann's narrative differs from the classic article written by Washburn and DeVore. As you read through this selection, pay particular attention to the details of Altmann's description of this encounter. In noting the differences, you'll find important clues about how the field of primatology developed following Washburn's initial investigations. Note also that Altmann's narrative is centered around a research problem—a specific question about baboon behavior—that she explores in her example. Try to identify that research question and state it in your own words. The central issue Altmann is exploring pertains to broader topics, such as social relationships, reproduction, and aging among savanna baboons. It points to some intriguing differences in sex roles among male and female baboons.

Some six years after Altmann recorded this scene, she published an update on this troop of Ambroseli baboons (see "Leading Ladies." In The Primate Anthology: Essays on Primate Behavior, Ecology, and Conservation from *Natural History, edited by Russell L. Ciochon and Richard A. Nisbett, 27. Upper Saddle River, NJ: Prentice Hall, 1998). Handle, the "leading lady" of this episode, had died, leaving behind some of her adult female offspring. According to Altmann, Handle's death signaled the "end of an era," for she had been the last of the Amboseli baboons to have been born before Altmann's work commenced in the 1970s. Most sobering of all, Altmann noted that the landscape of the park had been dramatically altered by the effects of global warming. Rising temperatures had radically transformed the landscape into more of an open savanna with fewer trees. She saw signs of the baboons adjusting to these environmental changes by spending more time looking for food, moving into more tree-filled niches to the south, and splitting up into smaller groups. Had she lived longer, would Handle's role as "leading lady" have been affected by the dramatically changing world of the Amboseli baboons? Hopefully, the devastating crisis of global warming will one day be met with as much human bravery and determination as our cousins the baboons have already demonstrated.*

SOURCE: Jeanne Altmann, "Leading Ladies," *Natural History*, February 1992, 48–51. Copyright © Natural History Magazine, Inc., 1992.

As her young infant alternately suckled and dozed in the shelter of her lap, the elderly baboon, known to us as Handle, stared intently toward the distant grove of trees. The five dozen members of her group sat tensely in clusters nearby. Indecision was in the air, and even the playful juveniles seemed to sense it, staying closer to their older relatives than they had all day. A short while before, as they were heading southward toward a grove of trees in which to spend the night, the group had spotted a leopard—the baboons' major predator. Although the leopard was no longer visible, the chatter of vervet monkeys in the distance, near the intended sleeping trees, confirmed that danger would await the baboons if they continued as planned. The sun was dropping rapidly now, and the short equatorial dusk would give the baboons little time to make a decision: stick to the original plan or strike out for one of the other groves—all farther away—scattered across their East African savanna home. If they didn't act fast, darkness would overtake them far from the safety of tall trees.

Occasionally, one young adult or another gave rapid, soft vocalizations and started moving tentatively toward the original grove or in another direction, but the other baboons remained in place and the initiator soon sat again. After ten long minutes, in a single, smooth motion, Handle stood, her infant still clutching her sides but now riding under her, and began to move decisively westward toward a grove still hidden in the dusty, dry-season haze. Barely a few seconds later, her daughter Heko followed with her own infant on her back. Handle paused as she looked back; throughout the group, baboons responded with soft grunts and moved to follow her. The rippling motion rapidly grew into a wave, and soon, all the baboons followed, silent except for the protests of tired youngsters for whom first the tension and now the sudden rapid pace were too much. By the time the baboons reached the grove, the light was nearly gone, and the animals were little more than silhouettes as they ascended the trees. I just barely made out Handle as, hunched stiffly over her sleeping infant, she settled onto a comfortable branch for the night.

During more than twenty years observing baboons in Amboseli National Park in southern Kenya, my colleagues and I have seen one elderly female after another serve as leaders at critical times in group movements. Actual fights with predators or other baboon groups usually involve many troop members; then, adult males are often in the fore, but each animal seems to know or decide for itself whether to flee, hang back, or threaten the intruders. In contrast, the decisive role of elderly females more often is seen at "controversial" moments in group movements, when all will take the same route, but just which route is not clear or agreed upon. At those times, elderly females (those over about fifteen years of age) seem to make the choices that are followed. We don't know for sure why the "opinions" of these females carry so much weight. Social rank is not the answer, for we have seen high-, low-, and mid-ranking individuals (such as Handle) lead the group. The permanent members of baboon society are the females, and many older females tend to have several daughters and other descendants in the group. Could the most influential females simply have the most descendants? Certain evidence seems to support this. Like Handle, elderly Alto had many offspring and she, too, was a leader at times. In contrast, we have never observed eighteen-year-old Dotty, who has few offspring, or Dotty's age-mate Janet, who has none, assume leadership roles.

The equation cannot be a simple one, however, for another elderly female, low-ranking Este, had few offspring and yet was often a leader at critical junctures in the troop's life. Perhaps the explanation lies in the extent to which the leaders are enmeshed in a longstanding, complex network of social relationships. Unlike males, who change group membership when they mature, females spend their whole lives in the group in which they are born. Certainly, twenty-three-year-old Handle has had a long time to build up a social network. Although none of her elders and few of her peers are still alive, all of the group's youngsters have grown up knowing her.

Few baboons live long enough to develop the kind of rich social network Handle enjoys. Less than half the baboons in the population survive infancy, and once they reach adulthood (at age six for females and eight for males) the annual death rate is about 10 percent. The rare elderly survivors like Handle usually seem somewhat slow and stiff. They sometimes drop to the rear of the group, especially in the morning cold, as the baboons set off for the day's six-mile foraging trek, and in the late afternoon, when the fatigued animals move to a sleeping grove. Although Handle actually still seems fairly spry, her teeth are very worn, and her weight seems to have declined in recent years, suggesting that she may need to spend more time feeding to obtain enough digestible food.

Not surprisingly, perhaps, Handle, like other elderly females, often seems to be somewhat separate from younger members of the group and to have less time to interact with them. And yet she is undeniably an active group member. Several factors of baboon life help keep it that way. Baboon females continue to bear young throughout their lives (although slightly less frequently), and when infants are born, relatives, friends, and just plain curious acquaintances cluster about the infant and its mother. Motherhood is a way of renewing and reinforcing social ties. These ties are further cemented by grooming, the baboons' way of keeping in close touch—calming one another down, sharing messages. Females groom their grown daughters, special unrelated male friends, and others in the troop. We think it significant that Handle has long been one of the group's most frequent, and most thorough, groomers.

The life of male baboons follows [a] quite different path. Even as two- or three-year-olds, they begin to move away from their mothers' world. Young females increasingly reciprocate their mothers' grooming; young males do not, and their mothers soon discontinue grooming them. In addition, the young males' social interactions involve more partners outside their maternal lineage, so that by the time males leave their birth group, at eight or nine years of age, they have experienced a broader range of social relationships than have their female peers. This is probably of great value, considering the tasks they face: those males that survive to immigrate into another group must deal with a hostile reception by the resident males. They must also develop all new relationships with both males and females, including potential sexual partners. And unlike females (who inherit their mother's social rank and retain it throughout adulthood), males must compete for the rank they attain and cannot expect to keep it: for males, status peaks in young adulthood and declines more or less rapidly soon thereafter. Social relationships may change even more for those males who, like Handle's firstborn son, Hans, switch groups several times. Moreover, males do much less grooming than females and, at least as young adults, do so primarily with potential sexual partners.

For all these reasons, we might expect to find that aging males are less socially integrated and have fewer social resources. However, studies increasingly document long-term friendships, involving grooming and some infant care, between mature males and females. Sometimes older males in these relationships have even greater success sexually than do dominant, younger males. Newly weaned youngsters may also benefit from the protective friendship of older males, who occasionally perform acts of heroism—defending the youngsters from injury by other adult males or rescuing and carrying them to safety when they cannot keep up with the group's rapid flight from predators.

Reaching old age may be rare in savanna baboon society, but those individuals that do survive are much more than decrepit hangers-on. As fellow primates, they suggest some of the many ways of growing old and contributing to a complex social world.

DISCUSSION QUESTIONS

1. How does this description of baboons differ from that provided in Washburn and DeVore's article (see Chapter 9)? What topics or behaviors did you see discussed in this reading that were not in the Washburn and DeVore article?

2. Do you see Altmann's observations as being relevant to the understanding of human evolution? In what ways might this study shed light on the origins of human behavior?

3. What is the central research problem that Altmann is addressing in this article? What are some observations that she draws upon to address this issue?

INTERNET RESOURCES

InfoTrac College Edition

(infotrac-college.com)
You can find many other readings pertinent to this topic by consulting online databases including InfoTrac College Edition. Some suggested search terms

for this article are as follows.

- Vervet monkey
- Nonhuman primate sex roles
- Female-dominated species
- Global warming

12

Dance of the Sexes

SHARON T. POCHRON AND PATRICIA C. WRIGHT

The primate order is exceedingly diverse. Taken as a whole, primates—a group that includes the major subdivisions of prosimians (lemurs and lorises), monkeys (from both the Old and New Worlds), and apes (lesser and greater)—are generalized mammals. They can eat practically anything from seeds to sap, or grass to grubs, as well as varying amounts of fruit, leaves, and animal protein. Some live in tropical forests, while others survive in near-desert conditions. Throughout their ancient history, primates moved into, and subsequently become better adapted for, a great array of environments. Thus, over time, and through natural selection, primates' generalized nature—their mammalian ability to function as the jack-of-all-trades in the natural world—supported their evolution into a diverse taxonomic order.

If we wanted to choose a primate that exemplifies that diversity, we'd certainly want to look among the lemurs of Madagascar. The primate featured in this article, the Milne-Edwards's sifaka, is no exception. Indeed, primatologists Pochron and Wright, the authors of this selection, remark that this species resembles something from The Muppet Show. *Their uniqueness among primates is attributed to several factors. It's hypothesized that the ancestors of modern lemurs rafted to Madagascar, the third largest island in the world, over 60 million years ago, thereby severing their kin ties with their original population. Once settled onto the island, members of the ancestral lineage moved into various econiches and subsequently evolved their distinctive features through natural selection. This phenomenon, known as an adaptive radiation, worked in concert with another force—isolation—to further shape the genetic makeup of lemurs. Consequently, Madagascar's lemurs demonstrate many unique behavioral and anatomical features.*

As you read this article, identify some distinguishing traits seen among various lemurs, while paying particular attention to the author's research questions about the Milne-Edwards's sifaka. The authors start with a seemingly simple question, "Why are females of this species dominant over males?" To answer this question, they must consider many variables, as is often the case in science. Variation in social behaviors, group size and composition, reproductive rate, longevity, and the environment all figure into an intriguing topic that is still under study.

The group of lemurs, known as Milne-Edwards's sifakas, was small—an adult male, an adult female, and two large offspring. With only four animals, distinguishing them should have been easy.

"That's the male," said Georges Rakotonirina, pointing. Rakotonirina was the lead field technician, a native of Madagascar who had been studying the sifakas with one of us (Wright) since 1986.

SOURCE: Sharon T. Pochran and Patricia C. Wright, "Dance of the Sexes," *Natural History* 114.5 (June 2005): 34–38.

"And that's the female." The novice among us (Pochron), new to the study in 2000, stared at the dark forms up in the tree and blinked. They all looked the same.

"Look," said Rakotonirina. "They're eating vahia-banikondro."

"What?" Pochron thought to herself. "How can he tell from down here what they're eating? And can I possibly learn to pronounce and spell . . . whatever it is?" Hearing chattering in the forest canopy, Pochron then asked aloud, "What bird is that?"

Rakotonirina laughed. "That's the sifaka," he said. "It means he wants to stop fighting." Pochron knew then and there she had some catching up to do, notwithstanding her previous experience studying baboons in Tanzania. But like Wright and many others whose first encounter with lemurs was life-changing, she was hooked.

The lemurs of Madagascar are the surviving members of a lineage that has been genetically isolated from the rest of the primate family for at least 65 million years. The island became separated from the African mainland 160 million years ago, and from the Indian landmass 80 million years ago. The ancestors of lemurs probably colonized the island by rafting there on drifting vegetation. Until relatively recently, lemurs lived in a separate world. Meanwhile, primates elsewhere evolved into monkeys, apes, and humans.

That ancient genetic split is surely one reason lemurs often boast such unusual traits, compared with humanity's closer primate relatives. For example, dwarf lemurs store up fat in their tails and then draw on it while hibernating; in contrast, no monkey or ape hibernates. Members of one lemur family, the indriids, maintain an upright, kangaroolike posture as they leap from one tree trunk and cling to another; monkeys, however, are quadrupedal, like squirrels. All lemurs have toothcombs—a set of teeth ideally shaped for grooming; monkey and ape teeth are shaped for biting and chewing.

Especially surprising to evolutionary biologists, in most groups of lemurs, females are dominant over males. In some lemur species female dominance becomes manifest only in conflicts over food; in other species it emerges in all social settings. Yet in monkeys and apes—indeed, in mammals generally—female dominance is rare. What has led to such an unusual social characteristic among lemurs, with its far-reaching implications?

Female mammals that do dominate males are usually well equipped physically to do so. Female spotted hyenas are often bigger than males. Female reindeer rule over males during the short season when males have shed their antlers prior to growing new ones and the females have not yet shed theirs. Female golden hamsters call the shots when they are fatter than males.

But female lemurs are not usually larger than males, nor do they have any special weapons for enforcing dominance, such as bigger teeth. Members of the two sexes are virtually monomorphic, or similar, when it comes to physical strength. How do females manage to get their way without the brawn to back up a threat? We and our colleagues do not yet have a definitive answer to that question, but after eighteen years studying one indriid species, we have some inklings.

The center of our universe is the Milne-Edwards's sifaka (*Propithecus edwardsi*). Until recently it was considered a subspecies of the diademed sifaka, but geneticists have now determined that it is a separate species. Weighing in at about thirteen pounds and looking like something out of the Muppet studio, the animal lives throughout Ranomafana National Park, a 170-square-mile emerald forest set in cloud-covered mountains, and in adjacent regions. . . . It has orange eyes and woolly, water-resistant fur (a useful trait in a rainforest), which is colored dark brown to black except for two large, white patches on the animal's back. The females have a lemony, maple-syrupy smell; the males, which have more glands for scent marking, smell muskier.

Active by day, Milne-Edwards's sifakas prefer to hang out some forty feet up in the trees, and they travel, as do other indriids, by leaping from one tree trunk to the next. Adults are mainly leaf eaters, but they also rely heavily on fruits and seeds.

Females and males do not often come into conflict, but when they do, the females win about 95 percent of the time. Apparently males are letting females win such altercations. What are they giving up by submitting? The answer may be calories. Adult females, for instance, appear to eat more seeds than adult males do. The difference is most pronounced during the mating season. Seeds are generally high in fat, and storing up fat is good preparation for a female on her way to becoming reproductively active. When you see males and females fighting, you will probably find tempting seeds nearby.

If males are allowing females to enjoy more seeds, what are they getting in return? The answers that jump to mind are: sex and offspring. And that would make sense in evolutionary terms. Unfortunately for the theory, the annual estrus cycle of the female lasts only ten hours, and in that short period she may mate with several males. None of those mating males is likely to know whose baby the female is having. If he allows a female to take his food, and she uses it to raise another male's offspring, he has not helped himself at all. So why would he allow her to win extra calories? Nature is hardly known for its generosity. In our years of field observations seeking answers to this question, we have found ourselves bumping into some other unusual and fascinating lemur traits. Our goal, then, is to find a coherent explanation that makes sense of it all: with apologies to the high-energy physicists, our holy grail is a kind of grand unified theory of the lemur.

Milne-Edwards's sifakas usually occur in small groups ranging from two to nine individuals. Typically, the groups include three adults (either two males and one female, or vice versa), infants, and older offspring. A female may come into her brief period of estrus at any time during the mating season, which runs from late November through mid-January. The babies are born in May, June, and July. A female gives birth to only one baby at a time, and nurses it attentively until the next mating season, if it survives until then. The cycle puts weaning at a propitious time, when food is most likely to be abundant. A mother that has nursed a baby that long is apt to skip a year before breeding again, most likely because it takes a while to store up enough fat.

Within a group of sifakas life is reasonably peaceful: members spend a lot more time grooming each other than they do squabbling. Males within a group get along most of the year. During the mating season, though, fights between males can be among the most aggressive in this species. There is little question that the fights are about sex, and the fact that fighters sometimes suffer injuries to their testicles may be no accident. You can tell that a threatening look, a swipe, or a bite has had an effect if you hear the intended target emit birdlike chatter, the equivalent of, "Stop picking on me! I'll leave now!"

Since the males are clearly competing with each other for access to fertile females, it is puzzling that males have not evolved to be larger than the females (or to have bigger teeth or other such endowments). According to classic behavioral ecology, when males compete, the larger or stronger males usually prevail. The larger males thus have more offspring, and those offspring carry the genes associated with being large. After several generations the repeated selection for large males should lead to males that are larger than the females. When the males and females of a species differ in such physical characteristics, the species is said to be sexually dimorphic.

Most large mammal species are sexually dimorphic. Monomorphism, where it is found, typically occurs in monogamous species, in which a single male and female pair up to raise their offspring together. To succeed evolutionarily, monogamy has to be a two-way street. The male has the genetic incentive to help feed, carry, and protect the young of a particular female only if the monogamous bond assures him the young are his. If the female needs a devoted mate to help raise her young, she has a genetic incentive of her own—to avoid mating with a male that beats up other males, because, despite winning the "right" to take many "wives," he cannot offer parental care to all his offspring. When male fighting is suppressed by such female preferences, so too is sexual dimorphism. Some lemurs such as indris (*Indri indri*) fit that pattern: they are monomorphic and monogamous. . . .

Paradoxically, though, most lemur species do not behave like indris: they mate promiscuously, and males provide little or no care for infants, which may or may not be theirs. In short, they look like monogamous species, but they act like nonmonogamous ones. The Milne-Edwards's sifaka fits that pattern, too. But how can it be a stable arrangement?

Our observations offer part of the solution to the puzzle. First, no male, even if he is stronger than other males, can prevent a female from mating promiscuously. Nor does a larger male have the advantage of producing more sperm, because during the breeding season the testicles of all the males are roughly the same size. Thus the ejaculate of a heavy male cannot, as has been observed in some mammalian and avian species, overwhelm the ejaculate of a light male: if they both mate with a particular female, each has an equal chance to father her offspring.

Aside from the competition between males over females, serious fighting may also erupt when a new adult animal joins a group. Such transitions in group membership shed additional light on the roles of males and females—and, in particular, the dominance of females—within lemur groups.

Milne-Edwards's sifaka groups are far less predictable in composition than those of monkey and ape species. A baboon troop, for instance, characteristically includes many adult males and females. Gorilla groups are generally polygynous, consisting of one silverback male, his harem of several adult females, their young, and one or more subordinate males. By contrast, sifaka groups can be polyandrous (one female and two or more males) or polygynous (one male and two or more females). They can include multiple males and multiple females—or just one adult pair. . . .

Not only do all such combinations turn up with roughly equal frequency, but a group may change in composition from one year to the next. A new member is most likely to join a group from August until October, just before the mating season. If a new male seeks to join a group, all the animals may coexist peacefully. Sometimes, though, the resident male and the newcomer fight, and one is driven away. And sometimes a female prefers the new male, and she may help force the old male to leave.

For any dependent offspring in the group, an incoming male poses great danger: he is likely to kill them, a measure that is evolutionarily adaptive because it speeds up his chance to father offspring. Such behavior is well documented in primates.

When an adult female tries to join a group, friction with the resident female seems inevitable. The two sometimes bite, slap, and chase each other. The resident female generally leaves, probably an indication that the incoming female has shrewdly judged her chances before attempting to gain entry. Just as males do, an incoming female may kill any dependent young. In other primates, at least, it is less common—and less easily explained as adaptive behavior—for the female to kill the young than it is for the male. The murderous action of the incoming female seems to hasten the departure of the resident female. When two adult females live together peaceably in a group, we suspect that they are closely related. Genetic studies currently under way should clarify this.

To investigate why the sifaka's social arrangements vary so widely, we compared sifaka survivorship and fertility patterns with those of some other primates. For example, tamarins and marmosets, both New World monkeys, suffer high mortality in their early years; sensibly, then, they reach sexual maturity and begin reproducing at an early age. By contrast, many Old World monkeys, such as baboons and macaques, live longer, start to reproduce later, and have more time between babies.

The mortality pattern of the Milne-Edwards's sifaka closely resembles that of the tamarins and marmosets: many die in their first few years of life. In fertility, however, Milne-Edwards's sifakas resemble baboons and macaques: the sifakas that do survive reach sexual maturity fairly late (about three and a half years for females, and four and a half years for males), and they reproduce at a slow rate over a span approaching thirty years. It is almost as if sifakas have deliberately chosen the most difficult of all the primate patterns ever observed: high mortality coupled with slow reproduction. By the end of her life, a female tamarin or marmoset will have three or four daughters; a baboon or macaque will have two or three. But by the end of her lifespan, a female sifaka will rarely have more than one daughter that survives to reproduce. The constraints on reproduction may be responsible for encouraging the sifakas' highly flexible group structures.

The sifaka's lifespan is unusual for a mammal its size. On average, the larger the species, the longer it lives. As we noted earlier, Milne-Edwards's sifakas weigh about thirteen pounds, yet they live nearly thirty years in the wild. Such longevity may have evolved in response to unpredictable environmental conditions. After all, a longer life gives the animals a better chance of reproducing during the years when conditions are most favorable. It is hard to imagine that food could ever be scarce in a place such as Ranomafana National Park, where greenery covers every surface. Yet the availability of food varies seasonally, with the rain. Furthermore, Madagascar is prone to cyclones and droughts, which can also lead to shortages.

Perhaps here too is part of the solution to our original question about lemurs: why are females the dominant sex? The behavioral pattern, in which males cede food to females, appears essential for balancing female and male reproductive needs. For females, fertility, pregnancy, and nursing all depend on sufficient body weight. Weight is less important for males, because their reproductive role is limited to copulation and, as we mentioned earlier, during the breeding season, the testes of small-bodied males are the same size as those of larger-bodied males. If the males did grow larger overall, Madagascar's unpredictable environment might prove fatal to them. In sum, neither having a small body size nor relinquishing high-calorie foods to females seems to compromise the fertility of males.

In the past few years we have considered a number of ways to account for these observations. Because the females mate promiscuously, perhaps each male simply defers to all females, on the grounds that there is always some chance that one of them will bear his offspring. Or a male may yield food to a female only when he has some good reasons for thinking he will sire her offspring. Or a male may defer to a close female relative (mother, sister, daughter), whose offspring would indirectly share some of his genes. Or maybe the reality is some combination of all those factors. . . .

One way to learn more about what is going on is to test offspring for paternity. Toni Lyn Morelli, one of Wright's graduate students, has been sampling blood of these sifakas and analyzing it genetically. In a species where the average number of adults in a group is three, however, discerning a statistically significant pattern may take some time. And—who knows?—the results may lead us to some new lemur mystery.

DISCUSSION QUESTIONS

1. How do relationships among males and females in Milne-Edwards's sifakas differ from those in other primate groups?

2. What kinds of social group structures have been observed among Milne-Edwards's sifakas?

3. How might environmental factors influence relationships among the sexes and variation in social groups among Milne-Edwards's sifakas?

4. What are some unusual behavioral and anatomical traits that have been seen among lemurs as compared to most other nonhuman primates such as monkeys and apes?

INTERNET RESOURCES

You can find additional information about primate species by searching for "animal diversity" on the web or visiting the website of the University of Wisconsin's National Primate Research Center at http://pin.primate.wisc.edu.

 **InfoTrac College Edition**

(infotrac-college.com)
You can find many other readings pertinent to this topic by consulting online databases including Info-Trac College Edition. Some suggested search terms for this article are as follows.

- Sexual dimorphism
- Polygynous and polyandrous groups
- Indriidae
- Lemuridae

13

Learning from the Chimpanzees: A Message Humans Can Understand

JANE GOODALL

In 1960, a young woman named Jane Goodall revolutionized the world of anthropology when she announced a landmark discovery from the Gombe Stream Reserve in Tanzania. She had watched a chimpanzee select a twig, clean it of leaves, and insert it into a termite mound. The chimp then removed the stick and ate what we can only assume was a tasty treat of termites.

Goodall, who at the time lacked formal training in animal behavior, had been investigating the common chimpanzee, Pan troglodytes, *at the request of Louis Leakey. Leakey and his wife, Mary, were busy studying their own finds—fossils and stone tools—from the famous site of Olduvai Gorge. Louis Leakey, ever passionate about reconstructing the earliest stages in human evolution, believed that our closest living relatives, the apes, could provide us with a more complete picture of our evolutionary journey.*

Prior to Goodall's observation, tool making was thought to be the sole province of human beings. Since that time, Leakey's expectations have been validated time and again. Other apes and some monkeys (not to mention other species of mammals) have been seen using natural objects for specific tasks. Meanwhile, other similarities between chimpanzees and humans have been noted, including food sharing and cooperative hunting as well as brutal interpersonal violence and seemingly unprovoked attacks. Though the idea of a chimp making a tool now seems commonplace, it still compels us to reconsider—as it did at the time—the meaning of our common ancestry with chimpanzees.

In this selection, Goodall reflects on her career, paying special attention to our changing attitudes about the mind and emotions of other species. As you read Goodall's article, ask yourself how she is defining the term "mind" with respect to chimpanzees. Also, think about the ways in which you could define humans *apart from those behaviors that we share with chimpanzees.*

Today, over four decades later, Dr. Jane Goodall is a deeply admired international figure who travels almost every day to speaking engagements and conferences. She also has written extensively both for general and scientific audiences. While the long-term studies of chimpanzees continue at Gombe, Goodall's energy and her mission are focused on broader causes involving conservation and global climate change. Also, she has fought to end the use of chimpanzees in biomedical research, while working tirelessly to ensure that both chimpanzees and humans will share a common future as well as an ancient past.

SOURCE: Jane Goodall, "Essays on Science and Society: Learning from the Chimpanzees: A Message Humans Can Understand," *Science* 282, no. 5397 (18 December 1998): 2184–2185. Reprinted with permission from AAAS.

When I began my study of wild chimpanzees in 1960 at Gombe Stream Research Center it was not permissible, at least not in ethological circles, to talk about an animal's mind. Only humans had minds. Nor was it quite proper to talk about animal personality. Of course everyone knew that they did have their own unique characters—everyone who had ever owned a dog or other pet was aware of that. But ethologists, striving to make theirs a "hard" science, shied away from the task of trying to explain such things objectively. One respected ethologist, while acknowledging that there was "variability between individual animals," wrote that it was best that this fact be "swept under the carpet."

How naïve I was. As I had not had an undergraduate science education, I did not realize that animals were not supposed to have personalities, or to think, or to feel emotions or pain. I had no idea that it would have been more appropriate—once I got to know him or her—to assign each of the chimpanzees a number rather than a name. I did not realize that it was unscientific to discuss behavior in terms of motivation or purpose. It was not respectable, in scientific circles, to talk about animal personality. That was something reserved for humans. Nor did animals have minds, so they were not capable of rational thought. And to talk about their emotions was to be guilty of the worst kind of anthropomorphism (attributing human characteristics to animals).

The editorial comments on the first paper that I wrote for publication demanded that every "he" or "she" be replaced with "it," and every "who" be replaced with "which." Incensed, I, in turn, crossed out the "it's" and "which's" and scrawled back the original pronouns. As I had no desire to carve out a niche for myself in the world of science but simply wanted to go on living among and learning about chimpanzees, the possible reaction of the editor of the learned journal did not trouble me. The paper, when finally published, did confer upon the chimpanzees the dignity of their appropriate genders and properly upgraded them from the status of mere "things" to essential beingness.

When I first began to read about human evolution I learned that one of the hallmarks of our own species was that we, and only we, are capable of making tools. I well remember writing to Louis Leakey about my first observations of the chimpanzees of Gombe, describing how David Greybeard not only used bits of straw to fish for termites but how he actually stripped leaves from a stem, and thus made a tool. And I remember, too, receiving the now oft-quoted telegram that Leakey sent in response to my letter: "Now we must redefine tool, redefine Man, or accept chimpanzees as humans." By and large, people were fascinated by this information and by the subsequent observations of other contexts in which the Gombe chimpanzees used objects as tools.

The mid-1960s saw the start of a project that, along with other similar research, was to teach us a great deal about the chimpanzee mind. This was Project Washoe, conceived by Trixie and Allen Gardner[,] who purchased an infant chimpanzee and began to teach her the signs of ASL, the American Sign Language used by the deaf. When news of Washoe's accomplishments first hit the scientific community it immediately provoked a storm of bitter protest. It implied that chimpanzees were capable of mastering a human language, and this, in turn, indicated mental powers of generalization, abstraction, concept formation, and an ability to understand and use abstract symbols. And so, with new incentive, psychologists began to test the mental abilities of chimpanzees in a variety of ways. Again and again the results confirmed that their minds are uncannily like our own.

As in Darwin's time, it is again fashionable to speak of and study the animal mind. This change came about gradually, and was, at least in part, due to the information collected during careful studies of animal societies in the field. As these observations became widely known, it was impossible to brush aside the complexities of social behavior that were revealed in species after species. A succession of experiments clearly proved that many intellectual abilities that had been thought unique to humans were actually present in nonhumans—particularly in the nonhuman primates and especially in chimpanzees—although in a less highly developed form.

Today, ethological thinking and methodology has softened, and it is generally recognized that the old, parsimonious explanations of complex behavior were inappropriate. The study of animal mentation is fashionable, and the examination of animal emotions is commonplace. This is without doubt due, in large part, to the information that came in from long-term field studies conducted during the 1960s. All of these careful observations, made in the natural habitat, helped to show that the societies and behavior of animals are far more complex than previously supposed by scientists. In light of the new information, overly simplistic explanations were generally abandoned, leading to a changed and expanded understanding of our fellow animals on Earth.

Of all the facts to emerge from my years of research on the chimpanzees at Gombe, it is their humanlike behaviors that most fascinate people: their tool-using and tool-making abilities; the close supportive bonds among family members, which can persist throughout a lifetime of 50 or more years; and their complex social interactions—the cooperation, the altruism, and the expression of emotions like joy and sadness. It is our recognition of these intellectual and emotional similarities between chimpanzees and ourselves that has, more than anything else, blurred the line, once thought so sharp, between human beings and other animals. Through observations of chimpanzees, people's attitudes toward nonhuman animals have definitely begun to change. In fact, the winds of change are blowing. There is finally, in our society, a growing concern for the plight of nonhuman animals. This changed attitude, among scientists and nonscientists alike, has unquestionably come about because chimps are so like us.

One of the unexpected rewards that I have found as I become increasingly involved in conservation and animal welfare issues, has been meeting so many dedicated, caring, and understanding people.

I cannot close this without sharing a story that, for me, has a truly symbolic meaning. The hero in this story is a human being named Rick Swope who visits the Detroit zoo once a year with his family. One day, as he watched the chimpanzees in their big new enclosure, a fight broke out between two adult males. Jojo, who had been at the zoo for years, was challenged by a younger and stronger newcomer, and Jojo lost. In his fear he fled into the moat which was brand new, and Jojo did not understand water. He had gotten over the barrier erected to prevent the chimpanzees from falling in—for they cannot swim—and the group of visitors and staff that happened to be there watched in horror as Jojo began to drown. He went under once, twice, three times. Rick Swope could bear it no longer. He jumped in to try to save the chimp, despite onlookers yelling at him about the danger. He managed to get Jojo's dead weight over his shoulder, and then crossed the barrier and pushed Jojo onto the bank of the island. Rick held him there—the bank was very steep and if he were to let go Jojo would slide back into the water—even when the other chimps charged toward him, screaming in excitement. Rick held Jojo until he raised his head, took a few staggering steps, and collapsed on more level ground.

The director of the institute called Rick. "That was a brave thing you did. You must have known how dangerous it was. What made you do it?"

"Well, I looked into his eyes. And it was like looking into the eyes of a man. And the message was, 'Won't anybody help me?'"

Rick Swope risked his life to save a chimpanzee, a nonhuman being who sent a message that a human could understand. Now it is up to the rest of us to join in too.

DISCUSSION QUESTIONS

1. What are some of the ways in which the study of animal behavior has changed since the beginning of Goodall's study of the Gombe chimpanzees?

2. What does it mean to be anthropomorphic? Have our definitions or use of this concept

changed since Goodall began her work? In what ways?

3. In evolutionary terms, what do common characteristics, or behavioral traits shared by human beings and chimpanzees, actually

represent? Does the fact that both species hunt or make tools mean that humans evolved directly from chimpanzees? Why or why not?

4. How much of our mind do you think we actually share with the chimpanzee? What is the basis for your reasoning? Are there ways to empirically test your ideas?

INTERNET RESOURCES

After reading this selection, you may want to research the following individuals.

- Washoe
- Allen Gardner
- Jane Goodall

You may also want to investigate the website of the Jane Goodall Institute at http://www.janegoodall.org/.

Trac College Edition. Some suggested search terms for this article are as follows.

- Chimpanzee
- Mind
- Altruism
- Anthropomorphism

InfoTrac College Edition

(infotrac-college.com)
You can find many other readings pertinent to this topic by consulting online databases including Info-

14

Why Are Some Animals So Smart?

CAREL VAN SCHAIK

We humans are awfully proud of our large, complex brains. When we reflect on those attributes that make us unique among the primates, our cognitive capacity—our intelligence—frequently is the first characteristic mentioned. Although there is wide agreement among physical anthropologists that the features that distinguish us from the apes are matters of degree *and not* kind, *our intellectual ability is recognized as a hallmark characteristic of modern humans. Many of the first scholars who speculated about human evolution believed that encephalization, expansion in the size of our brain relative to our body size, was actually the driving force of human evolution. These individuals included Sir Grafton Elliot Smith of the Natural History Museum in London. Central to this view is the idea that our high intelligence was a key event in our separation from the apes. Today we know that our hominid ancestors became fully encephalized only after the evolution of bipedal locomotion had commenced. There is no doubt, however, that the evolution of the hominid brain—both its size and complexity—is key to understanding our evolutionary journey.*

In this selection, primatologist Carel van Schaik takes up questions relating to the evolution of high intelligence using orangutans, our only great ape relative from Asia. In particular, van Schaik wants to know: What were the driving forces that led to higher intelligence among early hominids? What kinds of behaviors would select for a larger and more complex brain? Though he does not consider orangutans (or any other creature) to be as smart as we humans, he argues convincingly that orangutans are an appropriate model for understanding brain evolution. After a dozen or so years of observing orangutans in the wilds of Borneo and Sumatra, van Schaik encountered intensive tool-using behavior among orangutans inhabiting swampy environments of a region known as Suaq, as compared with orangutans residing in different areas. Based on this and other lines of evidence, van Schaik presents the intelligence-through-culture theory. He argues that tool use is a form of cultural behavior and that culture, in turn, both promotes intelligence and favors the evolution of greater intelligence.

This selection provides an excellent example of how scholars use new discoveries to advance scientific theory. As you read this article, pay particular attention to how van Schaik creates his scientific case, or argument, to support his ideas. What observations does he use to build his theory that tool use among the Suaq orangutans represents cultural behavior? Further, what evidence does he offer to support his intelligence-through-culture theory? As you read, try to imagine ways in which one could test his ideas. If possible, talk

SOURCE: Carel van Schaik, "Why Are Some Animals So Smart?" *Scientific American*, March 2006. Reprinted with permission. Copyright © 2006 by Scientific American, Inc. All rights reserved.

with some of your classmates and see what others think about van Schaik's theory. Did your understanding of the article improve following the discussion?

Even though we humans write the textbooks and may justifiably be suspected of bias, few doubt that we are the smartest creatures on the planet. Many animals have special cognitive abilities that allow them to excel in their particular habitats, but they do not often solve novel problems. Some of course do, and we call them intelligent, but none are as quick-witted as we are.

What favored the evolution of such distinctive brainpower in humans or, more precisely, in our hominid ancestors? One approach to answering this question is to examine the factors that might have shaped other creatures that show high intelligence and to see whether the same forces might have operated in our forebears. Several birds and nonhuman mammals, for instance, are much better problem solvers than others: elephants, dolphins, parrots, crows. But research into our close relatives, the great apes, is surely likely to be illuminating.

Scholars have proposed many explanations for the evolution of intelligence in primates, the lineage to which humans and apes belong (along with monkeys, lemurs and lorises). Over the past 13 years, though, my group's studies of orangutans have unexpectedly turned up a new explanation that we think goes quite far in answering the question.

INCOMPLETE THEORIES

One influential attempt at explaining primate intelligence credits the complexity of social life with spurring the development of strong cognitive abilities. This Machiavellian intelligence hypothesis suggests that success in social life relies on cultivating the most profitable relationships and on rapidly reading the social situation—for instance, when deciding whether to come to the aid of an ally attacked by another animal. Hence, the demands of society foster intelligence because the most intelligent beings would be most successful at making self-protective choices and thus would survive to pass their genes to the next generation. Machiavellian

traits may not be equally beneficial to other lineages, however, or even to all primates, and so this notion alone is unsatisfying.

One can easily envisage many other forces that would promote the evolution of intelligence, such as the need to work hard for one's food. In that situation, the ability to figure out how to skillfully extract hidden nourishment or the capacity to remember the perennially shifting locations of critical food items would be advantageous, and so such cleverness would be rewarded by passing more genes to the next generation.

My own explanation, which is not incompatible with these other forces, puts the emphasis on social learning. In humans, intelligence develops over time. A child learns primarily from the guidance of patient adults. Without strong social—that is, cultural—inputs, even a potential wunderkind will end up a bungling bumpkin as an adult. We now have evidence that this process of social learning also applies to great apes, and I will argue that, by and large, the animals that are intelligent are the ones that are cultural: they learn from one another innovative solutions to ecological or social problems. In short, I suggest that culture promotes intelligence.

I came to this proposition circuitously, by way of the swamps on the western coast of the Indonesian island of Sumatra, where my colleagues and I were observing orangutans. The orangutan is Asia's only great ape, confined to the islands of Borneo and Sumatra and known to be something of a loner. Compared with its more familiar relative, Africa's chimpanzee, the red ape is serene rather than hyperactive and reserved socially rather than convivial. Yet we discovered in them the conditions that allow culture to flourish.

TECHNOLOGY IN THE SWAMP

We were initially attracted to the swamp because it sheltered disproportionately high numbers of orangutans—unlike the islands' dryland forests, the moist swamp habitat supplies abundant food for the apes year-round and can thus support a large population. We worked in an area near Suaq Balimbing in the Kluet swamp . . . , which may have been paradise for orangutans but, with its sticky mud, profusion of biting insects, and oppressive heat and humidity, was hell for researchers.

One of our first finds in this unlikely setting astonished us: the Suaq orangutans created and wielded a variety of tools. Although captive red apes are avid tool users, the most striking feature of tool use among the wild orangutans observed until then was its absence. The animals at Suaq ply their tools for two major purposes. First, they hunt for ants, termites and, especially, honey (mainly that of stingless bees)—more so than all their fellow orangutans elsewhere. They often cast discerning glances at tree trunks, looking for air traffic in and out of small holes. Once discovered, the holes become the focus of visual and then manual inspection by a poking and picking finger. Usually the finger is not long enough, and the orangutan prepares a stick tool. After carefully inserting the tool, the ape delicately moves it back and forth and then withdraws it, licks it off and sticks it back in. Most of this "manipulation" is done with the tool clenched between the teeth; only the largest tools, used primarily to hammer chunks off termite nests, are handled.

The second context in which the Suaq apes employ tools involves the fruit of the Neesia. This tree produces woody, five-angled capsules up to 10 inches long and four inches wide. The capsules are filled with brown seeds the size of lima beans, which, because they contain nearly 50 percent fat, are highly nutritious—a rare and sought-after treat in a natural habitat without fast food. The tree protects its seeds by growing a very tough husk. When the seeds are ripe, however, the husk begins to split open; the cracks gradually widen, exposing neat rows of seeds, which have grown nice red attachments (arils) that contain some 80 percent fat.

To discourage seed predators further, a mass of razor-sharp needles fills the husk. The orangutans at Suaq strip the bark off short, straight twigs, which they then hold in their mouths and insert into the cracks. By moving the tool up and down inside the crack, the animal detaches the seeds from their stalks. After this maneuver, it can drop the seeds straight into its mouth. Late in the season, the orangutans eat only the red arils, deploying the same technique to get at them without injury.

Both methods of fashioning sticks for foraging are ubiquitous at Suaq. In general, "fishing" in tree holes is occasional and lasts only a few minutes, but when Neesia fruits ripen, the apes devote most of their waking hours to ferreting out the seeds or arils, and we see them grow fatter and sleeker day by day.

WHY THE TOOL USE IS CULTURAL

What explains this curious concentration of tool use when wild orangutans elsewhere show so little propensity? We doubt that the animals at Suaq are intrinsically smarter: the observation that most captive members of this species can learn to use tools suggests that the basic brain capacity to do so is present.

So we reasoned that their environment might hold the answer. The orangutans studied before mostly live in dry forest, and the swamp furnishes a uniquely lush habitat. More insects make their nests in the tree holes there than in forests on dry land, and Neesia grows only in wet places, usually near flowing water. Tempting as the environmental explanation sounds, however, it does not explain why orangutans in several populations outside Suaq ignore altogether these same rich food sources. Nor does it explain why some populations that do eat the seeds harvest them without tools (which results, of course, in their eating much less than the orangutans at Suaq do). The same holds for tree-hole tools. Occasionally, when the nearby hills—which have dryland forests—show massive fruiting, the Suaq orangutans go there to indulge, and while they are gathering fruit they use tools to exploit the contents of tree holes. The hill habitat is a dime a dozen throughout the orangutan's geographic range, so if tools can be used on the hillsides above Suaq, why not everywhere?

Another suggestion we considered, captured in the old adage that necessity is the mother of invention, is that the Suaq animals, living at such high density, have much more competition for provisions. Consequently, many would be left without food unless they could get at the hard-to-reach supplies—that is, they need tools in order to eat. The strongest argument against this possibility is that the sweet or fat foods that the tools make accessible sit very high on the orangutan preference list and should therefore be sought by these animals everywhere. For instance, red apes in all locations are willing to be stung many times by honeybees to get at their honey. So the necessity idea does not hold much water either.

A different possibility is that these behaviors are innovative techniques a couple of clever orangutans invented, which then spread and persisted in the population because other individuals learned by observing these experts. In other words, the tool use is cultural. A major obstacle to studying culture in nature is that, barring experimental introductions, we can never demonstrate convincingly that an animal we observe invents some new trick rather than simply applying a well-remembered but rarely practiced habit. Neither can we prove that one individual learned a new skill from another group member rather than figuring out what to do on its own. Although we can show that orangutans in the lab are capable of observing and learning socially, such studies tell us nothing about culture in nature—neither what it is generally about nor how much of it exists. So field-workers have had to develop a system of criteria to demonstrate that a certain behavior has a cultural basis.

First, the behavior must vary geographically, showing that it was invented somewhere, and it must be common where it is found, showing that it spread and persisted in a population. The tool uses at Suaq easily pass these first two tests. The second step is to eliminate simpler explanations that produce the same spatial pattern but without involving social learning. We have already excluded an ecological explanation, in which individuals exposed to a particular habitat independently converge on the same skill. We can also eliminate genetics because of the fact that most captive orangutans can learn to use tools.

The third and most stringent test is that we must be able to find geographic distributions of behavior that can be explained by culture and are not easily explained any other way. One key pattern would be the presence of a behavior in one place and its absence beyond some natural barrier to dispersal. In the case of the tool users at Suaq, the geographic distribution of Neesia gave us decisive clues. Neesia trees (and orangutans) occur on both sides of the wide Alas River. In the Singkil swamp, however, just south of Suaq and on the same side of the Alas River . . . , tools littered the floor, whereas in Batu-Batu swamp across the river they were conspicuously absent, despite our numerous visits in different years. In Batu-Batu, we did find that many of the fruits were ripped apart, showing that these orangutans ate Neesia seeds in the same way as their colleagues did at a site called Gunung Palung in distant Borneo but in a way completely different from their cousins right across the river in Singkil.

Batu-Batu is a small swamp area, and it does not contain much of the best swamp forest; thus, it supports a limited number of orangutans. We do not know whether tool use was never invented there or whether it could not be maintained in the smaller population, but we do know that migrants from across the river never brought it in because the Alas is so wide there that it is absolutely impassable for an orangutan. Where it is passable, farther upriver, Neesia occasionally grows, but the orangutans in that area ignore it altogether, apparently unaware of its rich offerings. A cultural interpretation, then, most parsimoniously explains the unexpected juxtaposition of knowledgeable tool users and brute-force foragers living practically next door to one another, as well as the presence of ignoramuses farther upriver.

TOLERANT PROXIMITY

Why do we see these fancy forms of tool use at Suaq and not elsewhere? To look into this question, we first made detailed comparisons among all the sites at which orangutans have been studied. We found that even when we excluded tool use, Suaq had the largest number of innovations that had spread throughout the population. This finding is probably not an artifact of our own interest in unusual behaviors, because some other sites have seen far more work by researchers eager to discover socially learned behavioral innovations.

We guessed that populations in which individuals had more chances to observe others in action would show a greater diversity of learned skills than would populations offering fewer learning opportunities. And indeed, we were able to confirm that sites in which individuals spend more time with others have greater repertoires of learned innovations—a relation, by the way, that also holds among chimpanzees. . . . This link was strongest for food-related behavior, which makes sense because acquiring feeding skills from somebody else requires more close-range observation than, say, picking up a conspicuous communication signal. Put another way, those animals exposed to the fewest educational opportunities have the smallest collection of cultural variants, exactly like the proverbial country bumpkin.

When we looked closely at the contrasts among sites, we noticed something else. Infant orangutans everywhere spend over 20,000 daylight hours in close contact with their mothers, acting as enthusiastic apprentices. Only at Suaq, however, did we also see adults spending considerable time together while foraging. Unlike any other orangutan population studied so far, they even regularly fed on the same food item, usually termite-riddled branches, and shared food—the meat of a slow loris, for example. This unorthodox proximity and tolerance allowed less skilled adults to come close enough to observe foraging methods, which they did as eagerly as kids.

Acquisition of the most cognitively demanding inventions, such as the tool uses found only at Suaq, probably requires face time with proficient individuals, as well as several cycles of observation and practice. The surprising implication of this need is that even though infants learn virtually all their skills from their mothers, a population will be able to perpetuate particular innovations only if tolerant role models other than the mother are around; if mom is not particularly skillful, knowledgeable experts will be close at hand, and a youngster will still be able to learn the fancy techniques that apparently do not

come automatically. Thus, the more connected a social network, the more likely it is that the group will retain any skill that is invented, so that in the end tolerant populations support a greater number of such behaviors.

Our work in the wild shows us that most learning in nature, aside from simple conditioning, may have a social component, at least in primates. In contrast, most laboratory experiments that investigate how animals learn are aimed at revealing the subject's ability for individual learning. Indeed, if the lab psychologist's puzzle were presented under natural conditions, where myriad stimuli compete for attention, the subject might never realize that a problem was waiting to be solved. In the wild, the actions of knowledgeable members of the community serve to focus the attention of the naive animal.

THE CULTURAL ROOTS
OF INTELLIGENCE

Our analyses of orangutans suggest that not only does culture—social learning of special skills—promote intelligence, it favors the evolution of greater and greater intelligence in a population over time. Different species vary greatly in the mechanisms that enable them to learn from others, but formal experiments confirm the strong impression one gets from observing great apes in the wild: they are capable of learning by watching what others do. Thus, when a wild orangutan, or an African great ape for that matter, pulls off a cognitively complex behavior, it has acquired the ability through a mix of observational learning and individual practice, much as a human child has garnered his or her skills. And when an orangutan in Suaq has acquired more of these tricks than its less fortunate cousins elsewhere, it has done so because it had greater opportunities for social learning throughout its life. In brief, social learning may bootstrap an animal's intellectual performance onto a higher plane.

To appreciate the importance of social inputs to the evolution of ever higher intelligence, let us do a thought experiment. Imagine an individual that grows up without any social inputs yet is provided with all the shelter and nutrition it needs. This situation is equivalent to that in which no contact exists between the generations or in which young fend for themselves after they emerge from the nest. Now imagine that some female in this species invents a useful skill—for instance, how to open a nut to extract its nutritious meat. She will do well and perhaps have more offspring than others in the population. Unless the skill gets transferred to the next generation, however, it will disappear when she dies.

Now imagine a situation in which the offspring accompany their mother for a while before they strike out on their own. Most youngsters will learn the new technique from their mother and thus transfer it—and its attendant benefits—to the next generation. This process would generally take place in species with slow development and long association between at least one parent and offspring, but it would get a strong boost if several individuals form socially tolerant groups.

We can go one step further. For slowly developing animals that live in socially tolerant societies, natural selection will tend to reward a slight improvement in the ability to learn through observation more strongly than a similar increase in the ability to innovate, because in such a society, an individual can stand on the shoulders of those in both present and past generations. But because the cognitive processes underlying social learning overlap with those producing innovations, improvements in social learning techniques should also bring improvements in innovation abilities. Hence, being cultural predisposes species with some innovative capacities to evolve toward higher intelligence. This, then, brings us to the new explanation for cognitive evolution.

This new hypothesis makes sense of an otherwise puzzling phenomenon. Many times during the past century people reared great ape infants as they would human children. These so-called enculturated apes acquired a surprising set of skills, effortlessly imitating complex behavior—understanding pointing, for example, and even some human language, becoming humorous pranksters and creating drawings. More recently, formal experiments such as those performed by Sue Savage-Rumbaugh of the Great Ape Trust of Iowa, involving the bonobo Kanzi, have revealed startling language abilities. . . . Though often dismissed as lacking in scientific rigor, these consistently replicated cases reveal the astonishing cognitive potential that lies dormant in great apes. We may not fully appreciate the complexity of life in the jungle, but I guess that these enculturated apes have truly become overqualified. In a process that encapsulates the story of human evolution, an ape growing up like a human can be bootstrapped to cognitive peaks higher than any of its wild counterparts.

The same line of thinking solves the long-standing puzzle of why many primates in captivity readily use—and sometimes even make—tools, when their counterparts in the wild seem to lack any such urges. The often-heard suggestion that they do not need tools is belied by observations of orangutans, chimpanzees and capuchin monkeys showing that some of this tool use makes available the richest food in the animals' natural habitats or tides the creatures over during lean periods. The conundrum is resolved if we realize that two individuals of the same species can differ dramatically in their intellectual performance, depending on the social environment in which they grew up.

Orangutans epitomize this phenomenon. They are known as the escape artists of the zoo world, cleverly unlocking the doors of their cages. But the available observations from the wild, despite decades of painstaking monitoring by dedicated field-workers, have uncovered precious few technological accomplishments outside Suaq. Wild-caught individuals generally never take to being locked up, always retaining their deeply ingrained shyness and suspicion of humans. But zoo-born apes happily consider their keepers valuable role models and pay attention to their activities and to the objects strewn around the enclosures, learning to learn and thus accumulating numerous skills.

The critical prediction of the intelligence-through-culture theory is that the most intelligent animals are also likely to live in populations in which the entire group routinely adopts innovations introduced by members. This prediction is not easily tested. Animals from different lineages vary so much in their senses and in their ways of life that a single yardstick for intellectual performance has traditionally been hard to find. For now, we can merely ask whether lineages that show incontrovertible signs of intelligence also have innovation-based cultures, and vice versa. Recognizing oneself in a mirror, for example, is a poorly understood but unmistakable sign of self-awareness, which is taken as a sign of high intelligence. So far, despite widespread attempts in numerous lineages, the only mammalian groups to pass this test are great apes and dolphins, the same animals that can learn to understand many arbitrary symbols and that show the best evidence for imitation, the basis for innovation-based culture. Flexible, innovation-based tool use, another expression of intelligence, has a broader distribution in mammals: monkeys and apes, cetaceans, and elephants—all lineages in which social learning is common. Although so far only these very crude tests can be done, they support the intelligence-through-culture hypothesis.

Another important prediction is that the propensities for innovation and social learning must have coevolved. Indeed, Simon Reader, now at Utrecht University in the Netherlands, and Kevin N. Laland, currently at the University of St. Andrews in Scotland, found that primate species that show more evidence of innovation are also those that show the most evidence for social learning. Still more indirect tests rely on correlations among species between the relative size of the brain (after statistically correcting for body size) and social and developmental variables. The well-established correlations between gregariousness and relative brain size in various mammalian groups are also consistent with the idea.

Although this new hypothesis is not enough to explain why our ancestors, alone among great apes, evolved such extreme intelligence, the remarkable bootstrapping ability of the great apes in rich cultural settings makes the gap seem less formidable. The explanation for the historical trajectory of change involves many details that must be painstakingly pieced together from a sparse and confusing fossil and archaeological record.

Many researchers suspect that a key change was the invasion of the savanna by tool-wielding, striding early *Homo*. To dig up tubers and deflesh and defend carcasses of large mammals, they had to work collectively and create tools and strategies. These demands fostered ever more innovation and more interdependence, and intelligence snowballed.

Once we were human, cultural history began to interact with innate ability to improve performance. Nearly 150,000 years after the origin of our own species, sophisticated expressions of human symbolism, such as finely worked nonfunctional artifacts (art, musical instruments and burial gifts), were widespread. . . . The explosion of technology in the past 10,000 years shows that cultural inputs can unleash limitless accomplishments, all with Stone Age brains. Culture can indeed build a new mind from an old brain.

DISCUSSION QUESTIONS

1. What ideas have scholars other than van Schaik proposed relating to the evolution of primate intelligence? How does van Schaik's theory match up to these explanations?

2. What are the criteria that demonstrate that tool use among the Suaq orangutans is cultural behavior?

3. What sort of predictions follow from van Schaik's intelligence-through-culture theory? Are these predictions testable?

4. How does this article demonstrate the characteristics of science? Which specific characteristics of science can you identify?

5. What would you expect to see in the remains of early hominids (fossils, stone tools, etc.) if the intelligence-through-culture hypothesis is correct?

 **INTERNET RESOURCES**

After reading this selection, you may want to re-search the following individuals.

- Sue Savage-Rumbaugh
- Roger Fouts
- Penny Patterson
- Kanzi, Washoe, and Koko

You may also want to visit the website of the Gorilla Foundation at http://www.koko.org.

InfoTrac College Edition

(infotrac-college.com)

You can find many other readings pertinent to this topic by consulting online databases including Info-Trac College Edition. Some suggested search terms for this article are as follows.

- Encephalization
- Tool use
- Culture

PART IV

Human Evolution

15

The Antiquity of Human Walking

JOHN NAPIER

Bipedalism—the ability to move about habitually on our hind limbs, or legs, in an upright posture—is one of the most distinctive human characteristics. Though chimpanzees and bonobos sometimes stand or walk bipedally, humans, alone among the primates, are habitually bipedal. Consequently, questions relating to when, where, why, and how our ancestors became bipedal have been matters of speculation and debate for decades.

The following article by John Napier is considered a classic in our field for several reasons. First, Napier brought together many different lines of evidence pertaining to the origins of bipedalism. This illustrates the need to approach research in biological anthropology (as in most other sciences) in an interdisciplinary manner. Questions in paleoanthropology, or the study of our early evolutionary ancestors, can't be solved just by studying fossils. In addition to paleontology, or the study of fossils themselves, research in human evolution usually requires a team approach consisting of specialists in anatomy, archaeology, and geology, to name just a few. As you read the article, therefore, take note of the different kinds of evidence that Napier brought to bear on bipedalism.

Second, Napier used a systematic and scientific approach to bipedalism. For example, look how carefully he defined bipedal locomotion by breaking this locomotory pattern into steps or phases. He also compared the relevant bones and musculature of modern humans and apes.

Third, Napier posed specific research questions about bipedalism. What questions was Napier addressing by comparing fossils—an australopithecine pelvis and a Homo habilis *foot? Why did Napier analyze striding (as opposed to walking)? What conclusions did he reach through using these methods?*

Bipedalism remains a hot topic in biological anthropology. Since the publication of Napier's article, a great many more fossils have been recovered through paleontological expeditions. Some of the most outstanding fossil finds generate more detailed ideas about the stages in the evolution of bipedalism. Interestingly, though, some of the basic questions still remain, including why *our ancestors became bipedal in the first place. Some scholars have suggested that bipedalism promoted a more efficient system for lowering body temperature, or thermoregulation. As you encounter hypotheses about the evolution of bipedalism, remember to ask what predictions would follow if the hypothesis is correct. In other words, what should the fossils show if the hypothesis is true?*

SOURCE: John Napier, "The Antiquity of Human Walking," *Scientific American*, April 1967. Reprinted with permission. Copyright © 1967 by Scientific American, Inc. All rights reserved.

Human walking is a unique activity during which the body, step by step, teeters on the edge of catastrophe. The fact that man has used this form of locomotion for more than a million years has only recently been demonstrated by fossil evidence. The antiquity of this human trait is particularly noteworthy because walking with a striding gait is probably the most significant of the many evolved capacities that separate men from more primitive hominids. The fossil evidence—the terminal bone of a right big toe discovered in 1961 in Olduvai Gorge in Tanzania—sets up a new signpost that not only clarifies the course of human evolution but also helps to guide those who speculate on the forces that converted predominantly quadrupedal animals into habitual bipeds.

Man's bipedal mode of walking seems potentially catastrophic because only the rhythmic forward movement of first one leg and then the other keeps him from falling flat on his face. Consider the sequence of events whenever a man sets out in pursuit of his center of gravity. A stride begins when the muscles of the calf relax and the walker's body sways forward (gravity supplying the energy needed to overcome the body's inertia). The sway places the center of body weight in front of the supporting pedestal normally formed by the two feet. As a result one or the other of the walker's legs must swing forward so that when his foot makes contact with the ground, the area of the supporting pedestal has been widened and the center of body weight once again rests safely within it. The pelvis plays an important role in this action: its degree of rotation determines the distance the swinging leg can move forward, and its muscles help to keep the body balanced while the leg is swinging.

At this point the "stance" leg—the leg still to the rear of the body's center of gravity—provides the propulsive force that drives the body forward. The walker applies this force by using muscular energy, pushing against the ground first with the ball of his foot and then with his big toe. The action constitutes the "push-off," which terminates the stance phase of the walking cycle. Once the stance foot leaves the ground, the walker's leg enters the starting, or "swing," phase of the cycle. As the leg swings forward it is able to clear the ground because it is bent at the hip, knee and ankle. This high-stepping action substantially reduces the leg's moment of inertia. Before making contact with the ground and ending the swing phase the leg straightens at the knee but remains bent at the ankle. As a result it is the heel that strikes the ground first. The "heel strike" concludes the swing phase; as the body continues to move forward the leg once again enters the stance phase, during which the point of contact between foot and ground moves progressively nearer the toes. At the extreme end of the stance phase, as before, all the walker's propulsive thrust is delivered by the robust terminal bone of his big toe.

A complete walking cycle is considered to extend from the heel strike of one leg to the next heel strike of the same leg; it consists of the stance phase followed by the swing phase. The relative duration of the two phases depends on the cadence or speed of the walk. During normal walking the stance phase constitutes about 60 percent of the cycle and the swing phase 40 percent. Although the action of only one leg has been described in this account, the opposite leg obviously moves in a reciprocal fashion; when one leg is moving in the swing phase, the other leg is in its stance phase and keeps the body poised. Actually during normal walking the two phases overlap, so that both feet are on the ground at the same time for about 25 percent of the cycle. As walking speed increases, this period of double leg-support shortens.

Anyone who has watched other people walking and reflected a little on the process has noticed that the human stride demands both an up-and-down and a side-to-side displacement of the body. When two people walk side by side but out of step, the alternate bobbing of their heads makes it evident that the bodies undergo a vertical displacement with each stride. When two people walk in step but with opposite feet leading, they will sway first toward each other and then away in an equally graphic demonstration of the lateral displacement at each stride. When both displacements are plotted sequentially, a pair of low-amplitude sinusoidal curves appear, one in the vertical plane and the other in the horizontal. . . . General observations of this kind were reduced to precise measurements during World War II when a group at the University of California at Berkeley led by H. D. Eberhart conducted a fundamental investigation of human walking in connection with requirements for the design of artificial legs. Eberhart and his colleagues found that a number of functional determinants interacted to move the human body's center of gravity through space with a minimum expenditure of energy. In all they isolated six major elements related to hip, knee and foot movement that, working together, reduced both the amplitude of the two sine curves and the abruptness with which vertical and lateral changes in direction took place. If any one of these six elements was disturbed, an irregularity was injected into the normally smooth, undulating flow of walking, thereby producing a limp. What is more important, the irregularity brought about a measurable increase in the body's energy output during each step.

THE EVIDENCE OF THE BONES

What I have described in general and Eberhart's group studied in detail is the form of walking known as striding. It is characterized by the heel strike at the start of the stance phase and the push-off at its conclusion. Not all human walking is striding; when a man moves about slowly or walks on a slippery surface, he may take short steps in which both push-off and heel strike are absent. The foot is simply lifted from the ground at the end of the stance phase and set down flat at the end of the swing phase. The stride, however, is the essence of human bipedalism and the criterion by which the evolutionary status of a hominid walker must be judged. This being the case, it is illuminating to consider how the act of striding leaves its distinctive marks on the bones of the strider.

To take the pelvis first, there is a well-known clinical manifestation called Trendelenburg's sign that is regarded as evidence of hip disease in children. When a normal child stands on one leg, two muscles connecting that leg and the pelvis—the gluteus medius and the gluteus minimus—contract; this contraction, pulling on the pelvis, tilts it and holds it poised over the stance leg. When the hip

is diseased, this mechanism fails to operate and the child shows a positive Trendelenburg's sign: the body tends to fall toward the unsupported side.

The same mechanism operates in walking, although not to the same degree. During the stance phase of the walking cycle, the same two gluteal muscles on the stance side brace the pelvis by cantilever action. Although actual tilting toward the stance side does not occur in normal walking, the action of the muscles in stabilizing the walker's hip is an essential component of the striding gait. Without this action the stride would become a slow, ungainly shuffle.

At the same time that the pelvis is stabilized in relation to the stance leg it also rotates to the unsupported side. This rotation, although small, has the effect of increasing the length of the stride. A familiar feature of the way women walk arises from this bit of anatomical mechanics. The difference in the proportions of the male and the female pelvis has the effect of slightly diminishing the range through which the female hip can move forward and back. Thus for a given length of stride women are obliged to rotate the pelvis through a greater angle than men do. This secondary sexual characteristic has not lacked exploitation; at least in our culture female pelvic rotation has considerable erotogenic significance. What is more to the point in terms of human evolution is that both the rotation and the balancing of the pelvis leave unmistakable signs on the pelvic bone and on the femur: the leg bone that is joined to it. It is by a study of such signs that the walking capability of a fossil hominid can be judged.

Similar considerations apply to the foot. One way the role of the foot in walking can be studied is to record the vertical forces acting on each part of the foot while it is in contact with the ground during the stance phase of the walking cycle. Many devices have been built for this purpose; one of them is the plastic pedograph. When the subject walks across the surface of the pedograph, a motion-picture camera simultaneously records the exact position of the foot in profile and the pattern of pressures on the surface. Pedograph analyses show that the initial contact between the striding leg and the ground is the heel strike. Because the foot is normally turned out slightly at the end of the swing phase of the walking cycle, the outer side of the back of the heel takes the brunt of the initial contact. . . . The outer side of the foot continues to support most of the pressure of the stance until a point about three-fifths of the way along the sole is reached. The weight of the body is then transferred to the ball of the foot and then to the big toe. In the penultimate stage of push-off the brunt of the pressure is under the toes, particularly the big toe. Finally, at the end of the stance phase, only the big toe is involved; it progressively loses contact with the ground and the final push-off is applied through its broad terminal bone.

The use of pedographs and similar apparatus provides precise evidence about the function of the foot in walking, but every physician knows that much the same information is recorded on the soles of everyone's shoes. Assuming that the shoes fit, their pattern of wear is a true record of the individual's habitual gait. The wear pattern will reveal a limp that one man is trying to hide, or unmask one that another man is trying to feign, perhaps to provide evidence for an insurance claim. In any case, just as the form of the pelvis and the femur can disclose the presence or absence of a striding gait, so can the form of the foot bones, particularly the form and proportions of the big-toe bones.

THE ORIGINS OF PRIMATE BIPEDALISM

Almost all primates can stand on their hind limbs, and many occasionally walk in this way. But our primate relatives are all, in a manner of speaking, amateurs; only man has taken up the business of bipedalism intensively. This raises two major questions. First, how did the basic postural adaptations that permit walking—occasional or habitual—arise among the primates? Second, what advantages did habitual bipedalism bestow on early man?

With regard to the first question, I have been concerned for some time with the anatomical proportions of all primates, not only man and the apes but also the monkeys and lower primate forms. Such consideration makes it possible to place the primates

in natural groups according to their mode of locomotion. Not long ago I suggested a new group, and it is the only one that will concern us here. The group comprises primates with very long hind limbs and very short forelimbs. At about the same time my colleague Alan C. Walker, now at Makerere University College in Uganda, had begun a special study of the locomotion of living and fossil lemurs. Lemurs are among the most primitive offshoots of the basic primate stock. Early in Walker's studies he was struck by the frequency with which a posture best described as "vertical clinging" appeared in the day-to-day behavior of living lemurs. All the animals whose propensity for vertical clinging had been observed by Walker showed the same proportions—that is, long hind limbs and short forelimbs—I had proposed as forming a distinct locomotor group.

When Walker and I compared notes, we decided to define a hitherto unrecognized locomotor category among the primates that we named "vertical clinging and leaping," a term that includes both the animal's typical resting posture and the essential leaping component in its locomotion. Since proposing this category a most interesting and important extension of the hypothesis has become apparent to us. Some of the earliest primate fossils known, preserved in sediments laid down during Eocene times and therefore as much as 50 million years old, are represented not only by skulls and jaws but also by a few limb bones. In their proportions and details most of these limb bones show the same characteristics that are displayed by the living members of our vertical-clinging-and-leaping group today. Not long ago Elwyn L. Simons of Yale University presented a reconstruction of the lemur-like North American Eocene primate *Smilodectes* walking along a tree branch in a quadrupedal position. . . . Walker and I would prefer to see *Smilodectes* portrayed in the vertical clinging posture its anatomy unequivocally indicates. The fossil evidence, as far as it goes, suggests to us that vertical clinging and leaping was a major primate locomotor adaptation that took place some 50 million years ago. It may even have been the initial dynamic adaptation to tree life from which the subsequent locomotor patterns of all the living primates, including man, have stemmed.

Walker and I are not alone in this view. In 1962 W. L. Straus, Jr., of Johns Hopkins University declared: "It can safely be assumed that primates early developed the mechanisms permitting maintenance of the trunk in the upright position. . . . Indeed, this tendency toward truncal erectness can be regarded as an essentially basic primate character." The central adaptations for erectness of the body, which have been retained in the majority of living primates, seem to have provided the necessary anatomical basis for the occasional bipedal behavior exhibited by today's monkeys and apes.

What we are concerned with here is the transition from a distant, hypothetical vertical-clinging ancestor to modern, bipedal man. The transition was almost certainly marked by an intermediate quadrupedal stage. Possibly such Miocene fossil forms as *Proconsul,* a chimpanzee-like early primate from East Africa, represent such a stage. The structural adaptations necessary to convert a quadrupedal ape into a bipedal hominid are centered on the pelvis, the femur, the foot and the musculature associated with these bones. Among the nonhuman primates living today the pelvis and femur are adapted for four-footed walking; the functional relations between hipbones and thigh muscles are such that, when the animal attempts to assume a bipedal stance, the hip joint is subjected to a stress and the hip must be bent. To compensate for the resulting forward shift of the center of gravity, the knees must also be bent. In order to alter a bent-hip, bent-knee gait into man's erect, striding walk, a number of anatomical changes must occur. These include an elongation of the hind limbs with respect to the forelimbs, a shortening and broadening of the pelvis, adjustments of the musculature of the hip (in order to stabilize the trunk during the act of walking upright), a straightening of both hip and knee and considerable reshaping of the foot.

Which of these changes can be considered to be primary and which secondary is still a matter that needs elucidation. Sherwood L. Washburn of the University of California at Berkeley has expressed the view that the change from four-footed to two-footed posture was initiated by a modification in the form and function of the gluteus maximus, a thigh muscle that is powerfully developed in man but weakly developed in monkeys and apes. . . . In a quadrupedal primate the principal extensors of the trunk are the "hamstring" muscles and the two upper-leg muscles I have already mentioned: the gluteus medius and gluteus minimus. In man these two muscles bear a different relation to the pelvis, in terms of both position and function. In technical terms they have become abductor muscles of the trunk rather than extensor muscles of the leg. It is this that enables them to play a critical part in stabilizing the pelvis in the course of striding. In man the extensor function of these two gluteal muscles has been taken over by a third, the gluteus maximus. This muscle, insignificant in other primates, plays a surprisingly unimportant role in man's ability to stand, or even to walk on a level surface. In standing, for example, the principal stabilizing and extending agents are the muscles of the hamstring group. In walking on the level the gluteus maximus is so little involved that even when it is paralyzed a man's stride is virtually unimpaired. The gluteus maximus comes into its own in man when power is needed to give the hip joint more play for such activities as running, walking up a steep slope or climbing stairs. . . . Its chief function in these circumstances is to correct any tendency for the human trunk to jackknife on the legs.

Because the gluteus maximus has such a specialized role I believe, in contrast to Washburn's view, that it did not assume its present form until late in the evolution of the striding gait. Rather than being the initial adaptation, this muscle's enlargement and present function appear to me far more likely to have been one of the ultimate refinements of human walking. I am in agreement with Washburn, however, when he states that changes in the ilium, or upper pelvis, would have preceded changes in the ischium, or lower pelvis. . . . The primary adaptation would probably have involved a forward curvature of the vertebral column in the lumbar region. Accompanying this change would have been a broadening and a forward rotation of the iliac portions of the pelvis. Together these early adaptations provide the structural basis for improving the posture of the trunk.

Assuming that we have now given at least a tentative answer to the question of how man's bipedal posture evolved, there remains to be answered the question of why. What were the advantages of habitual bipedalism? Noting the comparative energy demands of various gaits, Washburn points out that human walking is primarily an adaptation for covering long distances economically. To go a long way with a minimum of effort is an asset to a hunter; it seems plausible that evolutionary selection for hunting behavior in man was responsible for the rapid development of striding anatomy. Gordon W. Hewes of the University of Colorado suggests a possible incentive that, acting as an agent of natural selection, could have prompted the quadrupedal ancestors of man to adopt a two-footed gait. In Hewes's view the principal advantage of bipedalism over quadrupedalism would be the freeing of the hands, so that food could be carried readily from one place to another for later consumption. To assess the significance of such factors as survival mechanisms it behooves us to review briefly the ecological situation in which our prehuman ancestors found themselves in Miocene times, between 15 and 25 million years ago.

THE MIOCENE ENVIRONMENT

During the Miocene epoch the worldwide mountain-building activity of middle Tertiary times was in full swing. Many parts of the earth, including the region of East Africa where primates of the genus *Proconsul* were living, were being faulted and uplifted to form such mountain zones as the Alps, the Himalayas, the Andes and the Rockies. Massive faulting in Africa gave rise to one of the earth's major geological features: the Rift Valley, which extends 5,000 miles from Tanzania across East Africa to Israel and the Dead Sea. A string of lakes lies along the floor of the Rift Valley like giant stepping-stones. On their shores in Miocene times lived a fantastically rich fauna, inhabitants of the forest and of a new ecological niche—the grassy savanna.

These grasslands of the Miocene were the domain of new forms of vegetation that in many parts of the world had taken the place of rain forest, the dominant form of vegetation in the Eocene and the Oligocene. The savanna offered new evolutionary opportunities to a variety of mammals, including the expanding population of primates in the rapidly shrinking forest. A few primates—the ancestors of man and probably also the ancestors of the living baboons—evidently reacted to the challenge of the new environment.

The savanna, however, was no Eldorado. The problems facing the early hominids in the open grassland were immense. The forest foods to which they were accustomed were hard to come by; the danger of attack by predators was immeasurably increased. If, on top of everything else, the ancestral hominids of Miocene times were in the process of converting from quadrupedalism to bipedalism, it is difficult to conceive of any advantage in bipedalism that could have compensated for the added hazards of life in the open grassland. Consideration of the drawbacks of savanna living has led me to a conclusion contrary to the one generally accepted: I doubt that the advent of bipedalism took place in this environment. An environment neglected by scholars but one far better suited for the origin of man is the woodland-savanna, which is neither high forest nor open grassland. Today this halfway-house niche is occupied by many primates, for example the vervet monkey and some chimpanzees. It has enough trees to provide forest foods and ready escape from predators. At the same time its open grassy spaces are arenas in which new locomotor adaptations can be practiced and new foods can be sampled. In short, the woodland-savanna provides an ideal nursery for evolving hominids, combining the challenge and incentive of the open grassland with much of the security of the forest. It was probably in this transitional environment that man's ancestors learned to walk on two legs. In all likelihood, however, they only learned to stride when they later moved into the open savanna.

Moving forward many millions of years from Miocene to Pleistocene times, we come to man's most immediate hominid precursor: *Australopithecus*. A large consortium of authorities agrees that the shape of the pelvis in *Australopithecus* fossils indicates that these hominids were habitually bipedal, although not to the degree of perfection exhibited by modern man. A few anatomists, fighting a rear-guard action, contend that on the contrary the pelvis of *Australopithecus* shows that these hominids were predominantly quadrupedal. I belong to the first school but, as I have been at some pains to emphasize in the past, the kind of upright walking practiced by *Australopithecus* should not be equated with man's heel-and-toe, striding gait.

FROM BIPEDALIST
TO STRIDER

The stride, although it was not necessarily habitual among the earliest true men, is nevertheless the quintessence of the human locomotor achievement. Among other things, striding involves extension of the leg to a position behind the vertical axis of the spinal column. The degree of extension needed can only be achieved if the ischium of the pelvis is short. But the ischium of *Australopithecus* is long, almost as long as the ischium of an ape. . . . Moreover, it has been shown that in man the gluteus medius and the gluteus minimus are prime movers in stabilizing the pelvis during each stride; in *Australopithecus* this stabilizing mechanism is imperfectly evolved. The combination of both deficiencies almost entirely precludes the possibility that these hominids possessed a striding gait. For *Australopithecus* walking was something of a jog trot. These hominids must have covered the ground with quick, rather short steps, with their knees and hips slightly bent; the prolonged stance phase of the fully human gait must surely have been absent.

Compared with man's stride, therefore, the gait of *Australopithecus* is physiologically inefficient. It calls for a disproportionately high output of energy; indeed, *Australopithecus* probably found long-distance bipedal travel impossible. A natural question arises in this connection. Could the greater energy requirement have led these early representatives of the human family to alter their diet in the direction of an increased reliance on high-energy foodstuffs, such as the flesh of other animals?

The pelvis of *Australopithecus* bears evidence that this hominid walker could scarcely have been a strider. Let us now turn to the foot of what many of us believe is a more advanced hominid. In 1960 L. S. B. Leakey and his wife Mary unearthed most of the bones of this foot in the lower strata at Olduvai Gorge known collectively as Bed I, which are about 1.75 million years old. The bones formed part of a fossil assemblage that has been designated by the Leakeys, by Philip Tobias of the University of the Witwatersrand and by me as possibly the earliest-known species of man: *Homo habilis*. The foot was complete except for the back of the heel and the terminal bones of the toes; its surviving components were assembled and studied by me and Michael Day, one of my colleagues at the Unit of Primatology and Human Evolution of the Royal Free Hospital School of Medicine in London. On the basis of functional analysis the resemblance to the foot of modern man is close, although differing in a few minor particulars. Perhaps the most significant point of resemblance is that the stout basal bone of the big toe lies alongside the other toes. . . . This is an essentially human characteristic; in apes and monkeys the big toe is not exceptionally robust and diverges widely from the other toes. The foot bones, therefore, give evidence that this early hominid species was habitually bipedal. In the absence of the terminal bones of the toes, however, there was no certainty that *Homo habilis* walked with a striding gait.

Then in 1961, in a somewhat higher stratum at Olduvai Gorge (and thus in a slightly younger geological formation), a single bone came to light in an area otherwise barren of human bones. This fossil is the big-toe bone I mentioned at the beginning of this article. . . . Its head is both tilted and twisted with respect to its shaft, characteristics that are found only in modern man and that can with assurance be correlated with a striding gait. Day has recently completed a dimensional analysis of the bone, using a multivariate statistical technique. He is able to show that the fossil is unquestionably human in form.

There is no evidence to link the big-toe bone specifically to either of the two recognized hominids whose fossil remains have been recovered from Bed I at Olduvai: *Homo habilis* and *Zinjanthropus boisei*. Thus the owner of the toe remains unknown, at least for the present. Nonetheless, one thing is made certain by the discovery. We now know that in East Africa more than a million years ago there existed a creature whose mode of locomotion was essentially human.

DISCUSSION QUESTIONS

1. What is vertical clinging and leaping? Why is this locomotor pattern important to discussions of bipedalism and human evolution? How do basic body proportions differ in quadrupedalism, vertical clinging and leaping, and bipedalism?

2. What kinds of structural changes occurred in the skeleton and musculature of our ancestors in connection with bipedalism?

3. What did Napier conclude from his observations of the Australopithecine pelvis? What conclusions did he reach about the foot belonging to *Homo habilis* from Olduvai Gorge?

4. What did his analysis of striding lend to his understanding of the evolution of bipedalism?

5. What are some ideas relating to why bipedalism evolved during human evolution? Can you think of alternative explanations?

INTERNET RESOURCES

After reading this selection, you may want to research the following individuals.

- Louis Leakey
- Mary Leakey
- John Napier

InfoTrac College Edition

(infotrac-college.com)
You can find many other readings pertinent to this topic by consulting online databases including Info-

Trac College Edition. Some suggested search terms for this article are as follows.

- Bipedalism
- Australopithecine
- Olduvai Gorge

16

Lucy's Baby

KATE WONG

In 1974, paleoanthropologists Donald Johansen and Tim White discovered a fossilized skeleton in Ethiopia's Afar triangle. This skeleton, nicknamed Lucy *(after a song by the Beatles), was destined to rock the world of paleoanthropology. The spectacular nature of the find related to Lucy's geological age, degree of completeness, and anatomical characteristics. Lucy's date was estimated at 3.2 million years ago, and approximately 40 percent of her skeleton remained intact. Characteristics of her dental and cranial remains illustrated a unique combination of primitive and derived features. Lucy's os coxa, distal femur, and proximal tibia gave paleoanthropologists the opportunity to study the evolution of bipedalism. Lucy was placed in the genus* Australopithecus, *species* afarensis.

In 2000, paleoanthropologist Zeresenay Alemseged made an equally exciting and significant discovery of another member of Australopithecus afarensis, *just a short distance from where Lucy had been found. This article, a recent report by science writer Kate Wong, highlights the circumstances of the find and the analysis of this fossil, nicknamed* Selam, *which means* peace *in some of the native Ethiopian languages. As you read through Wong's article, you have the opportunity to focus on the ways in which paleoanthropologists assess the importance of a new find. While every hominin fossil contributes somewhat to our understanding of human evolution, some finds clearly have special significance. Moreover, individual bones and regions of a fossilized skeleton can help us delve more deeply into specific questions about our evolutionary heritage. As you read through this selection, pay particular attention to Selam's characteristics while asking yourself, "What makes this particular fossil significant?" Be sure to notice Selam's geological and biological age as well as the degree of preservation. At the same time, look to the discussion of certain bones—those from the hands, arms, and shoulder, for example—in the assessment of Selam's locomotor pattern. How do these remains shed light on the origins of bipedalism?*

Every field season, human paleontologists unearth new fossils. Physical anthropologists and their students know just how difficult it can be to keep up with the latest discoveries as our discipline advances. This article not only provides you with a glimpse of a significant new member of our family tree, it also gives you a feel for how paleoanthropologists evaluate each discovery. Imagine yourself with the sun bearing down as you walk across rocky, uneven ground. You know other remains from this location have dated to 3.2 million years ago. By a combination of skill, good eyesight, and a large helping of luck,

SOURCE: Kate Wong, "Lucy's Baby," *Scientific American*, December 2006, 78–85. Reprinted with permission.

you find yourself face to face with an almost complete fossilized skeleton of an adult hominin. What characteristics do you think you will see on close inspection?

The arid badlands of Ethiopia's remote Afar region have long been a favorite hunting ground for paleoanthropologists. Many hominins—the group that includes all the creatures in the human line since it branched away from that of the chimps—once called it home. The area is perhaps best known for having yielded "Lucy," the 3.2-million-year-old skeleton of a human ancestor known as *Australopithecus afarensis*. Now researchers have unveiled another incredible *A. afarensis* specimen from a site called Dikika, just four kilometers from where Lucy turned up. But unlike Lucy, who was well into adulthood by the time she died, the new fossil is that of an infant, one who lived 3.3 million years ago (and yet has nonetheless [been] dubbed "Lucy's baby").

No other hominin skeleton of such antiquity—including Lucy—is as complete as this one. Moreover, as the earliest juvenile hominin ever found, the Dikika child provides an unprecedented opportunity to study growth processes in our ancient relatives. "If Lucy was the greatest fossil discovery of the 20th century," says Donald C. Johanson of Arizona State University, who unearthed the famed fossil in 1974, "then this baby is the greatest find of the 21st thus far."

BUNDLE OF JOY

It was the afternoon of December 10, 2000, when fossil hunters led by Zeresenay Alemseged, now at the Max Planck Institute for Evolutionary Anthropology in Leipzig, Germany, spotted the specimen. Only part of its tiny face was visible; most of the rest of the skeleton was entombed in a melon-size block of sandstone. But "right away it was clear it was a hominin," Alemseged recollects, noting the smoothness of the brow and the small size of the canine teeth, among other humanlike characteristics. Further evaluation, however, would have to wait until the fossil was cleaned—a painstaking process in which the cementlike matrix is removed from the bone almost grain by grain with dental tools.

It took Alemseged five years to expose key elements of the child's anatomy; many more bones remain obscured by the sediment. Still, the find has already surrendered precious insights into a species that most researchers believe gave rise to our own genus, *Homo*. Alemseged and his colleagues described the fossil and its geologic and paleontological context in two papers published in the September 21 *Nature*. And at a press conference held in Ethiopia to announce the discovery, they christened the child Selam—"peace" in several Ethiopian languages—in hopes of encouraging harmony among the warring tribes of Afar.

The skeleton, judged to be that of a three-year-old girl, consists of a virtually complete skull, the entire torso, and parts of the arms and legs. Even the kneecaps—no larger than macadamia nuts—are preserved. Many of the bones are still in articulation. Hominin fossils this complete are incredibly rare, and ones of infants are rarer still because their bones are that much more fragile. Indeed, the next oldest skeleton of a juvenile that is comparably intact is a Neandertal baby dating to around 50,000 years ago.

WALKING VS. CLIMBING

The exceptional preservation of Selam, as well as that of other animals found at the site, indicates to team geologist Jonathan G. Wynn of the University of South Florida that her body was buried shortly after death by a flood event. Whether she perished in the flood or before it is unknown.

Although she was only three when she died, Selam already possessed the distinctive characteristics of her species. Her projecting snout and narrow nasal bones, for example, readily distinguish her from another ancient youngster, the so-called Taung child from South Africa, who was a member of the closely related *A. africanus* species. And her lower jaw resembles mandibles from Hadar, the site where Lucy and a number of other *A. afarensis* individuals were found.

Selam also exhibits the same mash-up of traits in her postcranial skeleton that has long vexed scientists interested in how *A. afarensis* moved around the landscape. Scholars agree that *A. afarensis* was a creature that got around capably on two legs. But starting in the 1980s, a debate erupted over whether the species was also adapted for life in the trees. The argument centered on the observation that whereas the species has clear adaptations to bipedal walking in its lower body, its upper body contains a number of primitive traits better suited to an arboreal existence, such as long, curved fingers for grasping tree branches. One camp held that *A. afarensis* had made a full transition to terrestrial life and that the tree-friendly features of the upper body were just evolutionary baggage handed down from an arboreal ancestor. The other side contended that if *A. afarensis* had retained those traits for hundreds of thousands of years, then tree climbing must have still formed an important part of its locomotor repertoire.

Like her conspecifics, Selam has legs built for walking and fingers built for climbing. But she also brings new data to the controversy in the form of two shoulder blades, or scapulae—bones previously unknown for this species. According to Alemseged, her scapulae look most like those of a gorilla. The upward-facing shoulder socket is particularly apelike, contrasting sharply with the laterally facing socket modern humans have. This orientation, Alemseged says, may have facilitated raising the hands above the head—something primates do when they climb. (Although gorillas do not climb as adults, they do spend time in the trees as youngsters.)

Further hints of arboreal tendencies reside in the baby's inner ear. Using computed tomographic imaging, the team was able to glimpse her semicircular canal system, which is important for maintaining balance. The researchers determined that Selam's semicircular canals are similar to those of African apes and *A. africanus*. This, they suggest, could indicate that *A. afarensis* was not as fast and agile on two legs as we modern humans are. It could also mean that *A. afarensis* was limited in its ability to decouple the movements of its head and torso, a feat that seems to play a key role in endurance running in our own species.

The conclusion that *A. afarensis* was a bipedal creature with an upper body at least partly adapted for life in the trees echoes what Jack T. Stern, Jr., of Stony Brook University and his colleagues wrote years ago in their reports on Lucy and her contemporaries. "I was happy to see that this paper suggests I might have been right," Stern comments. Johanson agrees that the case for a partly arboreal *A. afarensis* is stronger than it once was. "Early on I was a staunch advocate of strict terrestrial bipedalism in *afarensis*," he remarks. But taking more recent findings into consideration, Johanson says, "it's not out of the realm of possibility that they were still exploiting some of the arboreal habitats for getting off the ground at night and sleeping up there or going back to familiar food sources."

A combination of walking and climbing would fit neatly with the picture that is emerging from studies of the environments of early hominins, including Selam. Today Dikika is an expanse of dusty hills dotted with only the occasional tree or shrub. But 3.3 million years ago, it was a well-watered delta flanked by forests, with some grasslands nearby. "In this context, it is not surprising to have an 'ape' that spends time in the trees and on the ground," comments project member René Bobe of the University of Georgia.

Not everyone is persuaded by the arboreal argument. C. Owen Lovejoy of Kent State University disputes the claim that Selam's scapula looks like a gorilla's. "It's primitive, but it's really more humanlike than gorillalike," he remarks. Lovejoy, a leading proponent of the idea that *A. afarensis* was a dedicated biped, maintains that the forelimb features that are typically held up as indicators that *A. afarensis* spent time in the trees only provide "evidence that the animal has an arboreal history." The discovery of the famed Laetoli footprints in 1978 closed the debate, he states. The trail did not show a prehensile big toe, without which, Lovejoy says, *A. afarensis* simply could not move about effectively in the trees.

A HODGEPODGE HOMININ

Experts may disagree over the functional significance of Selam's apelike skeletal characteristics, but they concur that different parts of the hominin body were undergoing selection at different times. *A. afarensis* is "a good example of mosaic evolution," Johanson states. "You don't just magically flip some evolutionary switch somewhere and transmute a quadruped into an upright-walking bipedal human." It looks like natural selection is selecting for bipedalism in the lower limbs and pelvis first, and things that are not really used in bipedal locomotion, such as arms and shoulders, change at a later stage, he says. "We're getting to know more and more about the sequence of changes" that produced a terrestrial biped from a tree-dwelling, apelike creature.

Analysis of Selam's skull hints at a similarly piecemeal metamorphosis. The shape of the hyoid—a delicate, rarely preserved bone that helps to anchor the tongue and the voice box—indicates that *A. afarensis* had air sacs in its throat, which suggests that the species possessed an apelike voice box. Conversely, the child's brain shows a subtle sign of humanity. By studying the fossil's natural sandstone endocast, an impression of the braincase, Alemseged's team ascertained that Selam had attained only 65 to 88 percent of the adult brain size by the age of three. A chimp of comparable age, in contrast, has reached more than 90 percent of its adult brain size. This raises the tantalizing possibility that *A. afarensis* experienced a more humanlike pattern of brain growth.

More fossils are needed to discern whether the new skeleton is representative of *A. afarensis* infants, and scientists are doubtless eager to recover remains of other *A. afarensis* children of different ages—if they ever can—to see how they compare. But the little girl from Dikika still has more secrets to spill. "I think the impact of this specimen will be in its information of the growth and development of *Australopithecus,* not only for individual body parts but for rates of development among structures within one individual," observes Carol V. Ward of the University of Missouri–Columbia.

For his part, Alemseged estimates that it will take him several more years to finish removing the sandstone from Selam's bones. Once he does, however, he will be able to reconstruct nearly the entire body of an *A. afarensis* three-year-old—and begin to understand what growing up australopithecine was all about.

DISCUSSION QUESTIONS

1. Describe the overall significance of Selam. What is the geological and biological age of the specimen?

2. How does Selam compare with Lucy? If you have studied other early hominins, how does *Australopithecus afarensis* differ from other species of *Australopithecus* or *Homo?*

3. By referring to specific bones, what do paleoanthropologists believe about Selam's locomotor pattern? How have some scientists revised their opinion about the evolution of bipedalism based on *Australopithecus afarensis* fossils including Lucy and Selam?

4. What do you think about basing conclusions about evolution on the fossilized remains of a child? Are there any reasons for caution in using remains of individuals that were not fully grown when they died?

INTERNET RESOURCES

After reading this selection, you may want to research the following individuals.

- Donald Johanson
- Owen Lovejoy
- Zeresenay Alemseged
- Jack T. Stern, Jr.

 **InfoTrac College Edition**

(infotrac-college.com)
You can find many other readings pertinent to this topic by consulting online databases including Info-Trac College Edition. Some suggested search terms for this article are as follows.

- *Australopithecus afarensis*
- Conspecific
- Mosaic evolution
- Bipedalism

17

New Fossils Challenge Line of Descent in Human Family Tree

ANN GIBBONS

Since the 1920s, the search for our earliest direct ancestors—the hominins—has been concentrated in two major geographic areas: East Africa and South Africa. In this selection by science writer Ann Gibbons, you'll be introduced to some of the members of a famous family of fossil hunters from East Africa. Louis and Mary Leakey were the founders of a three-generation dynasty of paleoanthropologists. The Leakeys began their work at the well-known site of Olduvai Gorge in Tanzania in the 1930s. Although decades passed before Mary Leakey found their first hominin (an australopithecine they named Zin-janthropus boisei), stone tools were documented during their work at the site.

In 1960, Louis and Mary discovered a different sort of hominin at Olduvai, one that they ultimately placed in our genus Homo *with the species name of* habilis. *It differed from the australopithecine they had previously discovered by possessing a greater degree of encephalization (increase in brain size relative to body size) and molar teeth, which more resembled those of the genus* Homo *than the australopithecines. Eventually, many scholars came recognize* Homo habilis *as a direct ancestor of a hominin that was widely dispersed over Africa and Asia,* Homo erectus.

Gibbons's article fast-forwards us to the present in the East Lake Turkana region where the mother–daughter team of Meave and Louise Leakey has made some significant discoveries. Meave Leakey, a well-known paleoanthropologist in her own right, is married to Richard Leakey, who once worked actively in human paleontology and now is deeply involved in wildlife conservation. Meave and Louise have assigned the newest fossil they've discovered to Homo habilis. *As you read the article, look for the significance of this fossil in terms of our understanding of human evolution. The more traditional view of* Homo habilis *is that it was ancestral to later hominins. How does the date of the new specimen, as well as other hominin discoveries from this site, call this idea into question? What is the new interpretation for* Homo habilis *and* Homo erectus *based on the finds mentioned in this article?*

Many times, paleoanthropologists have faced similar situations. A new fossil is discovered, one that is inconsistent with earlier ideas relating to human origins. A novel interpretation of a fossil may be suggested by its date or another fossil. It might have an unusual combination of anatomical traits. Perhaps it seems out of place for the region where it's found.

SOURCE: Ann Gibbons, "New Fossils Challenge Line of Descent in Human Family Tree," *Science* 317 (August 2007): 733. Reprinted with permission from AAAS.

Although these situations may cause controversy, conflict between old ideas and new discoveries happens often in science. Such circumstances are what propel science forward. In our example, what is the most appropriate response for paleoanthropologists? Should they discard older ideas completely and think of alternative interpretations? Should they set aside the new find and "wait and see" until similar discoveries are made in the future?

Ever since the famous fossil hunter Louis Leakey found a skull of *Homo habilis* in Olduvai, Tanzania, in 1960, researchers have thought that this 2-million-year-old hominid was the first member of our own genus, *Homo.* This "handyman's" relatively big brain and association with flake tools eventually convinced many paleoanthropologists that *H. habilis* gave rise to *H. erectus* between 2 million and 1.6 million years ago, in a neat line of descent that led to modern humans.

Now, this gradual succession that dominated textbooks for decades is being challenged by none other than Leakey's daughter-in-law and grand-daughter, Meave and Louise Leakey. This week in *Nature,* the Leakeys and their international collaborators describe the discovery of a surprisingly recent upper jawbone of *H. habilis* in Kenya that persisted until 1.44 million years ago. The team also found an older skull of *H. erectus* in the same region, which, taken together with earlier discoveries of this species, extends the time that the two types of humans lived in the same Lake Turkana basin to half a million years. "Their coexistence makes it unlikely that *H. erectus* evolved from *H. habilis,*" says paleontologist Meave Leakey, an associate of the National Museums of Kenya in Nairobi.

Some other researchers agree. "Half a million years suggests that we are dealing with two lineages, not one with a bit of overlap," says paleoanthropologist Bernard Wood of George Washington University in Washington, D.C. But others question the identification of the jawbone as *H. habilis,* given that it depends on three worn teeth. When it comes to possible ancestors, "*Homo habilis* is all we've got," says paleoanthropologist Philip Rightmire of Harvard University. "I don't see any compelling reason to reject this species as the antecedent to *Homo erectus.*"

H. habilis arose during a time, 2 million to 3 million years ago, when there is a gap in the fossil record. As a result, no one knows where it came from or how it is related to the smaller-brained, more apelike australopithecines such as the fossil Lucy, whose species *Australopithecus afarensis* lived 3 million to 3.6 million years ago.

H. erectus appeared about 1.8 million years ago in Africa and Asia, in both places with a larger brain and other more modern features. The lineage of *H. habilis* to *H. erectus* had seemed straightforward, even though earlier discoveries showed overlap between them. But the new discoveries on the east side of Lake Turkana in Kenya suggest the two coexisted for so long that they must have adapted to different niches, says Leakey. If so, the team concludes, it's unlikely that *H. habilis* gave rise to *H. erectus.* "The unilineal picture, where you start with this smaller, more primitive thing and it gradually gets bigger brains, bodies, and limb proportions—that really doesn't work," says co-author Susan Antón of New York University.

A more likely scenario, Leakey says, is that both species arose from another, yet-to-be-identified ancestor. Several other fossils have been proposed as candidates for that role, but so far the evidence is "not satisfactory" to nail down a connection, says paleoanthropologist William Kimbel of Arizona State University in Tempe.

But Rightmire defends an early "*habilis*-like creature" as the most likely ancestor of early *H. erectus.* Fossils of early *H. erectus* that date to 1.7 million years from Dmanisi, Georgia, show affinities with *H. habilis* and lack some traits that appeared later in *H. erectus* in Africa, suggesting that *H. erectus* arose from one group of *H. habilis* in Asia and later migrated to Africa, Rightmire says (*Science,* 5 July 2002, p. 26).

Meanwhile, the new skull of *H. erectus* from the Ileret area east of Lake Turkana is revealing that this ancestor came in many sizes. "What is truly striking about this fossil is its size," says co-lead author Fred Spoor, a paleontologist at University College

London. With a cranial capacity of just 691 cubic centimeters, it is the smallest *H. erectus* ever found and is almost as small as some skulls of *H. habilis.* Yet it is not primitive or transitional from *H. habilis:* The new skull dates to 1.55 million years ago, which "nicely shows that there were big *H. erectus* and little ones for a long time," says Antón. Because the worldwide variation is greater than that between living male and female humans or chimpanzees but less than that between male and female gorillas, some researchers suspect that male *H. erectus* might have been significantly larger than female *H. erectus.*

The skull also shows features that had previously been seen only in Asian fossils of *H. erectus,* such as a keeling (or ridge) on its frontal and parietal bones.

These traits had persuaded a growing number of researchers in recent years to split the fossils of *H. erectus* into two species, with *H. erectus* from Asia and *H. ergaster* from Africa. But the skull's mix of traits shows *H. erectus* cannot be "easily divided between two species from Africa and Asia," says Spoor. Kimbel and Arizona State graduate student Claire Terhune reached a similar conclusion after studying the temporal bones of 15 *H. erectus* skulls, in a paper published in the July issue of the *Journal of Human Evolution.*

Others who have championed *H. ergaster* are taking note. "The new cranium blurs the distinction between *H. erectus* and *H. ergaster,*" says Wood. "I am not willing to sell my shares in *H. ergaster* just yet, but I am not relying on them for my retirement!"

DISCUSSION QUESTIONS

1. What is the more traditional interpretation of the relationship between *Homo habilis* and *Homo erectus?*

2. In what ways does the new discovery by Meave and Louise Leakey pose problems for the more traditional interpretations of *Homo habilis* and *Homo erectus?*

3. Would it be unusual for two different species of hominins to be living in the same region and time period? If this did occur, what kind of explanation would you provide?

INTERNET RESOURCES

After reading this selection, you may want to research the following individuals.

- Meave Leakey
- Richard Leakey
- Louise Leakey

Trac College Edition. Some suggested search terms for this article are as follows.

- *Homo habilis*
- *Homo erectus*
- Olduvai Gorge

InfoTrac College Edition

(infotrac-college.com)
You can find many other readings pertinent to this topic by consulting online databases including Info-

18

The Dawn of Stone Age Genomics

ELIZABETH PENNISI

We modern humans have always been fascinated by the stereotypical image of the traditional "cave man." Movies, television commercials, cartoons, and even a recent prime-time series have featured familiar images of a shaggy, dark-haired, largely human creature. In most such depictions, cave men (and women) demonstrate just enough difference from anatomically modern Homo sapiens to make them stand out in a crowd. This popular perception of an almost fully human cave man can be traced, in part, to the earliest discoveries of Neandertal fossils in Europe. This caricature—a heavily muscled, bent-kneed brute with a large, protruding brow—is largely the product of inaccurate interpretations of Neandertal remains.

A century and a half (and many more fossils) later, contemporary paleoanthropologists have a much better understanding of our Neandertal cousins. We know, for example, that Neandertals lived during the upper Pleistocene. They had big brains (in some cases bigger than ours) that were packaged in crania that were longer and lower than what we possess. Neandertals also had bigger, broader faces and wider noses than ours, and came equipped with heavy brow ridges. Beyond these phenotypic distinctions, however, some intriguing questions remain: just how different were Neandertals from modern Homo sapiens at a genetic level? How much of our genetic makeup did Neandertals share?

As reported in this selection by science writer Elizabeth Pennisi, several teams of scientists are now investigating these and other issues by sequencing the genome of Neandertal fossils. As you read through this selection, try to understand the range of questions that scientists hope to answer by comparing human and Neandertal DNA. Can genomic analysis help us determine what our relationship is to the Neandertals? Alternatively, will DNA tell when Neandertals branched from the lineage leading to modern Homo sapiens? Can we find out through genomic analysis whether Neandertals and Homo sapiens ever interbred? What do comparisons of chimp, Neandertal, and modern humans tell us?

Since its inception, physical anthropology has often taken great leaps forward with new and innovative technologies. On the downside, virtually every new technology presents challenges to its application. What are the difficulties scientists have had in applying DNA sequencing to ancient bones? Can we consider these issues as resolved, or are there ongoing concerns?

When German quarry workers chipped the first Neandertal bones out of a limestone cave in 1856, DNA analysis wasn't even a glimmer in any scientist's mind. Now, two reports . . . describe the first successes in sequencing nuclear DNA from a Neandertal bone—a feat once considered

SOURCE: Elizabeth Pennisi, "The Dawn of Stone Age Genomics," *Science* 314 (November 2006): 1068–1071. Reprinted with permission from AAAS.

impossible. The results from the two groups, working collaboratively but using different approaches, support the view that Neandertals are a separate branch of the hominid family tree that diverged from our own ancestors perhaps 450,000 years ago or more.

Because the extinct Neandertals are our closest relatives, comparing their DNA to ours may one day reveal the mutations that set *Homo sapiens* apart from all other species, as well as the timing of key evolutionary changes. But it's early days yet, and this week's papers chiefly suggest the potential of Neandertal genomics. They also fan the flames of the debate about how different Neandertals were from modern humans, and whether the two groups interbred during the thousands of years they coexisted in Eurasia. . . . "This is great stuff," says molecular evolutionist Alan Cooper of the University of Adelaide, Australia. "It opens the way for much more work on identifying uniquely human genetic changes."

Coming on the heels of dramatic sequencing successes with ancient mammoth and cave bear DNA, the papers also herald a renaissance for a field that has been stymied by issues of poor sample quality and contamination. The Neandertal studies use metagenomics, which makes unnecessary the onerous task of purifying ancient DNA. They also employ faster, cheaper sequencing methods, and their achievement demonstrates the feasibility of deciphering ancient genetic material. "It has people talking about new ideas, new extraction techniques, new ways to prepare samples, new ways to think about old DNA," says Beth Shapiro, an ancient DNA specialist at the University of Oxford in the U.K.

Both teams are planning major additional projects. In July [2006], the team led by Svante Pääbo, a paleogeneticist at the Max Planck Institute for Evolutionary Anthropology in Leipzig, Germany, announced that it plans to produce a very rough draft of the entire Neandertal genome in 2 years. With that draft, he and others will be better able to tell which of the 35 million bases that differ between chimp and humans are mutations that occurred in just the past 500,000 years and therefore

likely define our species. "Perhaps we can find that last little bit that made us special," says Pääbo.

Meanwhile, the other team, led by Edward Rubin, head of the Department of Energy Joint Genome Institute in Walnut Creek, California, has support from the U.S. National Institutes of Health to gather DNA from several Neandertal fossils to study specific regions deemed key to understanding human evolution. At least one other team, led by Cooper, has its own Neandertal project and is working to gather DNA from other ancient humans as well. "A whole new world has opened up with regard to what can be done with ancient DNA," says Thomas Gilbert, a paleogeneticist at the University of Copenhagen, Denmark. But despite the seductive promise of new techniques, researchers warn that ancient DNA has been a fickle mistress. Over the past 20 years, successes have been followed by frustration after frustration. It's hard to find suitable DNA, and it's also quite tricky to avoid contamination with modern genetic material and to cull errors. These issues may come back to haunt Pääbo and Rubin, says genomicist Stephan Schuster of Pennsylvania State University in State College. "The divergence [between living people and Neandertals] is so small compared to the DNA damage and the sequencing error" that it's hard to be confident of any results, he says. "If we've learned anything, it is that we generally haven't perceived the full extent of the problems and complexities of ancient DNA research," admits Cooper. "We're still very much in the learning curve."

UPS AND DOWNS

Ancient DNA made its first appearance in 1984, when Allan Wilson of the University of California (UC), Berkeley, was able to tease out 100 bases from a quagga, an extinct species that looked like a cross between a horse and a zebra. A year later, Pääbo succeeded in extracting genetic material from a 2400-year-old Egyptian mummy.

The world was wowed by these successes, "but there was not much future in the field or the approach," Pääbo recalls. DNA degrades after death, as water, oxygen, and microbes attack it, and the sequencing methods of the time demanded more DNA than was readily available from ancient specimens.

The polymerase chain reaction (PCR), which uses an enzyme to make millions of copies of a particular DNA fragment, seemed to be just what the field needed, offering a way to amplify and read a tiny bit of sequence. The technique powered analyses of quagga, Tasmanian wolves, moas, and other extinct species during the 1990s.

But reliable results from more ancient specimens proved hard to come by. The reaction also amplified age-induced errors and extraneous DNA. A few spectacular failures cast doubt on the whole field: Supposedly 25-million-year-old DNA from amber-encased bees and even older DNA from dinosaurs turned out to be from living humans instead. Ancient human remains were especially problematic because of the specter of contamination: Anyone who handled bone could leave traces of their DNA upon it, and it was impossible to distinguish old from modern sequence.

Then in 1997, following new methodological guidelines, a team led by Pääbo, then at the University of Munich in Germany, and his student Matthias Krings restored the appeal of ancient DNA by decoding 379 bases of Neandertal mitochondrial DNA (mtDNA) (*Science,* 11 July 1997, p. 176). The bases were quite different from the equivalent modern human DNA, suggesting that Neandertals were a distinct species that split off from a common ancestor a half-million years ago and did not interbreed with modern humans. That and subsequent mtDNA and fossil studies supported the leading view that *H. sapiens* arose in Africa and spread around the globe, replacing other kinds of humans.

But in part because modern humans and Neandertals overlapped in Europe and west Asia for at least a few thousand years, and perhaps up to 10,000 years, some researchers had continued to argue that the two species interbred. They pointed out that 379 base pairs were too few to be conclusive. Also, because mitochondria are passed on only by the mother, nuclear DNA is needed to rule out the possibility of mixing.

MAKING THE DREAM REAL

But getting nuclear DNA from ancient bones was a tall order. Back in 1997, "it was just a dream," Pääbo recalls. Because the amount of nuclear DNA in a cell is just 0.05% that of mitochondrial DNA, it's even harder to get enough nuclear DNA to sequence, particularly because often the DNA has disintegrated. Also, Neandertal bones are rare, and curators are reluctant to provide samples. But Pääbo's team devised a hierarchy of tests that required just a tiny amount of material to begin with.

First they tested a tiny, 10-milligram sample for intact proteins, as their presence suggests that DNA was preserved as well. Then they examined 150 milligrams to determine the ratio of Neandertal to modern human DNA, using existing Neandertal mtDNA as a guide. Two of the 70 samples they examined passed both tests with flying colors. So Pääbo's team sliced out a larger piece of one, a 38,000-year-old bone from Croatia, and extracted the DNA.

Meanwhile, Rubin had begun to think that the metagenomics approaches that he was pioneering to study microbial diversity would work with fossil DNA too. He suggested to Pääbo that Neandertal genomics might now be possible. After Rubin's postdoc James Noonan successfully sequenced 26,861 bases of cave bear DNA (*Science,* 22 July 2005, p. 597), Pääbo gave a sample of the Neandertal DNA to Noonan to work on.

The two teams embarked on parallel but independent analyses using different methods. Noonan first created a library of Neandertal DNA incorporated into live bacteria. As each bacterium replicated, it made copies of a particular fragment. The team employed a new, massively parallel technique called pyrosequencing, which uses pulses of light to read the sequence of thousands of bases at once. Sophisticated computer programs then compared the sequence fragments to available DNA databases and identified the potential Neandertal ones based on their similarity to modern human sequence. The team used several tests to rule out contamination with modern human DNA, such as checking that fragments had the correct flanking sequence and the expected amount of DNA damage for their size. In all, Rubin's team was able to extract 65,000 bases of Neandertal DNA.

Pääbo employed pyrosequencing too, but he used a different method to prepare the DNA. Schuster and Hendrik Poinar of McMaster University in Hamilton, Canada, had successfully used this technique to read an astonishing 13 million bases from a 27,000-year-old mammoth (*Science*, 20 January [2006], p. 392). This procedure avoids using bacteria, which for unknown reasons sometimes fail to incorporate certain stretches of DNA and so may not provide a complete sequence. Instead, Pääbo's team coated tiny beads with Neandertal DNA fragments, one fragment per bead. Then each bead's DNA was amplified, independently, by PCR, and read using pyrosequencing.

Ed Green of Pääbo's lab and his colleagues sequenced 225,000 fragments of DNA, totaling millions of bases. But by comparing the sequences with those in existing databases, they found that "the vast majority [of the DNA]—94%—has nothing to do with the human genome," says Pääbo, and came from sources such as soil microbes. Still, they identified a staggering 1 million bases of Neandertal DNA.

Green kept tabs on contamination in part by comparing stretches of mtDNA that showed up in the sequencing to known modern human and Neandertal mtDNA. They found little modern human mitochondrial sequence and say they are confident their Neandertal DNA is genuine.

Both teams compared the new sequences to the modern human genome and to the chimp genome and tallied the sequence differences between each pair of species. Places where the two human genomes match but the chimp's differs likely mark mutations that resulted in uniquely human changes, perhaps including our upright skeletons, bigger brains, lack of hair, and so forth. Differences between the two humans are signposts to changes that were key to their individual evolution. Eventually those changes could lead researchers to the genetic basis of *H. sapiens* speciation.

As expected, the Neandertal and human genomes proved more than 99.5% identical. Rubin's team's analysis of 65,000 bases revealed that the two humans shared 502 mutations that were different

from chimp bases. And 27 bases varied between modern humans and Neandertals, indicating sites where evolution occurred after the two species diverged. Assuming that chimps and humans split 6.5 million years ago, the most recent common ancestor of the two human species lived 468,000 to 1 million years ago, most likely dating back 700,000 years, Noonan and his colleagues report.

In Green and Pääbo's much larger analysis, 10,167 bases were shared by just the modern human and Neandertal, and 434 were unique to modern humans. Taking a slightly different approach from Rubin, the Leipzig team found a more recent divergence time, about 465,000 to 569,000 years ago. This matches the mtDNA analyses, too, but doesn't quite settle the question. Not everyone agrees with the 6.5-million-year-old divergence date for humans and chimps, and a different date would change the timing of the split between modern humans and Neandertals.

As to the question of admixture, Rubin's group found no sign of it. There were no sites where the Neandertal possessed a rare single nucleotide polymorphism (SNP) found only in Europeans, which one would expect had interbreeding occurred. However, given the size of the study, there's still a chance that such shared SNPs exist but haven't yet been found, Rubin explains. So his study refutes the notion that Neandertals were major contributors to the modern human genome but can't rule out a modest amount of gene flow.

In contrast, the Leipzig group did find some evidence of hanky-panky between the two humans—although it's far from conclusive. They used the HapMap and another large catalog of modern human variation developed by a private company to guide them to potential SNP sites in the Neandertal. They found that at 30% of those sites, the Neandertal had the same base as living people, but the chimp had a different base. That's too much similarity, given how long ago the two lineages split. "Taken at face value, our data can be explained by gene flow from modern humans into Neandertals," says Pääbo. He thinks there may have been one-sided mating: Modern human males invaded the Neandertal gene pool by sometimes fathering children with Neandertal females, but not necessarily vice versa.

To those who have long argued for Neandertal admixture—and been in the minority— this is vindication. "These comprise some of the strongest genetic evidence of interbreeding with Neandertals that we have yet seen," says Milford Wolpoff, a biological anthropologist at the University of Michigan, Ann Arbor. But Stanford paleoanthropologist Richard Klein disagrees. "I don't think either paper bears much on the issue of admixture," he says. Schuster is even more circumspect: "Both papers are overinterpreting the data."

Rubin hopes that other researchers will do their own analyses on these publicly available data to help clarify the results. But Montgomery Slatkin, a theoretical population geneticist at UC Berkeley, thinks that even with more studies and more sequence, "it will be very difficult to distinguish between a low level of admixture and no admixture at all."

CONCERN ABOUT CONTAMINATION

Anxiety about the sequence being wrong fuels this pessimism. Researchers need to be sure that what they called "Neandertal" isn't really "technician" DNA. And contamination is hard to avoid. "Bone acts like a sponge; a drop of sweat on the surface will penetrate very deep," Schuster explains.

With nonhuman ancient DNA, researchers can easily pick out and discard modern sequences, but that's not possible with Neandertal DNA, which is nearly identical to our own, notes paleogeneticist Carles Lalueza-Fox of the University of Barcelona, Spain. He is not convinced that the tests for contamination are foolproof. "It might never be possible to determine if the amplified sequence is real or one of the many potential sources of contamination," agrees Shapiro.

All the same, researchers are making some headway. Lalueza-Fox sequenced mtDNA from everyone who had ever touched a Neandertal specimen and compared it to the DNA obtained from the

Neandertal. He found that most of the contamination came from the field, not the lab. His solution: Treat the excavation site like a crime scene. Archaeologists in his team now wear face masks, coveralls, and sterile gloves; they use sterile blades and quickly freeze bones destined for DNA sampling. The dress code has reduced human contamination from about 95% to 5%, says Lalueza-Fox.

Even if contamination can be contained, ancient DNA studies must contend with errors. Sequencing itself makes mistakes. And that's where Rubin's bacterial libraries come in handy. With an ever-reproducing source of DNA, his team can sequence the same fragment multiple times and therefore tell right from wrong bases. With Pääbo's method, the sample gets used up.

More problematic are those errors that have arisen from age-related decay. "Many, and perhaps most, observed differences between a Neandertal genome sequence and the human reference will be caused by [ancient] chemical damage to the Neandertal sample," says Webb Miller, a computer scientist at Pennsylvania State University. One way to detect such errors is to sequence and compare several different specimens, because each fossil should have a unique pattern of DNA damage, says Miller.

Here, too, Rubin's methods can help. He envisions several libraries, each from a different Neandertal. Researchers would pull out the same fragment from each library to compare with each other and with living people. A pilot project has already demonstrated probes that ferret out specific target sequences, so the team needn't analyze the billions of bases shared by Neandertals and living humans, or among different Neandertals. "We will be able to identify and confirm sequence changes in more than one Neandertal without having to sequence several Neandertals to completion," Rubin says. "Seeing the same change in multiple Neandertals will give us confidence that we got [the sequence] right."

Such talk of multiple sequencing has some fossil guardians anxious. "If everybody that wanted a chunk of Neandertal got a chunk of Neandertal, that would put the whole Neandertal fossil record at risk," warns paleoanthropologist Tim White of UC Berkeley.

At this point, however, even the paleontologists seem eager to see what genomic studies can do. This month, Lalueza-Fox will bring one of his "clean-room excavated" bones to Pääbo to see whether its DNA qualifies for sequencing, and he's thrilled

with the potential of sequencing. "For the [150th] Neandertal anniversary, we are moving from paleo-genetics to paleogenomics," Lalueza-Fox explains. "It is incredible considering this was impossible just a few years ago."

DISCUSSION QUESTIONS

1. How can analysis of chimpanzee DNA help us answer questions about the role of Neandertals in the evolution of modern *Homo sapiens?*

2. What is the state of our knowledge now, based on genomic evidence? Do most of the experts who work with genomic sequences think that Neandertals were ancestral to modern *Homo sapiens?* Is there any indication of the presumed time that Neandertals branched off from the

lineage leading to modern humans? Is there any indication of interbreeding between Neandertals and *Homo sapiens?*

3. What are some problems in using ancient DNA to shed light on human evolution?

4. Do you think that genomic analyses will actually replace the need for fossils to reconstruct human evolution? Explain your answer.

INTERNET RESOURCES

After reading this selection, you may want to research the following individuals.

- Svante Pääbo
- Allan Wilson
- Edward Rubin

Trac College Edition. Some suggested search terms for this article are as follows.

- Neandertal
- Ancient DNA
- Polymerase chain reaction (or PCR)

InfoTrac College Edition

(infotrac-college.com)
You can find many other readings pertinent to this topic by consulting online databases including Info-

19

Beyond Stones and Bones

SHARON BEGLEY WITH MARY CARMICHAEL

We live in a rapidly changing, technology-driven society. In other words, much of the change that comes about in our contemporary world involves technological innovation, either directly or indirectly. Physical anthropologists have often seized upon promising new methods to help us learn more about human biology in the human past and present. It's not uncommon for biological anthropologists to perform CT scans on a mummy or subject a piece of bone to microscopic or chemical analyses. When it comes to the study of ancient human evolution, just how far can new scientific instruments and methods take us? In this selection, science writer Sharon Begley describes some of the ways new techniques can help us learn about the key events, or turning points, during the course of human evolution.

Begley focuses on two general areas of investigation. The first, molecular anthropology, involves studies of genomes, chromosomes, or specific genes. Back in the 1950s, anthropologists initially used proteins to estimate the degree of biological difference between humans, apes, and nonhuman primates. Today, as Begley reports, studies of DNA and specific chromosomes are replacing such indirect measures. The timing of the last common ancestor of modern humans and chimpanzees can be estimated by comparing our species' genomes. Pay close attention to how the current estimates for the branching of the human-chimpanzee lineages compares with some recently discovered fossils, including Sahelanthropus tchadensis. *What have we learned about the human-chimpanzee evolutionary split? What do we still need to know?*

Begley also describes the field of paleoneurology. Paleoneurologists may focus, for example, on specific genes that are involved in brain growth or function among humans and chimpanzees. Such comparisons have been made for the HAR1 gene, which is involved in embryonic development of brain tissue. What have we learned from studies such as these? How might investigations involving brain chemicals such as oxytocin teach us about the evolution of cultural practices?

As you read, identify the research questions that are being addressed through new scientific techniques. Look also at the actual type of material that is subjected to study. Notice that not all of the techniques are applied directly to fossils. In some instances, for example, studies involving living peoples can help answer questions about the past. Finally, what do we do when the results of a new method conflict with what has been hypothesized previously based on the fossil record?

When we talk about ancient DNA, paleoneurology, and comparative genomics we are not only assessing the present situation in paleoanthropology, we are getting a glimpse

SOURCE: Sharon Begley with Mary Carmichael, "Beyond Stones and Bones," *Newsweek*, 19 March 2007.

of the future of our field. Someday we may know a lot more about our ancestry than we can even imagine today.

Unlike teeth and skulls and other bones, hair is no match for the pitiless ravages of weather, geologic upheaval and time. So although skulls from millions of years ago testify to the increase in brain size as one species of human ancestor evolved into the next, and although the architecture of spine and hips shows when our ancestors first stood erect, the fossil record is silent on when they fully lost their body hair and replaced it with clothing. Which makes it fortunate that Mark Stoneking thought of lice.

Head lice live in the hair on the head. But body lice, a larger variety, are misnamed: they live in clothing. Head lice, as a species, go back millions of years, while body lice are a more recent arrival. Stoneking, an evolutionary anthropologist, had a hunch that he could calculate when body lice evolved from head lice by comparing the two varieties' DNA, which accumulates changes at a regular rate. (It's like calculating how long it took a typist to produce a document if you know he makes six typos per minute.) That fork in the louse's family tree, he and colleagues at Germany's Max Planck Institute for Evolutionary Anthropology concluded, occurred no more than 114,000 years ago. Since new kinds of creatures tend to appear when a new habitat does, that's when human ancestors must have lost their body hair for good—and made up for it with clothing that, besides keeping them warm, provided a home for the newly evolved louse.

If you had asked paleoanthropologists a generation ago what lice DNA might reveal about how we became human, they would have laughed you out of the room. But research into our origins and evolution has come a long way. Starting with the first discovery of a fossil suggesting that a different sort of human once lived on this planet—it was a Neanderthal skull, unearthed in a mine in Germany's Neander Valley in 1856—our species' genealogy was inferred from stones and bones. Fossils and tools testified to our ancestors' origins in Africa, the emergence of their ability to walk upright, the development of toolmaking and more. But now two new storytellers have begun speaking: DNA and brains.

The science of human evolution is undergoing its own revolution. Although we tend to see the march of species down through time as a single-file parade, with descendant succeeding ancestor in a neat line, the emerging science shows that the story of our species is far more complicated than Biblical literalists would have it—but also more complex than secular science suspected. By analyzing the DNA of today's humans as well as chimps and other species (even lice), scientists are zeroing in on turning points in evolution, such as when and how language and speech developed, and when our ancestors left Africa. DNA can even reveal how many pilgrims made that trek. At the new Hall of Human Origins at the American Museum of Natural History in New York, DNA gets equal billing with fossils. And by comparing the impressions that brains left on the inside of skulls, "paleoneurology" is documenting when structures that power the human mind arose, shedding light on how our ancestors lived and thought. Whether or not you believe the hand of God was guiding these changes, the discoveries are overturning longstanding ideas about how we became human.

Not that fossils are passé. New discoveries are pruning and reshaping humankind's family tree as radically as bonsai. The neat traditional model in which one species gave rise to another like Biblical "begats" has been replaced by a profusion of branches, representing species that lived at the same time as our direct ancestors but whose lines died out. It's like discovering that your great-great-grandfather was not an only child as you'd thought, but had a number of siblings who, for unknown reasons, left no descendants. New research also shows that "progress" and "human evolution" are only occasional partners. More than once in human prehistory, evolution created a modern trait such as a face without jutting, apelike brows and jaws, only to let it go extinct, before trying again a few million years later. Our species' travels through time proceeded in fits and starts, with long periods when "nothing much happened," punctuated by bursts of dizzying change, says paleontologist Ian Tattersall, co-curator of the American Museum's new hall.

As its exhibits show, humankind's roots are sunk deep in the East African savanna. There, the last creature ancestral to humans as well as chimps—our closest living cousins—lived, standing at a fork in the family tree as momentous as it is contentious. Fossils never resolved when the lineages split. DNA might. Human DNA and chimp DNA differ by no more than 1.2 percent, and DNA changes at a fairly regular rate. That lets scientists use this rate to calibrate a "molecular clock" whose tick-tocks measure how long ago a genetic change occurred. The fact that the DNA of living chimps and humans differ by about 35 million chemical "letters," for instance, implies that the two lineages split 5 million to 6 million years ago. That fits with the discovery that Earth became cruelly colder and drier 6.5 million years ago, just the sort of climate change that coaxes new species into being. The apes that stayed in the forests hardly changed; they are the ancestors of today's chimps. Those that ventured into the newly formed habitat of dry grasslands had taken the first steps toward becoming human.

Now the contentious part. In 2001, a team digging in Chad unearthed what it claimed was the oldest fossil of an ancestor of humans but not chimps. If so, it must have lived after the two lineages split. Trouble was, *Sahelanthropus tchadensis* (nicknamed Toumai, the local word for "child") lived close to 7 million years ago. The genetic data, pointing to a human-chimp split at least 1 million years later, suggest that Toumai is not the ur-hominid—the first creature ancestral only to humans and not our chimp cousins—after all.

If Toumai is not our ancestor, what is he doing with such a humanlike face and teeth, which look like those of species 5 million years his junior? "A 7-million-year-old hominid should be just starting to look like a hominid, not have a trait you see so much later in the fossil record," says paleoanthropologist Bernard Wood of George Washington University. Even if he is not our ancestor, Toumai is valuable because he undermines the "begat" model of human evolution—that Toumai begat *Australopithecus* who begat *Homo habilis* who begat *Homo erectus* who begat *Homo sapiens*. That model assumes that each biological innovation, whether bipedality or a large brain or any other, evolved only once and stuck.

Instead, evolution played Mr. Potato Head, putting different combinations of features on ancient hominids then letting them vanish until a later species evolved them. "Similar traits evolved more than once, which means you can't use them as gold-plated evidence that one fossil is descended from another or that having an advanced trait means a fossil was a direct ancestor of modern humans," says Wood. "Lots of branches in the human family tree don't make it to the surface."

In fact, starting 4 million years ago half a dozen hominids belonging to the genus *Australopithecus* called Africa home. Best-known for the fossil named Lucy, which was discovered in 1974, *Australopithecus afarensis* had apelike features such as a large jaw and jutting face, and probably scrambled up trees for safety and shelter. But she also strode the grasslands erect, a hallmark of modern humans. Footprints preserved in volcanic ash 3.6 million years old are mute testimony to how one larger *afarensis* and a smaller companion—woman and mate, or parent and child—walked across a plain in what is now Tanzania.

What triggered this abrupt change—what set us on the road to becoming fully human—has long stumped experts. Where stones and bones were of little help, however, genes and brains have begun to speak. Last summer scientists discovered a gene called HAR1 (for human accelerated region) that is present in animals from chickens to chimps to people. It had changed in only two of its 118 chemical "letters" from 310 million years ago (when the lineages of chickens and chimps split) to 5 million years ago. But 18 letters changed in the (relative) blink of an eye since the human lineage split from chimps', Katherine Pollard of the University of California, Davis, and colleagues reported. That high rate of change is a sign of a gene whose evolution keeps conferring advantages on those who carry it, perhaps starting with *Australopithecus*.

The brain, more than any other organ, may have reaped those genetic advantages. HAR1 reaches a peak of activity from the seventh to ninth week of gestation in humans, apparently spurring brain growth. And it is plentiful in cells that create the six layers of neurons in the human cortex. "HAR1 is present in neurons that play a role in the geometry and layout of the cortex," says Pollard. It likely helped the cortexes of our ancestors develop the elaborate folds characteristic of a complex brain.

Besides making brain structure more complex, genetic change also advanced the brain's chemistry. In 2005, Matthew Rockman of Duke University and colleagues discovered that a gene called PDYN began accumulating changes 7 million years ago, soon after our oldest direct ancestor appeared. This gene regulates production of a molecule called prodynorphin, which is like the brain's soup stock: depending on what other ingredients are added, it can change into neurochemicals that underlie perception, behavior or memory. "Fossils can tell us a lot, but it is genomes that tell us what was involved in making language possible and in making brains the way they are today," says Rob DeSalle, co-curator of the American Museum's new hall.

It surely took more than prodynorphin's magic to modernize a brain and thus jump-start the creation of new species. To find what else made us human, scientists led by neurogeneticist Daniel Geschwind of UCLA are examining which combinations of genes are active in the cortex, the seat of higher thinking, of chimps and people. Among the genes turned to "high" in people, they reported last year, are those that influence how fast electrical signals jump from neuron to neuron and therefore how fast the brain can process information, those that enhance connections between the cells and thus learning and memory, and those that promote brain growth. This pattern of gene activity, it appears, began emerging when *Australopithecus* species did.

And it helps explain why Lucy's kind were the way they were. *Afarensis* women and men stood three to five feet tall and weighed 60 to 100 pounds. They had small teeth good for fruits and nuts, but not meat. (The available prey was enough to make one a confirmed vegetarian: hyenas the size of bears, sabertoothed cats and other mega-reptiles and raptors.) That suggests that early humans were more often prey than predators, says anthropologist Robert Sussman of Washington University, coauthor of the 2005 book *Man the Hunted*. The evidence is as stark as the many fossil skulls containing holes made by big cats and talon marks from raptors.

The realization that early humans were the hunted and not hunters has upended traditional ideas about what it takes for a species to thrive. For decades the reigning view had been that hunting prowess and the ability to vanquish competitors was the key to our ancestors' evolutionary success (an idea fostered, critics now say, by the male domination of anthropology during most of the 20th century). But prey species do not owe their survival to anything of the sort, argues Sussman. Instead, they rely on their wits and, especially, social skills to survive. Being hunted brought evolutionary pressure on our ancestors to cooperate and live in cohesive groups. That, more than aggression and warfare, is our evolutionary legacy.

Both genetics and paleoneurology back that up. A hormone called oxytocin, best-known for inducing labor and lactation in women, also operates in the brain (of both sexes). There, it promotes trust during interactions with other people, and thus the cooperative behavior that lets groups of people live together for the common good. By comparing the chimp genome with the human, scientists infer that oxytocin existed in the ancestor of both. But it has undergone changes since then, perhaps in how strongly the brain responds to it and in how much is produced. The research is still underway, but one possibility is that the changes occurred around the time our ancestors settled into a system based on enduring bonds between men and women, about 1.7 million years ago.

That was a formula for success, and one that may have also left a mark on the brain. Besides revealing the size of a brain, paleoneurology examines impressions of surface features that the brain leaves on the inside of the skull. That yields clues to its organization. Comparing the shapes of the brains of two hominids that lived 2.5 million years ago, *Australopithecus africanus* and *Paranthropus,* scientists find major differences in the shape of the frontal lobe, which controls higher cognition. "*Paranthropus* has a teardrop shape, whereas *africanus* is more squared off, and *africanus* has a swooping down on the bottom where *Paranthropus* is sort of peaked," says Dean Falk of Florida State University. That configuration suggests that *africanus* had a better-developed region called area 10, which plays a key role in decision-making, taking initiative and advance planning. It may be why *africanus* evolved while *Paranthropus* came to a dead end.

Paleoneurology promises to do what simplistic studies of ancient brains—which asked only how big they were—could not: explain our ancestors' great leaps forward. About 2.5 million years ago a new genus, *Homo habilis,* appeared in Africa. Discovered by the legendary Louis and Mary Leakey, *habilis* was the first hominid with a brain bigger than a chimp's, and was the first toolmaker: stone tools—sharp flakes of rock—appeared when *habilis* did. Their direct descendant, *Homo erectus,* took an equally momentous step: venturing beyond Africa. In the Republic of Georgia at a site called Dmanisi, scientists have unearthed 1.8-million-year-old fossils of *erectus,* "the first outpost we know of beyond Africa," says G. Philip Rightmire of Binghamton University. "It looks like these people got out and materialized everywhere in Eurasia," showing up as Java man and Peking man, among others. (None of the original fossils of Peking man survived World War II. Packed for shipment to the United States for safekeeping, they disappeared in transit; only casts remain.) Ancient humans didn't just walk: they reached Australia 60,000 years ago, across miles of open ocean.

Erectus shows that brain size is too crude a measure of a species' talents. At Dmanisi, the brains range from 600 to 770 cubic centimeters, comparable to the more primitive *habilis.* But while *erectus* did not distinguish themselves in brain size, brain structure is more telling. They were the first of our ancestors to have an asymmetric brain, as modern humans do; *Australopithecus* species do not. Asymmetry is a mark of increasing specialization and therefore complex cognitive ability. *Erectus* used it to, among other things, discover and tame fire. What they did not use it for is technology. Tools found with the Dmanisi fossils include cutting flakes, rock "cores" from which flakes were made and a chopper, all primitive even for their time. "The old idea that you needed a master's degree in stone tools to leave Africa is crazy," says Bernard Wood.

Although *erectus* spread across Eurasia between 2 million and 1 million years ago, DNA makes clear that the species was almost certainly a dead end and not our ancestor, as some scientists had argued. According to this idea, groups of *erectus* scattered across the Old World all accrued the same mutations and underwent the same natural selection that led to *Homo sapiens.* The Y chromosome begs to differ. The Y is passed intact from father to son; in that sense, it's like a last name and so can be used to trace ancestries. But like surnames that got Anglicized at Ellis Island, sometimes a Y changes, with the altered version being passed to all male descendants. Peter Underhill, a molecular anthropologist at Stanford University, tracked 160 such changes in the Y's of 1,062 men from 21 populations across the world. Applying the molecular-clock technique, he concludes that the most recent common ancestor of all men alive today lived 89,000 years ago in Africa. The first modern humans—and therefore, unlike the earlier wave of *Homo erectus* into Asia a million years ago, the ancestors of everyone today—departed Africa about 66,000 years ago.

These pilgrims were strikingly few. From the amount of variation in Y chromosomes today, population geneticists infer how many individuals were in this "founder" population. The best estimate: 2,000 men. Assuming an equal number of women, only 4,000 brave souls ventured forth from Africa. We are their descendants.

A curious thing about early *Homo* species is that they looked quite human early on. "By 600,000 years ago everyone had a big brain, and by 200,000 years ago people in Africa looked like modern humans," says archeologist Richard Klein of Stanford. "But there was no representational art, no figurines, no jewelry until 50,000 years ago. Some kind of cognitive advance was required, probably in language or working memory. But since size hardly changed, the brain change that produced behaviorally modern humans must have been in structure."

The source of such structural changes must come, like every aspect of our physiology, from genes. Combing the genome for genes that emerged just when language, art, culture and other products of higher intelligence did, researchers have found three with the right timing.

The first, called FOXP2, plays a role in human speech and language, but it must do something else in other species, because the decidedly nonverbal mouse has a version of it. Using the standard molecular-clock tactic, Svante Pääbo and colleagues at the Max Planck Institute estimate that the human version of FOXP2 appeared less than 200,000 years ago—about when anatomically modern humans stepped onto the world stage—and maybe as recently as 50,000. If so, then it is only humans as modern as those in the last diaspora out of Africa who developed advanced, spoken language. Another gene with interesting timing is microcephalin, which affects brain size. It carries a time stamp of 37,000 years ago, again when symbolic thinking was taking hold in our most recent ancestors. The third, called

ASPM and also involved in brain size, clocks in at 5,800 years. That was just before people established the first cities in the Near East and is well after *Homo sapiens* attained their modern form. It therefore suggests that we are still evolving.

The fossils have not finished speaking, of course. These countless postcards from the past surely still lie encased in the rocks of the Old World. But now, as ancient DNA and gray matter give up their secrets, they are adding life to the age-old quest to understand where humankind came from and how we got here.

DISCUSSION QUESTIONS

1. A friend says to you, "There's no point in studying the characteristics of fossils any more. You should drop your comparative anatomy and osteology classes and just learn more about molecular genetics." Do you run to drop the courses or argue that fossils will always be relevant to the study of human evolution?

2. Can you think of a molecular mechanism that would account for the multiple branches Begley refers to in the evolution of modern *Homo sapiens?* What other circumstances might account for similar anatomical adaptations found among species of *Homo* that eventually became extinct?

3. What is a molecular clock? How is a molecular clock used? What do molecular clocks teach us about the timing of the human-chimpanzee split?

4. In what ways have studies of the Y chromosome furthered our knowledge of the evolution of modern *Homo sapiens?*

5. What has paleoneurology contributed to our understanding of the evolution of brain size and structure? In what ways might it help us learn about cultural practices among the early hominids?

www INTERNET RESOURCES

After reading this article, you might wish to learn more about the research and writings of other individuals such as:

- Mark Stoneking
- Dean Falk
- Bernard Wood

 InfoTrac College Edition

(infotrac-college.com)
You can find many other readings pertinent to this topic by consulting online databases including Info-

Trac College Edition. Some suggested search terms for this article are as follows.

- Oxytocin
- Molecular clock
- FOXP2
- Paleoneurology
- *Sahelanthropus tchadensis*

PART V

Modern Human Variation

20

Lactose and Lactase

NORMAN KRETCHMER

Got milk? When was the last time you drank a glass? If you enjoyed milk recently, perhaps you're unaware that many adult humans don't share your taste. In fact, their physiology precludes their ability to digest lactose, or milk sugar. In this classic article, Norman Kretchmer takes us on a scientific investigation of this paradoxical question: why do some adult humans retain the ability to digest milk from infancy when virtually all other adult mammals (including humans) lose this ability? Today we know that people who maintain the ability to digest lactose continue, as adults, to produce lactase, the enzyme that breaks lactose down into two simpler sugars, glucose and galactose. Such people are said to be lactose tolerant *or to have* lactase persistence. *People who don't produce lactase as adults are said to be lactose intolerant or to have lactase deficiency.*

Before you read the article, scan it to note the wide variety of information that Kretchmer brings together on the topic of lactose digestion. While he provides new data and insights, he also, as in most classic articles, first lays a solid and broad foundation for the new ideas. Ultimately, Kretchmer evaluates two alternative hypotheses relating to why adults from some populations retain their ability to break down lactose while other adults lose it. First, however, he reviews evidence relating to lactose intolerance among mammals as well as the mechanisms for lactase persistence into adulthood. Although the chemistry in this article may be somewhat difficult to understand, the most important principle is this: in order for milk to be digested, milk sugar, or lactose, must be broken down by lactase.

Kretchmer also demonstrates that there is a pattern to lactose tolerance among various ancestral groups. Adults of northern European ancestry are most likely to show lactose tolerance. Furthermore, among African populations, those who are pastoralists, or herding peoples, are the most likely to show lactose tolerance.

Kretchmer's paper evaluates two alternative hypotheses. The first is that certain individuals can adapt to milk drinking during their lifetime by the activation of a specific gene or genes. The second, which focuses on development of lactase persistence over the course of evolution, postulates that individuals who possessed a mutation allowing for lactose tolerance would have been favored through natural selection. To weigh these hypotheses, Kretchmer and his team studied different ethnic groups in Nigeria that differed in terms of their subsistence pattern and therefore their dependence on milk. As you read, pay special attention to the description of how these groups varied with respect to lactose tolerance and how Kretchmer explained these results. What findings did he make that had a bearing on

*his hypotheses? How does this study illustrate the way natural selection acted upon human pop-
ulations in the past? What factors may have selected for the evolution of lactase persistence?*

Milk is the universal food of newborn mammals, but some human infants cannot digest
it because they lack sufficient quantities of lactase,
the enzyme that breaks down lactose, or milk sugar.
Adults of all animal species other than man also lack
the enzyme—and so, it is now clear, do most human beings after between two and four years of
age. That this general adult deficiency in lactase
has come as a surprise to physiologists and nutri-
tionists can perhaps be attributed to a kind of ethnic
chauvinism, since the few human populations in
which tolerance of lactose has been found to ex-
ceed intolerance include most northern European
and white American ethnic groups.

Milk is a nearly complete human food, and in
powdered form it can be conveniently stored and
shipped long distances. Hence it is a popular source
of protein and other nutrients in many programs of
aid to nutritionally impoverished children, including
American blacks. The discovery that many of these
children are physiologically intolerant to lactose is
therefore a matter of concern and its implications
are currently being examined by such agencies as the
U.S. Office of Child Development and the Protein
Advisory Group of the United Nations System.

Lactose is one of the three major solid components of milk and its only carbohydrate; the other
components are fats and proteins. Lactose is a disaccharide composed of the monosaccharides glucose
and galactose. It is synthesized only by the cells of
the lactating mammary gland, through the reaction
of glucose with the compound uridine diphosphate
galactose. . . . One of the proteins found in milk,
alpha-lactalbumin, is required for the synthesis of lactose. This protein apparently does not actually enter
into the reaction; what it does is "specify" the action
of the enzyme galactosyl transferase, modifying the
enzyme so that in the presence of alpha-lactalbumin
and glucose it catalyzes the synthesis of lactose.

In the nonlactating mammary gland, where
alpha-lactalbumin is not present, the enzyme synthesizes instead of lactose a more complicated carbohydrate, N-acetyl lactosamine. Test-tube studies have
shown that alpha-lactalbumin is manufactured only
in the presence of certain hormones: insulin, corti-
sone, estrogen and prolactin; its synthesis is inhibited
by the hormone progesterone. It is when progesterone levels decrease late in pregnancy that the manufacture of alpha-lactalbumin, and thus of lactose, is
initiated. . . .

The concentration of lactose in milk from different sources varies considerably. Human milk is the
sweetest, with 7.5 grams of lactose per 100 milliliters
of milk. Cow's milk has 4.5 grams per 100 milliliters.
The only mammals that do not have any lactose—or
any other carbohydrate—in their milk are certain of
the Pinnipedia: the seals, sea lions and walruses of the
Pacific basin. If these animals are given lactose in any
form, they become sick. (In 1933 there was a report
of a baby walrus that was fed cow's milk while being
shipped from Alaska to California. The animal suf-
fered from severe diarrhea throughout the voyage
and was very sick by the time it arrived in San
Diego.) Of these pinnipeds the California sea lion
has been the most intensively studied. No alpha-
lactalbumin is synthesized by its mammary gland.
When alpha-lactalbumin from either rat's milk or
cow's milk is added to a preparation of sea lion mammary gland in a test tube, however, the glandular
tissue does manufacture lactose.

In general, low concentrations of lactose are associated with high concentrations of milk fat (which
is particularly useful to marine mammals). The
Pacific pinnipeds have more than 35 grams of fat
per 100 milliliters of milk, compared with less than
four grams in the cow. In the whale and the bear (an
ancient ancestor of which may also be an ancestor of
the Pacific pinnipeds) the lactose in milk is low and
the fat content is high.

Lactase, the enzyme that breaks down lactose
ingested in milk or a milk product, is a specific intestinal beta-galactosidase that acts only on lactose,
primarily in the jejunum, the second of the small
intestine's three main segments. The functional units
of the wall of the small intestine are the villus
(composed of metabolically active, differentiated,

nondividing cells) and the crypt (a set of dividing cells from which those of the villus are derived). Lactase is not present in the dividing cells. It appears in the differentiated cells, specifically within the brush border of the cells at the surface of the villus. . . . Lactase splits the disaccharide lactose into its two component monosaccharides, glucose and galactose. Some of the released glucose can be utilized directly by the cells of the villus; the remainder, along with the galactose, enters the bloodstream, and both sugars are metabolized by the liver. Neither Gary Gray of the Stanford University School of Medicine nor other investigators have been able to distinguish any qualitative biochemical or physical difference among the lactases isolated from the intestine of infants, tolerant adults and intolerant adults. The difference appears to be merely quantitative; there is simply very little lactase in the intestine of a lactose-intolerant person. In the intestine of Pacific pinnipeds, Philip Sunshine of the Stanford School of Medicine found, there is no lactase at all, even in infancy.

Lactase is not present in the intestine of the embryo or the fetus until the middle of the last stage of gestation. Its activity attains a maximum immediately after birth. Thereafter it decreases, reaching a low level, for example, immediately after weaning in the rat and after one and a half to three years in most children. The exact mechanism involved in the appearance and disappearance of the lactase is not known, but such a pattern of waxing and waning activity is common in the course of development; in general terms, one can say that it results from differential action of the gene or genes concerned.

Soon after the turn of the century the distinguished American pediatrician Abraham Jacobi pointed out that diarrhea in babies could be associated with the ingestion of carbohydrates. In 1921 another pediatrician, John Howland, said that "there is with many patients an abnormal response on the part of the intestinal tract to carbohydrates, which expresses itself in the form of diarrhea and excessive fermentation." He suggested as the cause a deficiency in the hydrolysis, or enzymatic breakdown, of lactose.

The physiology is now well established. If the amount of lactose presented to the intestinal cells exceeds the hydrolytic capacity of the available lac-

tase (whether because the lactase level is low or because an unusually large amount of lactose is ingested), a portion of the lactose remains undigested. Some of it passes into the blood and is eventually excreted in the urine. The remainder moves on into the large intestine, where two processes ensue. One is physical: the lactose molecules increase the particle content of the intestinal fluid compared with the fluid in cells outside the intestine and therefore by osmotic action draw water out of the tissues into the intestine. The other is biochemical: the glucose is fermented by the bacteria in the colon. Organic acids and carbon dioxide are generated and the symptoms can be those of any fermentative diarrhea, including a bloated feeling, flatulence, belching, cramps and a watery, explosive diarrhea.

At the end of the 1950's Paolo Durand of the University of Genoa and Aaron Holzel and his colleagues at the University of Manchester reported detailed studies of infants who were unable to digest lactose and who reacted to milk sugar with severe diarrhea, malnutrition and even death. This work stimulated a revival of interest in lactose and lactase, and there followed a period of active investigation of lactose intolerance. Many cases were reported, including some in which lactase inactivity could be demonstrated in tissue taken from the patient's intestine by biopsy. It became clear that intolerance in infants could be a congenital condition (as in Holzel's two patients, who were siblings) or, more frequently, could be secondary to various diseases and other stresses: cystic fibrosis, celiac disease, malnutrition, the ingestion of certain drugs, surgery and even non-specific diarrhea. During this period of investigation, it should be noted, intolerance to lactose was generally assumed to be the unusual condition and the condition worthy of study.

In 1965 Pedro Cuatrecasas and his colleagues and Theodore M. Bayless and Norton S. Rosensweig, all of whom were then at the Johns Hopkins School of Medicine, administered lactose to American blacks and whites, none of whom had had gastrointestinal complaints, and reported some startling findings. Whereas only from 6 to 15 percent of the whites showed clinical symptoms of intolerance, about 70 percent of the blacks were intolerant. This immediately suggested that many human adults might be unable to digest lactose and, more specifically, that there might be significant differences among ethnic groups. The possibility was soon confirmed: G. C. Cook and S. Kajubi of Makerere University College examined two different tribes in Uganda. They found that only 20 percent of the adults of the cattle-herding Tussi tribe were intolerant to lactose but that 80 percent of the non-pastoral Ganda were intolerant. Soon one paper after another reported a general intolerance to lactose among many ethnic groups, including Japanese, other Orientals, Jews in Israel, Eskimos and South American Indians.

In these studies various measures of intolerance were applied. One was the appearance of clinical symptoms—flatulence and diarrhea—after the ingestion of a dose of lactose, which was generally standardized at two grams of lactose per kilogram (2.2 pounds) of body weight, up to a maximum of either 50 or 100 grams. Another measure was a finding of low lactase activity (less than two units per gram of wet weight of tissue) determined through an intestinal biopsy after ingestion of the same dose of lactose. A third was an elevation of blood glucose of less than 20 milligrams per 100 milliliters of blood after ingestion of the lactose. Since clinical symptoms are variable and the biopsy method is inconvenient for the subject being tested, the blood glucose method is preferable. It is a direct measure of lactose breakdown, and false-negative results are rare if the glucose is measured 15 minutes after lactose is administered.

By 1970 enough data had been accumulated to indicate that many more groups all over the world are intolerant to lactose than are tolerant. As a matter of fact, real adult tolerance to lactose has so far been observed only in northern Europeans, approximately 90 percent of whom tolerate lactose, and in the members of two nomadic pastoral tribes in Africa, of whom about 80 percent are tolerant. Although many other generally tolerant groups will be found, they will always belong to a minority of the human species. In this situation it is clearly more interesting and potentially more fruitful to focus the investigation on tolerant people in an effort to explain adult tolerance, a characteristic in which man differs from all other mammals.

There are two kinds of explanation of adult tolerance to lactose. The first, and perhaps the most immediately apparent, originates with the fact that most people who tolerate lactose have a history of drinking milk. Maybe the mere presence of milk in the diet suffices to stimulate lactase activity in the individual, perhaps by "turning on" genes that encode the synthesis of the enzyme. Individual enzymatic adaptation to an environmental stimulus is well known, but it is not transferable genetically. The other explanation of tolerance is based on the concept of evolution through natural selection. If in particular populations it became biologically advantageous to be able to digest milk, then the survival of individuals with a genetic mutation that led to higher intestinal lactase activity in adulthood would have been favored. An individual who derived his ability to digest lactose from this classical form of Darwinian adaptation would be expected to be able to transfer the trait genetically.

These two points of view have become the subject of considerable controversy. I suspect that each of the explanations is valid for some of the adult tolerance being observed, and I should like to examine both of them.

The possibility of individual adaptation to lactose has been considered since the beginning of the century, usually through attempts to relate lactase activity to the concentration of milk in the diet of animals. Almost without exception the studies showed that although there was a slight increase in lactase activity when a constant diet of milk or milk products was consumed, there was no significant change in the characteristic curve reflecting the developmental rise and fall of enzymatic activity. Recently there have been reports pointing toward adaptation, however. Some studies, with human subjects as well as rats, indicated that continued intensive feeding of milk or lactose not only made it possible for the individual to tolerate the sugar but also resulted in a measurable increase in lactase activity. The discrepancy among the findings could be partly attributable to improvement in methods for assaying the enzyme activity.

On balance it would appear that individual adaptation may be able to explain at least some cases of adult tolerance. I shall cite two recent studies. John

Godell, working in Lagos, selected six Nigerian medical students who were absolutely intolerant to lactose and who showed no physiological evidence of lactose hydrolysis. He fed them increasing amounts of the sugar for six months. Godell found that although the students did develop tolerance for the lactose, there was nevertheless no evidence of an increase of glucose in the blood—and thus of enzymatic adaptation—following test doses of the sugar. The conjecture is that the diet brought about a change in the bacterial flora in the intestine, and that the ingested lactose was being metabolized by the new bacteria.

In our laboratory at the Stanford School of Medicine Emanuel Lebenthal and [Philip] Sunshine found that in rats given lactose the usual pattern of a developmental decrease in lactase activity is maintained but the activity level is somewhat higher at the end of the experiment. The rise in activity does not appear to be the result of an actual increase in lactase synthesis, however. We treated the rats with actinomycin, which prevents the synthesis of new protein from newly activated genes. The actinomycin had no effect on the slight increase in lactase activity, indicating that the mechanism leading to the increase was not gene activation. It appears, rather, that the presence of additional amounts of the enzyme's substrate, lactose, somehow "protects" the lactase from degradation. Such a process has been noted in many other enzyme-substrate systems. The additional lactase activity that results from this protection is sufficient to improve the rat's tolerance of lactose, but that additional activity is dependent on the continued presence of the lactose.

Testing the second hypothesis—that adult lactose tolerance is primarily the result of a long-term process of genetic selection—is more complicated. It involves data and reasoning from such disparate areas as history, anthropology, nutrition, genetics and sociology as well as biochemistry.

As I have noted, the work of Cuatrecasas, of Bayless and Rosensweig and of Cook and Kajubi in the mid-1960's pointed to the likelihood of significant differences in adult lactose tolerance among ethnic groups. It also suggested that one ought to study in particular black Americans and their ancestral populations in Africa. The west coast of Africa was the primary source of slaves for the New World.

With the objective of studying lactose tolerance in Nigeria, we developed a joint project with a group from the University of Lagos Teaching Hospital headed by Olikoye Ransome-Kuti.

The four largest ethnic groups in Nigeria are the Yoruba in western Nigeria, the Ibo in the east and the Fulani and Hausa in the north. These groups have different origins and primary occupations. The Yoruba and the Ibo differ somewhat anthropometrically, but both are Negro ethnic groups that probably came originally from the Congo Basin; they were hunters and gatherers who became farmers. They eventually settled south of the Niger and Benue rivers in an area infested with the tsetse fly, so that they never acquired cattle (or any other beast of burden). Hence it was not until recent times that milk appeared in their diet beyond the age of weaning. After the colonization of their part of Nigeria by the British late in the 19th century, a number of Yoruba and Ibo, motivated by their intense desire for education, migrated to England and northern Europe; they acquired Western dietary habits and in some cases Western spouses, and many eventually returned to Nigeria.

The Fulani are Hamites who have been pastoral people for thousands of years, originally perhaps in western Asia and more recently in northwestern Africa. Wherever they went, they took their cattle with them, and many of the Fulani are still nomads who herd their cattle from one grazing ground to another. About 300 years ago the Fulani appeared in what is now Nigeria and waged war on the Hausa. (The Fulani also tried to invade Yorubaland but were defeated by the tsetse fly.) After the invasion of the Hausa region some of the Fulani moved into villages and towns.

As a result of intermarriage between the Fulani and the Hausa there appeared a new group known as the town-Fulani or the Hausa-Fulani, whose members no longer raise cattle and whose ingestion of lactose is quite different from that of the pastoral Fulani. The pastoral Fulani do their milking in the early morning and drink some fresh milk. The milk reaches the market in the villages and towns only in a fermented form, however, as a kind of yogurt called *nono*. As the *nono* stands in the morning sun it becomes a completely fermented, watery preparation, which is then thickened with millet or some other cereal. The final product is almost completely free of lactose and can be ingested without trouble even by a person who cannot digest lactose.

We tested members of each of these Nigerian populations. Of all the Yorubas above the age of four who were tested, we found only one person in whom the blood glucose rose to more than 20 milligrams per 100 milliliters following administration of the test dose of lactose. She was a nurse who had spent six years in the United Kingdom and had grown accustomed to a British diet that included milk. At first, she said, the milk disagreed with her, but later she could tolerate it with no adverse side effects. None of the Ibos who were studied showed an elevation of glucose in blood greater than 20 milligrams per 100 milliliters. (The major problem in all these studies is determining ethnic purity. All the Yorubas and Ibos who participated in this portion of the study indicated that there had been no intermarriages in their families.) Most of the Hausa and Hausa-Fulani (70 to 80 percent) were intolerant to lactose. In contrast most of the nomadic Fulani (78 percent) were tolerant to it. In their ability to hydrolyze lactose they resembled the pastoral Tussi of Uganda and northern Europeans more than they resembled their nearest neighbors.

Once the distribution of lactose intolerance and tolerance was determined in the major Nigerian populations, we went on to study the genetics of the situation by determining the results of mixed marriages. One of the common marriages in western Nigeria is between a Yoruba male and a British or other northern European female; the reverse situation is less common. Our tests showed that when a tolerant northern European marries a lactose-intolerant Yoruba, the offspring are most likely to be lactose-tolerant. If a tolerant child resulting from such a marriage marries a pure Yoruba, then the children are also predominantly tolerant. There is no sex linkage of the genes involved: in the few cases in which a Yoruba female had married a northern European male, the children were predominantly tolerant.

On the basis of these findings one can say that lactose tolerance is transmitted genetically and is dominant, that is, genes for tolerance from one of the parents are sufficient to make the child tolerant. On the other hand, the children of two pure Yorubas are always intolerant to lactose, as are the children of a lactose-intolerant European female and a Yoruba male. In other words, intolerance is also transmitted genetically and is probably a recessive trait, that is, both parents must be lactose-intolerant to produce an intolerant child. When the town-dwelling royal line of the Fulani was investigated, its members were all found to be unable to digest lactose—except for the children of one wife, a pastoral Fulani, who were tolerant.

Among the children of Yoruba-European marriages the genetic cross occurred one generation ago or at the most two generations. Among the Hausa-Fulani it may have been as much as 15 generations ago. This should explain the general intolerance of the Hausa-Fulani. Presumably the initial offspring of the lactose-tolerant Fulani and the lactose-intolerant Hausa were predominantly tolerant. As the generations passed, however, intolerance again became more prevalent. The genes for lactase can therefore be considered incompletely dominant.

The blacks brought to America were primarily Yoruba or Ibo or similar West African peoples who were originally intolerant to lactose. American blacks have been in this country for between 10 and 15 generations, in the course of which a certain complement of white northern European genes has entered the black population. Presumably as a result lactose intolerance among American blacks has been reduced to approximately 70 percent. One can speculate that if this gene flow eventually stopped, lactose intolerance would approach 100 percent among American blacks.

What events in human cultural history might have influenced the development of tolerance to lactose in the adults of some groups? Frederick J. Simoons of the University of California at Davis has proposed a hypothesis based on the development of dairying. It would appear that the milking of cattle, sheep, goats or reindeer did not begin until about 10,000 years ago, some 100 million years after the origin of mammals and therefore long after the mammalian developmental pattern of lactase activity had been well established. Man presumably shared that pattern, and so adults were intolerant to lactose.

When some small groups of humans began to milk animals, a selective advantage was conferred on individuals who, because of a chance mutation, had high enough lactase activity to digest lactose. A person who could not digest lactose might have difficulty in a society that ingested nonfermented milk or milk products, but the lactose-tolerant individual was more adaptable: he could survive perfectly well in either a milk-drinking or a non-milk-drinking society.

The genetic mutation resulting in the capability to digest lactose probably occurred at least 10,000 years ago. People with the mutation for adult lactase activity could be members of a dairying culture, utilize their own product for food (as the Fulani do today) and then sell it in the form of a yogurt (as the Fulani do) or cheese to the general, lactose-intolerant population. These statements are presumptions, not facts, but they are based soundly on the idea that tolerance to lactose is a mutation that endowed the individual with a nutritional genetic advantage and on the basic assumption, which is supported by fact, that lactose intolerance is the normal genetic state of adult man and that lactose tolerance is in a sense abnormal.

What are the implications of all of this for nutrition policy? It should be pointed out that many people who are intolerant to lactose are nevertheless able to drink some milk or eat some milk products; the relation of clinical symptoms to lactose ingestion is quantitative. For most people, even after the age of four, drinking moderate amounts of milk has no adverse effects and is actually nutritionally beneficial. It may well be, however, that programs of indiscriminate, large-scale distribution of milk powder to intolerant populations should be modified, or that current moves toward supplying lactose-free milk powder should be encouraged.

DISCUSSION QUESTIONS

1. Why did Kretchmer begin his article by discussing lactose intolerance among other mammals? What relevance do other mammals have for human populations with respect to lactose and lactase?

2. Describe the different subsistence patterns documented among the four African ethnic groups. How did lactose tolerance vary with the different subsistence patterns?

3. What kinds of cultural or environmental factors may have selected for the ability to digest milk as an adult?

INTERNET RESOURCES

After reading this selection, you may want to research the following individuals.

- Norman Kretchmer
- Frederick J. Simoons

InfoTrac College Edition

(infotrac-college.com)
You can find many other readings pertinent to this topic by consulting online databases including Info-

Trac College Edition. Some suggested search terms for this article are as follows.

- Lactose
- Lactase persistence
- Pastoralism

21

How Africa Learned to Love the Cow

ERIKA CHECK

In contemporary physical anthropology, new technologies are providing novel ways to approach old research questions. By the 1970s physical anthropologists knew that a majority of the world's adults lack lactase, the enzyme that breaks down lactose, or milk sugar. Therefore people who can digest lactose are exceptions. Northern Europeans and some African ethnic groups are distinguished by having the highest known frequencies of the mutations necessary to continue metabolizing lactose as adults. When did the genes involved in lactose digestion mutate and become more frequent in human evolution? How do these genes relate to cultural or environmental factors? Why did natural selection favor genes that control lactase production in adults? While previous scientists have long speculated on these things, we can now put genomic studies to work in our quest to identify the exact gene or genes responsible for the adult production of lactase.

In this selection, science writer Erika Check provides a progress report in finding the genes responsible for lactase persistence based on the work of Dr. Sarah Tishkoff. Tishkoff and her students have spent several years traveling around Africa collecting and analyzing blood samples from eastern African herding peoples. Tishkoff and her team identified several mutations responsible for lactase retention among the East Africans. As you read this article, notice that the frequencies of these mutations vary among the different East Africans sampled. Even more interesting, the African mutations for lactase retention are distinctly different from one previously identified in an investigation of northern Europeans.

What does this suggest about the evolutionary process? Tishkoff's study produced several interesting findings. Calculation of the rate of these mutations suggested that they arose rapidly around the time of cattle domestication. Moreover, differences between East Africans and northern Europeans provide evidence for convergent evolution, or the independent evolution of lactase retention in the two regions.

The article also provides a sense of the realities and hardships of fieldwork in some parts of the world. As you read about the work and adventures of Tishkoff's team, you may find yourself imagining yourself in the role of student researcher working with living peoples in some faraway lands. What kinds of questions do you think you would like to ask using the biocultural perspective? Do you have any concerns about conducting research investigations on contemporary peoples? Given our changing world, what kinds of research problems or discoveries can you imagine for physical anthropologists of the future?

SOURCE: Erika Check, "How Africa Learned to Love the Cow," *Nature* 444 (December 2006): 994–996.
Reprinted by permission.

The Dinka people of southern Sudan, it is said, have 400 different words to refer to the cattle that they prize above all other things. The Maasai, who live in Kenya and northern Tanzania, have traditionally believed that all cattle on Earth were given to them by the gods, and value those in their possession accordingly. The Zulu, Xhosa and Swazi in South Africa devote themselves to their strikingly patterned Nguni cattle, whose hides are now prized by high-end interior designers.

And in all these pastoralist or semi-pastoralist groups, which rely on herding for survival, people drink milk—which is something of a puzzle. Most adult humans (those of European stock are largely an exception) find the sugar in milk, called lactose, indigestible. The gene for lactase, the enzyme that breaks lactose down into the more digestible forms of glucose and galactose, is normally switched off as children are weaned. Without lactase, lactose is of little use to a milk drinker; but it is still a valid food for some stomach bacteria, which can have unsettling and unpleasant results. Thus, most adults tend not to drink much milk.

Now, genetic detective work is showing how, in parts of Africa, evolution found a way round this problem—just as it did a few thousand years earlier in northern Europe. The results should help clarify the origins and spread of cattle rearing in Africa, and provide a textbook illustration of the ways in which the same social innovation can write its consequences into the human genome in different times and places.

A DRINKING GAME

Sarah Tishkoff of the University of Maryland, College Park, first heard the story of "lactase persistence"—the ability to continue making lactase throughout adult life—in an introductory anthropology course she took at college in the late 1980s. In the 1960s, anthropologists first started noticing that groups of humans that raise cattle also tended to be the same ones that could drink milk as adults.[1] In the 1970s, a genetic basis for lactose intolerance was established, although the nature of the mutation has remained a mystery.[2] Drinking milk thus came to

be seen as a metabolic, not merely cultural, proclivity. People whose ancestors had herded cattle had evolved to make use of their milk. In places where lactase persistence is rare, the milk that is drunk is frequently sour—its lactose content lowered by hungry bacteria.

But it was not until 1997, when Tishkoff was doing postdoctoral research with Andy Clark at Pennsylvania State University, that she began thinking about lactase persistence as a focus for her own work. Tishkoff visited geneticist Trevor Jenkins at the University of Witwatersrand in Johannesburg, South Africa, to help him study an extensive collection of DNA samples from southern Africans. She began to wonder whether she could trace the genetic origin and history of lactase persistence by studying the DNA of Africa's cattle herders. If so, it would be a neat piece of genetics. And it would also be of interest to anthropologists interested in cattle domestication itself. Had the ancestral aurochs been domesticated just once, in the middle East, and the practice then spread to Europe and Africa? Or had Africans learned to domesticate cattle on their own?

Tishkoff designed a project to collect DNA samples from 43 ethnic groups in three East African countries and to correlate the data with various physiological characteristics relevant to taste perception, disease susceptibility and other things—including lactose metabolism. It was an ambitious plan at best— a foolhardy undertaking at worst. Few researchers, if any, had ever collected such a large, diverse set of genetic samples from Africa. Many of the groups she wanted to study were in remote locations, isolated by choice or by circumstance. And although she started to apply for permission to research in Tanzania in 1999, she didn't get permission to work there until 2001.

LIVING ON THE EDGE

Tishkoff set out with a 30-year-old Land Rover full of cases of energy bars and camping gear. Over the next three years, on and off, she and her students roamed around Tanzania, Kenya and Sudan, collecting data in some dangerous as well as out of the way places—

such as parts of Kenya where carjacking was rampant and everyone carried semi-automatic weapons. The team also had a close call once, on a journey near Lake Eyasi in Tanzania, when a bus rounded a corner and smashed head-on into the Land Rover; miraculously, no one was hurt. Tishkoff credits her students—especially Jibril Hirbo and Alessia Ranciaro, who collected samples in the most dangerous parts of Kenya—with persistence and courage. "Those guys literally risked their lives for this work," Tishkoff says.

At most stops, Tishkoff's group hired a translator to explain the purpose of her research, get permission from local leaders, and recruit people for their research. In all, they took samples from 470 people. To test for lactase, the team members stirred powdered lactose into cups of water, gave it to each person, and took a series of timed blood samples. That told the researchers how well each person could digest lactose, as well as providing samples of the individual's DNA.

In 2002, while the work was under way, a team of Finnish researchers reported that it had found a genetic mutation that seemed to cause lactase persistence in North Europeans.[3] A small change in an "enhancer" region upstream of the lactase gene seemed to keep the gene from being switched off after infancy. All of the 137 lactase-persistent Finns studied had the mutation in question, and studies of other populations showed that the frequency of the mutation matched that of the lactase persistence. But two years later, another team reported that the Finns' genetic variant was not found in East Africans, even though some are lactase persistent.[4]

Tishkoff's team showed why this was. Ranciaro sequenced DNA from her subjects and noticed several mutations close to the lactase gene. A collaborator at the Wellcome Trust Sanger Institute in Cambridge, UK, Panos Deloukas, checked for the mutations in the full set of 470 people, and Tishkoff and a postdoctoral fellow working with her, Floyd Reed, noticed that one of these mutations was tightly linked to lactase persistence in Tanzanians and Kenyans. The team also found that two other mutations were associated with lactase persistence in peo-

ple in northern Kenya and Sudan, though not as strongly.[5] It was immediately clear that these mutations had arisen independently from the one found in Finland.

QUICK START

The DNA also showed evidence that the mutation seen in the Tanzanians had spread very quickly. DNA accumulates small, random imperfections over the generations, and yet the stretches of DNA surrounding the lactase persistence mutation were identical in most of those who had it. This uniformity shows that the gene evolved recently and spread rapidly—which in turn means that it must have conferred an advantage strongly selected for by evolution. Statistical models of Tishkoff's data suggest that the mutation arose between 3,000 and 7,000 years ago—a blink of an eye in evolutionary time.

Tishkoff and Reed conclude that lactase persistence bears one of the strongest signatures of positive selection ever observed in the human genome. Mutations that favour malaria resistance, such as the sickle-cell gene and an inability to make the enzyme glucose-6-phosphate dehydrogenase, or G6PD, are also strongly favoured and spread rapidly. (They seem to have got going at about the same time, too, and are also related to domestication—malaria is thought to have first become a major problem for Africans when they started to live in settlements.) But the positive selection for lactase persistence seems even stronger, perhaps because the costs of the mutation are less severe than those for malaria. Tishkoff and Reed suspect that the advantage might go beyond the extra calories that could be gained from the lactose. Lactase persistence might also have allowed people to stay alive during times of drought, when those benefiting from the mutation would have been able to drink milk without the risk of diarrhoea, which exacerbates dehydration.

The study, and subsequent follow-up, should help to elucidate the origins of East African cultures and traditions. Anthropologists such as Diane

Gifford-Gonzalez from the University of California, Santa Cruz, one of the world's experts on the origins of herding, say that these genetic data are changing the way they think about human history. "Until the geneticists contributed to the data, the rest of us always thought about evolution happening very slowly and gradually."

HERDING ALONG EVOLUTION

And the genes provide data even in places, such as East Africa, where the archaeological data are poor. "That is why this article is so interesting to people like me," says Gifford-Gonzalez. "This gives us a totally independent line of evidence about the origins of dairying, and gives us a much better way of homing in on when these major nutritional transitions occurred." The human genetic data might thus in some ways complement the genetic data on cattle, which in the decade since Tishkoff began thinking about the issue have come down in favour of multiple domestications, including one in Africa.

Tishkoff's work also highlights the incredible genetic diversity in African people, a diversity that as yet has been studied very little. For example, the African DNA samples in the Haplotype Map[6]—the catalogue of genetic diversity published last year—come from only one ethnic group: the Yoruba of West Africa. But, traditionally, the Yoruba don't herd cattle, and Tishkoff didn't discover any mutations for lactase persistence in them (although in some populations of West African pastoralists, fewer people have the "European" lactase persistence mutation). Such blind spots could be a problem, because scientists hunting for the genetic causes of diseases often rely on HapMap data. "There's such a huge amount of genetic diversity in Africa that we're clearly going to have to look at all the ethnic groups in different regions to find all the variants," Tishkoff says. "Otherwise,

we could be completely missing things that are important in disease." She worries that the fragmentation and disappearance of traditional cultures will make it harder to access and understand that diversity in the future.

The lactose work still leaves a lot of questions unanswered, and the possibility of more adaptations still to be found. A particularly intriguing question surrounds the Hadza of Tanzania, who show a surprisingly high level of lactase persistence despite having very little to do with cattle. One possibility is that, though they are now mainly hunter-gatherers, their ancestors might have been pastoralists. Another is that lactase may offer some other benefits besides the ability to drink milk—perhaps aiding in the digestion of some specific local foods.

A TEXTBOOK CASE

But if there are still questions, there's also a significant achievement. Scientists have to date found little genetic evidence for convergent evolution in people: "This is the best example of convergent evolution in humans that I've ever seen," says Joel Hirschhorn, a geneticist and paediatrician at Children's Hospital Boston, Massachusetts. "Lactase persistence has always been a textbook example of selection, and now it'll be a textbook example in a totally different way."

Convergent evolution is not unknown in humans; lighter skin colour seems to have evolved independently in Europe and Asia, and a range of different malaria adaptations are known. But lactase persistence offers a particularly simple and tractable example: there's a single gene involved, with different mutations in different parts of the world having similar effects. The challenge now is to learn from this textbook example how to spot more subtle convergences that have been forced on human biology by shared experiences and cultural innovations—or that are still under way today.

NOTES

1. Swallow, D. M. *Annu. Rev. Genet.* 37, 197–219 (2003).

2. Sahi, T. *Scand. J. Gastroenterol. Suppl.* 1–73 (1974).

3. Enattah, N. S., et al. *Nature Genet.* 30, 233–237 (2002).

4. Mulcare, C. A., et al. *Am. J. Hum. Genet.* 74, 1102–1110 (2004).

5. Tishkoff, S. A., et al. *Nature Genet.* doi:10.1038/ng1946 (2006).

6. The International HapMap Consortium. *Nature* 437, 1299–1320 (2005).

DISCUSSION QUESTIONS

1. What were some possible advantages of being lactase persistent among East Africans and northern Europeans?

2. When and under what circumstances is lactase persistence thought to have evolved in human populations?

3. What is convergent evolution? How do the studies of northern Europeans and East Africans described in this article suggest a role for convergent evolution with respect to lactase persistence in human populations?

 **INTERNET RESOURCES**

After reading this selection, you may want to research the following individuals.

- Sarah Tishkoff
- Diane Gifford-Gonzalez

 **InfoTrac College Edition**

(infotrac-college.com)
You can find many other readings pertinent to this topic by consulting online databases including Info-

Trac College Edition. Some suggested search terms for this article are as follows.

- Convergent evolution
- Haplotype map
- Lactase persistence

22

Skin Deep

NINA G. JABLONSKI AND GEORGE CHAPLIN

Modern humans have sometimes been referred to as naked apes *because our exposed skin is a distinctive feature that sets us apart from our closest evolutionary cousins. As shown in this article, our species also exhibits a wide variety of skin colors, which has long attracted the attention of physical anthropologists. For the last few decades, explanations of variation in skin color have been related to the fact that, in the tropics, increased pigmentation shields the skin from the more damaging effects of the sun's ultraviolet (UV) radiation, a known carcinogen. But darker skin can be a liability in northern latitudes, where exposure to sunlight is reduced, because deeply pigmented skin can filter out too much sunlight. This is a problem because some UV light is necessary for the formation of vitamin D in the skin, and, in turn, vitamin D is essential for calcium absorption and bone mineralization. This explanation, called the "vitamin D hypothesis," has been largely accepted for a few decades.*

In this selection, Jablonski and Chaplin offer another, not necessarily conflicting, explanation of skin color variation. First, they stipulate that the earliest hominins—like apes today—had fairly thick body hair covering a light skin. They argue that selection began to favor darker skin as reduction of body hair occurred, which may have begun when hominins started to occupy more open, sunnier savanna habitats. Reduced body hair facilitated body cooling by exposing more of the skin's surface. But this would have increased their exposure to UV radiation, and increased pigmentation compensated for the loss of protection once provided by hair. Jablonski and Chaplin propose that, although there is little question that increasing melanin protected individuals from skin cancers, protection against folate deficiency exerted an even more powerful selective force for darker skin color. In other words, early hominins with more skin pigmentation had higher folate levels.

Folate is a vitamin that is essential for the embryonic formation of the brain and spinal cord, and plays a critical role in synthesizing cellular DNA and in rapid cell proliferation. Jablonski and Chaplin argue that once modern Homo sapiens *left Africa and settled in more northerly latitudes, their dark skins became a liability because of lower levels of UV radiation. Under those circumstances, lighter skins and enhanced vitamin D synthesis were selected for.*

Applying a new biomedical discovery involving folate to the mystery of skin pigmentation is innovative, and the Jablonski and Chaplin article can rightfully be called a new classic. As you read through this selection, note the ways in which the authors use biological, cultural, and environmental factors to investigate skin color variation. In taking this tack, they are applying a biocultural perspective to explain the evolution of skin pigmentation.

SOURCE: Nina G. Jablonski and George Chaplin, "Skin Deep," *Scientific American,* October 2002. Reprinted with permission. Copyright © 2002 by Scientific American, Inc. All rights reserved.

Among primates, only humans have a mostly naked skin that comes in different colors. Geographers and anthropologists have long recognized that the distribution of skin colors among indigenous populations is not random: darker peoples tend to be found nearer the equator, lighter ones closer to the poles. For years, the prevailing theory has been that darker skins evolved to protect against skin cancer. But a series of discoveries has led us to construct a new framework for understanding the evolutionary basis of variations in human skin color. Recent epidemiological and physiological evidence suggests to us that the worldwide pattern of human skin color is the product of natural selection acting to regulate the effects of the sun's ultraviolet (UV) radiation on key nutrients crucial to reproductive success.

The evolution of skin pigmentation is linked with that of hairlessness, and to comprehend both these stories, we need to page back in human history. Human beings have been evolving as an independent lineage of apes since at least seven million years ago, when our immediate ancestors diverged from those of our closest relatives, chimpanzees. Because chimpanzees have changed less over time than humans have, they can provide an idea of what human anatomy and physiology must have been like. Chimpanzees' skin is light in color and is covered by hair over most of their bodies. Young animals have pink faces, hands, and feet and become freckled or dark in these areas only as they are exposed to sun with age. The earliest humans almost certainly had a light skin covered with hair. Presumably hair loss occurred first, then skin color changed. But that leads to the question, When did we lose our hair?

The skeletons of ancient humans—such as the well-known skeleton of Lucy, which dates to about 3.2 million years ago—give us a good idea of the build and the way of life of our ancestors. The daily activities of Lucy and other hominids that lived before about three million years ago appear to have been similar to those of primates living on the open savannas of Africa today. They probably spent much of their day foraging for food over three to four miles before retiring to the safety of trees to sleep.

By 1.6 million years ago, however, we see evidence that this pattern had begun to change dramati-

cally. The famous skeleton of Turkana Boy—which belonged to the species *Homo ergaster*—is that of a long-legged, striding biped that probably walked long distances. These more active early humans faced the problem of staying cool and protecting their brains from overheating. Peter Wheeler of Liverpool John Moores University has shown that this was accomplished through an increase in the number of sweat glands on the surface of the body and a reduction in the covering of body hair. Once rid of most of their hair, early members of the genus *Homo* then encountered the challenge of protecting their skin from the damaging effects of sunlight, especially UV rays.

BUILT-IN SUNSCREEN

In chimpanzees, the skin on the hairless parts of the body contains cells called melanocytes that are capable of synthesizing the dark-brown pigment melanin in response to exposure to UV radiation. When humans became mostly hairless, the ability of the skin to produce melanin assumed new importance. Melanin is nature's sunscreen: it is a large organic molecule that serves the dual purpose of physically and chemically filtering the harmful effects of UV radiation; it absorbs UV rays, causing them to lose energy, and it neutralizes harmful chemicals called free radicals that form in the skin after damage by UV radiation.

Anthropologists and biologists have generally reasoned that high concentrations of melanin arose in the skin of peoples in tropical areas because it protected them against skin cancer. James E. Cleaver of the University of California at San Francisco, for instance, has shown that people with the disease xeroderma pigmentosum, in which melanocytes are destroyed by exposure to the sun, suffer from significantly higher than normal rates of squamous and basal cell carcinomas, which are usually easily treated. Malignant melanomas are more frequently fatal, but they are rare (representing 4 percent of skin cancer diagnoses) and tend to strike only light-skinned people. But all skin cancers typically arise later in life, in most cases after the first reproductive years, so they could not have exerted enough evolutionary pressure for skin protection alone to account for darker skin colors. Accordingly, we began to ask what role melanin might play in human evolution.

THE FOLATE CONNECTION

In 1991 one of us (Jablonski) ran across what turned out to be a critical paper published in 1978 by Richard F. Branda and John W. Eaton, now at the University of Vermont and the University of Louisville, respectively. These investigators showed that light-skinned people who had been exposed to simulated strong sunlight had abnormally low levels of the essential B vitamin folate in their blood. The scientists also observed that subjecting human blood serum to the same conditions resulted in a 50 percent loss of folate content within one hour.

The significance of these findings to reproduction—and hence evolution—became clear when we learned of research being conducted on a major class of birth defects by our colleagues at the University of Western Australia. There Fiona J. Stanley and Carol Bower had established by the late 1980s that folate deficiency in pregnant women is related to an increased risk of neural tube defects such as spina bifida, in which the arches of the spinal vertebrae fail to close around the spinal cord. Many research groups throughout the world have since confirmed this correlation, and efforts to supplement foods with folate (folic acid) and to educate women about the importance of the nutrient have become widespread.

We discovered soon afterward that folate is important not only in preventing neural tube defects but also in a host of other processes. Because folate is essential for the synthesis of DNA in dividing cells, anything that involves rapid cell proliferation, such as spermatogenesis (the production of sperm cells), requires folate. Male rats and mice with chemically induced folate deficiency have impaired spermatogenesis and are infertile. Although no comparable studies of humans have been conducted, Wai Yee Wong and his colleagues at the University Medical Center of Nijmegen in the Netherlands have recently reported that folic acid treatment can boost the sperm counts of men with fertility problems.

Such observations led us to hypothesize that dark skin evolved to protect the body's folate stores from destruction. Our idea was supported by a report published in 1996 by Argentine pediatrician Pablo Lapunzina, who found that three young and otherwise healthy women whom he had attended gave birth to infants with neural tube defects after using sun beds to tan themselves in the early weeks of pregnancy. Our evidence about the breakdown of folate by UV radiation thus supplements what is already known about the harmful (skin-cancer-causing) effects of UV radiation on DNA.

HUMAN SKIN ON THE MOVE

The earliest members of *Homo sapiens,* or modern humans, evolved in Africa between 120,000 and 100,000 years ago and had darkly pigmented skin adapted to the conditions of UV radiation and heat that existed near the equator. As modern humans began to venture out of the tropics, however, they encountered environments in which they received significantly less UV radiation during the year. Under these conditions their high concentrations of natural sunscreen probably proved detrimental. Dark skin contains so much melanin that very little UV radiation, and specifically very little of the shorter-wavelength UVB radiation, can penetrate the skin. Although most of the effects of UVB are harmful, the rays perform one indispensable function: initiating the formation of vitamin D in the skin. Dark-skinned people living in the tropics generally receive sufficient UV radiation during the year for UVB to penetrate the skin and allow them to make vitamin D. Outside the tropics this is not the case. The solution, across evolutionary time, has been for migrants to northern latitudes to lose skin pigmentation.

The connection between the evolution of lightly pigmented skin and vitamin D synthesis was elaborated in 1967 by W. Farnsworth Loomis of Brandeis University. He established the importance of vitamin D to reproductive success because of its role in enabling calcium absorption by the intestines, which in turn makes possible the normal development of the skeleton and the maintenance of a healthy immune system. Research led by Michael Holick of the Boston University School of Medicine has, over the past 20 years, further cemented the significance of vitamin D in development and immunity. His team also showed that not all sunlight contains enough UVB to stimulate vitamin D production. In Boston, for instance, which is located at about 42 degrees north latitude, human skin cells begin to produce vitamin D only after mid-March. In the wintertime there isn't enough UVB to do the job. We realized that this was another piece of evidence essential to the skin color story.

During the course of our research in the early 1990s, we sought in vain to find sources of data on actual UV radiation levels at the earth's surface. We were rewarded in 1996, when we contacted Elizabeth Weatherhead of the Cooperative Institute for Research in Environmental Sciences at the University of Colorado at Boulder. She shared with us a database of measurements of UV radiation at the earth's surface taken by NASA's Total Ozone Mapping Spectrophotometer satellite between 1978 and 1993. We were then able to model the distribution of UV radiation on the earth and relate the satellite data to the amount of UVB necessary to produce vitamin D.

We found that the earth's surface could be divided into three vitamin D zones: one comprising the tropics, one the subtropics and temperate regions, and the last the circumpolar regions north and south of about 45 degrees latitude. In the first, the dosage of UVB throughout the year is high enough that humans have ample opportunity to synthesize vitamin D all year. In the second, at least one month during the year has insufficient UVB radiation, and in the third area not enough UVB arrives on average during the entire year to prompt vitamin D synthesis. This distribution could explain why indigenous peoples in the tropics generally have dark skin, whereas people in the subtropics and temperate regions are lighter-skinned but have the ability to tan, and those who live in regions near the poles tend to be very light-skinned and burn easily.

One of the most interesting aspects of this investigation was the examination of groups that did not precisely fit the predicted skin color pattern. An example is the Inuit people of Alaska and northern Canada. The Inuit exhibit skin color that is somewhat darker than would be predicted given the UV levels at their latitude. This is probably caused by two factors. The first is that they are relatively recent inhabitants of these climes, having migrated to North America only roughly 5,000 years ago. The second is that the traditional diet of the Inuit is extremely high in foods containing vitamin D, especially fish and marine mammals. This vitamin D-rich diet offsets the problem that they would otherwise have with vitamin D synthesis in their skin at northern latitudes and permits them to remain more darkly pigmented.

Our analysis of the potential to synthesize vitamin D allowed us to understand another trait related to human skin color: women in all populations are generally lighter-skinned than men. (Our data show that women tend to be between 3 and 4 percent lighter than men.) Scientists have often speculated on the reasons, and most have argued that the phenomenon stems from sexual selection—the preference of men for women of lighter color. We contend that although this is probably part of the story, it is not the original reason for the sexual difference. Females have significantly greater needs for calcium throughout their reproductive lives, especially during pregnancy and lactation, and must be able to make the most of the calcium contained in food. We propose, therefore, that women tend to be lighter-skinned than men to allow slightly more UVB rays to penetrate their skin and thereby increase their ability to produce vitamin D. In areas of the world that receive a large amount of UV radiation, women are indeed at the knife's edge of natural selection, needing to maximize the photoprotective function of their skin on the one hand and the ability to synthesize vitamin D on the other.

WHERE CULTURE AND BIOLOGY MEET

As modern humans moved throughout the Old World about 100,000 years ago, their skin adapted to the environmental conditions that prevailed in different regions. The skin color of the indigenous people of Africa has had the longest time to adapt because anatomically modern humans first evolved there. The skin color changes that modern humans underwent as they moved from one continent to another—first Asia, then Austro-Melanesia, then Europe and, finally, the Americas—can be reconstructed to some extent. It is important to remember, however, that those humans had clothing and shelter to help protect them from the elements. In some places, they also had the ability to harvest foods that were extraordinarily rich in vitamin D, as in the case of the Inuit. These two factors had profound effects on the tempo and degree of skin color evolution in human populations.

Africa is an environmentally heterogeneous continent. A number of the earliest movements of contemporary humans outside equatorial Africa were into southern Africa. The descendants of some of these early colonizers, the Khoisan (previously known as Hottentots), are still found in southern Africa and have significantly lighter skin than indigenous equatorial Africans do—a clear adaptation to the lower levels of UV radiation that prevail at the southern extremity of the continent.

Interestingly, however, human skin color in southern Africa is not uniform. Populations of Bantu-language speakers who live in southern Africa today are far darker than the Khoisan. We know from the history of this region that Bantu speakers migrated into this region recently—probably within the past 1,000 years—from parts of West Africa near the equator. The skin color difference between the Khoisan and Bantu speakers such as the Zulu indicates that the length of time that a group has inhabited a particular region is important in understanding why they have the color they do.

Cultural behaviors have probably also strongly influenced the evolution of skin color in recent human history. This effect can be seen in the indigenous peoples who live on the eastern and western banks of the Red Sea. The tribes on the western side, which speak so-called Nilo-Hamitic languages, are thought to have inhabited this region for as long as 6,000 years. These individuals are distinguished by very darkly pigmented skin and long, thin bodies with long limbs, which are excellent biological adaptations for dissipating heat and intense UV radiation. In contrast, modern agricultural and pastoral groups on the eastern bank of the Red Sea, on the Arabian Peninsula, have lived there for only about 2,000 years. These earliest Arab people, of European origin, have adapted to very similar environmental conditions by almost exclusively cultural means—wearing heavy protective clothing and devising portable shade in the form of tents. (Without such clothing, one would have expected their skin to have begun to darken.) Generally speaking, the more recently a group has migrated into an area, the more extensive its cultural, as opposed to biological, adaptations to the area will be.

PERILS OF RECENT MIGRATIONS

Despite great improvements in overall human health in the past century, some diseases have appeared or reemerged in populations that had previously been little affected by them. One of these is skin cancer, especially basal and squamous cell carcinomas, among light-skinned peoples. Another is rickets, brought about by severe vitamin D deficiency, in dark-skinned peoples. Why are we seeing these conditions?

As people move from an area with one pattern of UV radiation to another region, biological and cultural adaptations have not been able to keep pace. The light-skinned people of northern European origin who bask in the sun of Florida or northern Australia increasingly pay the price in the form of premature aging of the skin and skin cancers, not to mention the unknown cost in human life of folate depletion. Conversely, a number of dark-skinned people of southern Asian and African origin now living in the northern U.K., northern Europe or the northeastern U.S. suffer from a lack of UV radiation and vitamin D, an insidious problem that manifests itself in high rates of rickets and other diseases related to vitamin D deficiency.

The ability of skin color to adapt over long periods to the various environments to which humans have moved reflects the importance of skin color to our survival. But its unstable nature also makes it one of the least useful characteristics in determining the evolutionary relations between human groups. Early Western scientists used skin color improperly to delineate human races, but the beauty of science is that it can and does correct itself. Our current knowledge of the evolution of human skin indicates that variations in skin color, like most of our physical attributes, can be explained by adaptation to the environment through natural selection. We look ahead to the day when the vestiges of old scientific mistakes will be erased and replaced by a better understanding of human origins and diversity. Our variation in skin color should be celebrated as one of the most visible manifestations of our evolution as a species.

DISCUSSION QUESTIONS

1. In what ways does the Jablonski and Chaplin hypothesis about skin color illustrate a biocultural approach? What other topics could be investigated in this way?

2. According to the article, what were some of the environmental and physiological challenges that faced the early hominins? When do the authors believe that hominins became capable of bipedal striding?

3. You know a very light-skinned woman who has moved to equatorial Africa, where she will have a job working in the sunlight all day. What kinds of hazards do you foresee for her?

4. You know a very dark-skinned woman who has moved to the New York inner city, where she has an office job in a building without any windows. Do you have any health concerns for her or for her potential offspring?

 **INTERNET RESOURCES**

After reading this selection, you may want to research the following individuals.

- Nina Jablonski
- Peter Wheeler
- George Chaplin

InfoTrac College Edition

(infotrac-college.com)
You can find many other readings pertinent to this topic by consulting online databases including Info-

Trac College Edition. Some suggested search terms for this article are as follows.

- Melanin
- *Homo ergaster*
- Vitamin D
- Folate

23

Ancient DNA Reveals Neanderthals with Red Hair, Fair Complexions

ELIZABETH CULOTTA

Just how much like modern humans were the Neandertals? If a Neandertal wearing con-temporary clothing took the seat next to you on a jumbo jet, would you notice anything unusual? What characteristics would give her away? In what ways would a Neandertal look similar to (or different from) you? While we can anticipate certain features based on Neandertal skulls and other fossilized bones, we have had limited ways to predict what their soft tissues, such as skin and hair, must have looked like. This is changing, however.

As Elizabeth Culotta reports in this selection, our ways of reconstructing our ancient cousins are changing. Paleoanthropologists are now identifying specific genes in fossils and trying to interpret their corresponding characteristics. For example, several teams of inves-tigators are studying Neandertal genes. Most notable is the MC1R gene (otherwise known as the melanocortin cell receptor), which is involved in skin and hair color. The gene helps reg-ulate the amounts of two kinds of melanin—phaeomelanin and eumelanin—in skin and hair. Recent studies demonstrated a mutation, unique to Neandertals, that would have af-fected the relative quantities of phaeomelanin and eumelanin. As a result, Neandertals who had two copies of this mutated gene would have had red hair and fair skin. What factors would have selected for light skin among the Neandertals? What do we know about the inheritance of these traits among modern humans?

Culotta's article shows that it's now possible to anticipate a day when we'll be able to sequence entire genomes from fossil forms. As you read this article, note the other gene that's been documented in Neandertal DNA. What does its presence imply about Neandertal behavior or appearance? What did we learn about the evolution of these traits, or evolutionary processes in general, in modern Homo sapiens? *Thinking more broadly, if you were able to investigate ancient DNA, what questions about human evolution would you be interested in researching? Would you want to test any specific hypotheses? If so, what would those research questions involve?*

W hat would it have been like to meet a Neandertal? Researchers have hypothesized answers for decades, seeking to put flesh on an-cient bones. But fossils are silent on many traits, from hair and skin color to speech and personality.

Personality will have to wait, but in a paper pub-lished online in *Science* . . . (www.sciencemag.org/

SOURCE: Elizabeth Culotta, "Ancient DNA Reveals Neanderthals with Red Hair, Fair Complexions," *Science* 318 (26 October 2007): 546–547. Reprinted with permission from AAAS.

cgi/content/abstract/1147417), an international team announces that it has extracted a pigmentation gene, *mc1r,* from the bones of two Neandertals. The researchers conclude that at least some Neandertals had pale skin and red hair, similar to some of the *Homo sapiens* who today inhabit their European homeland. The paper comes on the heels of one that used similar techniques to show that Neandertals shared the modern human form of the only gene so far known to influence human speech, *FOXP2.* Although researchers are working to sequence the entire Neandertal genome (*Science,* 17 November 2006, p. 1068), these are the first specific nuclear genes to be retrieved. "These are the two genes you'd most like to see from a Neandertal," explains Svante Pääbo of the Max Planck Institute for Evolutionary Anthropology in Leipzig, Germany, who led the *FOXP2* study.

The *mc1r* paper is "logical, elegant, and convincing," says anthropologist Nina Jablonski of Pennsylvania State University in University Park. "It's a great paper," agrees molecular geneticist and pigmentation expert Rick Sturm of the University of Queensland in St. Lucia, Australia.

Many of the Neandertals cavorting in museum dioramas around the world already have pale skin or red hair, because anthropologists have long predicted this coloration on the basis of evolutionary theory. The dark skin beneficial in Africa offers no advantage at high latitudes, and in cloudy Europe, pale skin facilitates vitamin D production, Jablonski says. But there was no proof of Neandertals' looks until a team led by Carles Lalueza-Fox of the University of Barcelona in Spain and Holger Römpler of the University of Leipzig in Germany set out to retrieve the *mc1r* gene from a 43,000-year-old Neandertal from El Sidrón, Spain, and a 50,000-year-old specimen from Monti Lessini, Italy.

MC1R is a cell membrane receptor that helps regulate the balance between red-and-yellow-colored phaeomelanin and black-and-brown-colored eumelanin. Living people with variations that make the receptor work poorly tend to have red hair and pale skin, although other pigmentation genes also have strong effects (*Science,* 2 March [2007], p. 1215).

Using the polymerase chain reaction (PCR) to target and amplify the gene, the researchers found a point mutation not seen in living humans. They checked about 3700 people, including everyone involved in the project, to be sure that the variant was unique to Neandertals. Next, they explored the variant's function by expressing it in human cells and found that it impaired the receptor's activity. "If you have a variant with this low action in modern humans, you get classically Irish-looking red hair and pale skin" in homozygotes, people with two copies of the variant, says team member Michael Hofreiter of the Max Planck Institute in Leipzig. The researchers calculate that at least 1 in 100 Neandertals would have been homozygotes. Thus Neandertals and *Homo sapiens* in Europe followed independent evolutionary paths to a similar phenotype, Lalueza-Fox says.

"I'm convinced that what they're saying is real," says Sturm, who has used similar functional assays to check *mc1r* variants in living people. Lalueza-Fox adds that Neandertals may have carried a variety of changes in *mc1r,* as we do, and so may have had a spectrum of skin and hair colors.

Pääbo and colleagues also used targeted PCR to isolate the *FOXP2* gene. They chose *FOXP2* because people with mutations in the gene have impaired speech. Pääbo's team had previously traced the gene in living people and suggested that the unique human variant was selected relatively recently, less than 200,000 years ago—long after Neandertals and modern humans had diverged (*Science,* 16 August 2002, p. 1105). The implication was that Neandertals lacked the modern human form, Pääbo says.

But to their surprise, that's not what they found when they sequenced the gene from two bones from El Sidrón, where Lalueza-Fox runs a "clean" excavation for DNA analysis. Both bones carried the modern human version of *FOXP2.* That doesn't necessarily mean Neandertals spoke as we do, because many genes presumably influence speech. But "from the point of view of the one gene we know, there's nothing to say that Neandertals were different from us" in their language abilities, Pääbo says.

Because the Neandertal *FOXP2* gene matched that found in living people, Pääbo's team used extra controls to try to rule out contamination with modern human DNA. For example, they sequenced the Neandertal Y chromosome and found that it differed from that of living men at five key sites. No contamination of the Y chromosome strengthens the case that the *FOXP2* result is real, Pääbo says.

The Y chromosome finding also argues against interbreeding between Neandertals and the modern humans then entering Europe. "I find it paradoxical in some ways," says Lalueza-Fox, who is an author of both studies. "The papers make Neandertals more like modern Europeans, with light skin and hair color and language abilities, and yet there are no signs of interbreeding with modern humans."

But others aren't yet ready to concede that either contamination or mixing has been completely ruled out. "The additional controls give one more confidence that contamination is not a problem, but we can't be 100% sure," says evolutionary ge-

neticist Jeff Wall of the University of California, San Francisco, who in August reported what he saw as contamination in Pääbo's group's bulk Neandertal sequencing (*Science*NOW, 29 August [2007], sciencenow.sciencemag.org/cgi/content/full/2007/829/4).

Wall adds that if the *FOXP2* result is real, it's possible that Neandertals acquired the human *FOXP2* variant by mixing. "If there was admixture, it wasn't very much. But we can't tell if there was a small amount." Pääbo says he can't rule out that scenario but considers it "unlikely," given the genetic data so far.

DISCUSSION QUESTIONS

1. How does the inheritance of fair skin and red hair among modern humans differ from the way these traits were inherited among Neandertals? What does this tell us about the evolution of these characteristics in both Neandertals and modern humans?

2. How many fossils were analyzed in the pigmentation gene study presented by Culotta? What difference does the number of analyzed bones—or sample size—actually make?

3. What is FOXP2? What does its presence in modern *Homo sapiens* tell us? What do we

know at this point about FOXP2 in Neandertals?

4. Are there aspects of human evolution that we *won't* learn about through studying ancient DNA? Alternatively, which research questions do you think we will learn the most about by investigating ancient genomes?

5. What are the kinds of melanin that determine skin and hair color? What do we know about how these traits are inherited in modern *Homo sapiens?*

INTERNET RESOURCES

After reading this selection, you may want to research the following individuals.

■ Nina Jablonski

■ Svante Pääbo

■ Rick Sturm

InfoTrac College Edition

(infotrac-college.com)
You can find many other readings pertinent to this topic by consulting online databases including Info-

Trac College Edition. Some suggested search terms for this article are as follows.

■ Polymerase chain reaction

■ FOXP2

■ Eumelanin

■ Phaeomelanin